A Muslim American Slave

Ambrotype of Omar ibn Said (North Carolina Collection, University of North Carolina at Chapel Hill)

A Muslim American Slave

The Life of Omar Ibn Said

Translated from the Arabic,
edited,
and with an introduction by
ALA ALRYYES

The University of Wisconsin Press

Publication of this volume has been made possible, in part, through support from the
FREDERICK W. HILLES FUND of Yale University.

The University of Wisconsin Press
1930 Monroe Street, 3rd Floor
Madison, Wisconsin 53711-2059
uwpress.wisc.edu

3 Henrietta Street
London WC2E 8LU, England
eurospanbookstore.com

Printed in the United States of America

Library of Congress Cataloging-in-Publication Data
Said, Omar ibn, 1770?–1863 or 4.
A Muslim American slave : the life of Omar ibn Said / translated from the Arabic,
edited, and with an introduction by Ala Alryyes.
p.   : ill, facsim., maps; cm.—(Wisconsin studies in autobiography)
English translations on pages facing facsim. pages of Arabic text.
Includes bibliographical references and index.
ISBN 978-0-299-24954-0 (pbk.: alk. paper)
ISBN 978-0-299-24953-3 (e-book)
1. Said, Omar ibn, 1770?–1863 or 4.   2. Slave narratives—North Carolina.   3. Slaves' writings, American.
4. Slaves—North Carolina—Biography.   5. African American Muslims—North Carolina—History—Sources.
6. Slavery—United States—History—Sources.
I. Alryyes, Ala A., 1963-   II. Title.   III. Series: Wisconsin studies in autobiography.
E444.S25 2011
306.3′62092—dc22
[B]
2010044625

"Autobiography of Omar Ibn Said, Slave in North Carolina, 1831," translated by Isaac Bird, first appeared in *American Historical Review* 30, no. 4 (July 1925): 787–95. Copyright © 1925 by the American Historical Review. Used by permission of the University of Chicago Press.

"Muslims in Early America," by Michael A. Gomez, first appeared in *Journal of Southern History* 60, no. 4 (November 1994): 671–710. Copyright © 1994 by the Southern Historical Association. Used by permission of the Editor.

"Representing the West in the Arabic Language: The Slave Narrative of Omar Ibn Said," by Ghada Osman and Camille F. Forbes, first appeared in the *Journal of Islamic Studies* 15, no. 3 (September 2004): 331–43. Used by permission of Oxford University Press.

Appendix 1 is used by permission of Charles E. Merrill Department of Rare Books and Special Collections, Franklin Trask Library, Andover Newton Theological School. John Hunwick's translation first appeared in "'I Wish to Be Seen in Our Land Called Afrika': 'Umar b. Sayyid's Appeal to Be Released from Slavery (1819)," *Journal of Arabic and Islamic Studies* 5 (2003): 62–77. Used by permission of *Journal of Arabic and Islamic Studies*.

Contents

The *Life*

Contextual Essays

Contents

Illustrations

Acknowledgments

I am indebted to many people for their help with this book. My project had its seed in a conference on Omar ibn Said held at Houghton Library, Harvard University, under the auspices of the Longfellow Institute, which supports the study of non-English writings in what is now the United States. I am deeply grateful to Werner Sollors and Marc Shell, who organized that conference, for their invaluable interest and encouragement during the beginning stages of this project. Early parts of the book were published with the support of the Longfellow Institute. I warmly thank Yota Batsaki for her help in that process. I am very grateful to Derrick Beard, the owner of the manuscript, for generously providing full access to it and for allowing it to be reproduced here. Special thanks are due to the contributors of this volume.

For their insights and comments, I thank Anthony K. Appiah, Srinivas Aravamudan, Ian Baucom, Natalie Zemon Davis, Henry Louis Gates Jr., Muhsin al-Musawi, Gregory Nagy, Allen F. Roberts, and Jan Ziolkowski. I am also grateful to Jonathan Curiel, John Hunwick, Sulayman Nyang, Muhammed al-Ahari, and the late Thomas C. Parramore.

My book benefited from questions and comments at invited talks and conferences. I particularly thank the Instituto de Filosofía de Ciências Sociais, Universidade Federal do Rio de Janeiro, Brazil; Wellesley College; the organizers of the Textual Culture Conference, the University of Stirling, Scotland; and participants in the "Non-English Literatures of the United States" seminar at the American Comparative Literature Association conference in Puerto Vallarta, Mexico, especially Alicia Borinsky, Dan Duffy, Peter Fenves, Melinda Gray, Gönül Pultar, Steven Rowan, and Ted Widmer.

A Morse fellowship at Yale University provided financial assistance and time off, which helped in the development of the project. I am grateful to the members of the Yale's Working Group in Cross-Lingual Poetics and the Yale Arabic Colloquium for helpful comments, and thank Wai Chee Dimock and Beatrice Gruendler, respectively, for invitations to speak to these two colloquia. For valuable discussions and suggestions, I also thank my colleagues Rolena Adorno, Nigel

Acknowledgments

Alderman, Hazel Carby, Vilashini Cooppan, Benjamin Foster, Moira Fradinger, Dimitri Gutas, Chris Hill, Michael Holquist, Edward Kamens, John MacKay, Christopher L. Miller, Haun Saussy, Robert Stepto, Lamin Sanneh, Joseph Roach, and the late Richard Maxwell.

My research assistant, Ross Powell, helped greatly with this project; I thank him for his enthusiasm and energy. My book would not have seen the light without the dedicated help of various librarians. Special thanks to Diana Yount, Archives and Special Collections, Franklin Trask Library, Andover Newton Theological School; Keith Longiotti, North Carolina Collection, University of North Carolina at Chapel Hill; Abraham Parrish, Map Department, Yale University Library; and Diane E. Kaplan and Steve Ross, Manuscripts and Archives, Yale University Library.

I am very grateful to the anonymous readers who reviewed my manuscript for the University of Wisconsin Press, as well as to William Broadway, Nicole Kvale, Katie Malchow, Adam Mehring, Nicole Rodriguez, and Raphael Kadushin at the Press. I heartily thank Amy Johnson, who copyedited the manuscript with meticulousness and intelligence. I am also deeply grateful to William L. Andrews for his enthusiasm, counsel, and example.

Above all, I thank Aya and Amy for their love and support.

I dedicate this book to the memory of my friend William Nathan Alexander.

Chronology

1770	Omar is born.
1807	Omar captured in Bure at age 37.
1819	Two-page manuscript sent to Francis Scott Key, accompanied by letter by a John Louis Taylor of Raleigh, North Carolina. A melding of Hadith and Qur'anic excerpts. Taylor requests an Arabic Bible for *Moreau*.
1823–35	Isaac Bird (1793–1876) in Syria.
1825	*Christian Advocate* article, "Prince Moro."
1828–30	Jim Owen governor of North Carolina.
1828	Omar's Lord Prayer, opens "thus you pray you."
1831	Omar's *Life*.
1835	Lahmen Kebby liberated.
1836	Omar's manuscript mailed to Kebby; Kebby passes it to Theodore Dwight (1838), founder of the American Ethnological Society.
1837	Ralph Gurley, secretary of the American Colonization Society (ACS), reports Kebby is about to embark for Liberia at New York, in a letter from Augusta, Georgia. Gurley meets Omar and mentions Jonas King. Gurley reports in the *African Repository*.
1844	William B. Hodgson's *Notes on Northern Africa, the Sahara, and Soudan*.
1847	*Wilmington Chronicle* article refers to seventy-five years old "Monroe."
1848	Alexander Cotheal's translation (first translation).
1857	*Surat al-Nasr*
1854–9	Rev. Mathew B. Grier expresses doubt regarding Omar's conversion.
1857	Dred Scott decision.
1862	Isaac Bird's letter to Dwight regarding manuscripts (second translation).
1863	Dwight informs Rev. Daniel Bliss, president of the Syria Protestant College, of Omar's Arabic; Bliss offers to send Bibles printed in

Beirut to Liberia. They send Bibles with Arabic message in the fly-leaf requesting information from tribes.

1863   Death of Omar ibn Said. He is buried in plantation's graveyard of General Owen.

1864   Dwight's essay on Kebby in *Methodist Review.*

A Muslim American Slave

Introduction

"Arabic Work," Islam, and American Literature

Ala Alryyes

In 1831, Omar ibn Said, then a slave in the United States, was asked to write "his Life."[1] Omar composed his narrative in North Carolina, having escaped from Charleston, South Carolina, where he was sold in 1807 after his transportation from Africa. His *Life*, which he wrote in formal Arabic in a West African (Maghribi) script, is a unique text.[2] Several North American slaves wrote in Arabic.[3] Some of these writings even became famous in their writers' lifetimes. Nor were these Arabic texts limited to the United States. Muslim slaves came to other regions of the Americas, leaving Arabic writings in Panama, Colombia, Trinidad, Mexico, and especially Brazil, where Muslim slaves led the great revolt of 1835 in Bahia, in which "the bodies of the fallen rebels . . . [carried] Muslim amulets with prayers and passages from the *Koran*."[4] Omar's manuscript is of singular importance, however, not only because it is the only extant autobiography written by a slave in Arabic in the United States, but also because it thus raises the question of how the *Life* compares to the numerous narratives written by escaped slaves. In this introductory essay, I investigate these connections both by analyzing Omar's text and by exploring the influence of the network of contemporary "editors" and translators who worked on Omar's text. Omar's *Life* straddles two genres: the familiar slave narrative and the largely unfamiliar genre of Arabic writings collected and circulated by Omar's editors.

Omar ibn Said was born to a wealthy father around 1770 in a West African region then called Futa Toro, between the Senegal and Gambia rivers. After early Qur'anic schooling during which he learnt Arabic, Omar became a teacher. He was enslaved in 1807, possibly in the course of a military campaign, and transported to Charleston.[5] According to Thomas Parramore, "after working for two years as a slave in Charleston and on a South Carolina rice plantation, he escaped in 1810 and made his way to Fayetteville, N.C., near which he was recaptured" and jailed. Omar became the property of General James Owen of Bladen County, and later moved with the Owen family during the Civil War to "Owen Hill, a Cape Fear farm formerly the home of General Owen's brother, Governor John Owen," where Omar died in 1864.[6] Omar came to the attention of the Owens after filling "the walls of his room [jail cell] with piteous petitions to be released, all written in the Arabic language."[7] Omar's facility with Arabic made him a local celebrity. A contemporary account notes that he "wrote in a masterly hand, writing from right to left, in what was to [local observers] an unknown language."[8] Another article describes him as "an Arabic scholar" and stresses his devoted reading of his Arabic Bible. Allan Austin observes a similar strategic hybridity: "Omar was regularly willing and able to reassure all visiting Christians that he was a true convert, as he often wrote in Arabic what he called 'The Lord's Prayer' and the Twenty-Third Psalm."[9]

The *Life* was neither Omar's first nor his only Arabic text. In addition to this 1831 manuscript, a number of his other Arabic inscriptions survive. In a particularly moving example, intimating his desire to go home, Omar writes in 1819, "I want to be seen in a place called Africa in a place called Kaba in Bewir."[10] It is this knowledge of Arabic that set Omar apart then and continues to matter prominently in our reappraisals of him.

The *Life* is not our only source for the life of Omar ibn Said. There are, as the discussion above shows, many other references to him—Omar lived for about thirty-five years after he wrote his autobiographical narrative—ranging from newspaper stories to accounts of personal interviews, published nineteenth-century scholarly articles, and family archives. Many who met him noted his distinguished bearing. "Meroh's fingers are very well tapered. His whole person and gait bear marks of considerable refinement," wrote a visiting pastor.[11]

This volume, it is worth stating at the outset, is a critical study of the text and contexts of Omar's *Life* and not a biography of the man. Omar's literacy enabled his own words to figure centrally in what we know about a former slave. Most slaves, after all, left no written records. But Omar's narrative is also an important instance of what Werner Sollors has called "the long multilingual history in all genres of American literature."[12] Omar's knowledge of Arabic plays a part in American literary and cultural history. As this essay shows, the *Life* is a document no less fundamental to the reconstruction of a singular life than to the understanding of an important, and largely unstudied, episode in the annals of American slave thought.

Like the meaning of all texts, Omar's autobiography's meaning—its place in literary history—varies with time, context, and readers. This book includes and

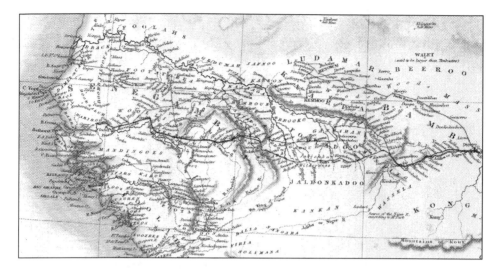

Western Africa, 1929 (Map Collection, Sterling Memorial Library, Yale University)

considers the work of three sets of interpreters. Omar's Arabic literacy made his story important for a number of nineteenth-century missionaries, ethnographers, and intellectuals, a group that will prove central to our understanding of his *Life*. This first set of readers is explored in this essay, while my translation and the "Contextual Essays" belong to our own period and reflect our literary and cultural interests. An earlier translation of Omar's *Life*, published in 1925 in the *American Historical Review*, reveals different concerns but more importantly, perhaps, a different cultural viewpoint. One distinction between the two translations is worth stressing. Despite the earlier translation's editor's learning and knowledge of the context of Omar's autobiography evidenced in his introductory text, it is clear that the editor does not see the "literate Mohammedans" he introduces in the company of Omar as part and parcel of America's antebellum literature.

Remarkably, the most recent round of attention paid to the *Life* resulted from the manuscript's reappearance after having vanished for most of the twentieth century. The editor of the 1925 text states that the manuscript was in the possession of the curator of the American Numismatic Society in New York. It later disappeared. It was discovered in an old trunk in Virginia in 1995 and purchased at an auction by a private collector who displayed it in various libraries and museums and made it accessible to scholars.[13] The manuscript's discovery also caused a flurry of recent media attention.[14] In our age of desktop publishing and memory sticks, we take for granted the ability of almost any writer to preserve and disseminate his or her words in permanent forms. Yet all students of literature and history ought to keep in mind that this ghostly permanence of the written word is recent. Omar wrote his narrative almost forty years before the invention of the typewriter, and he wrote it by hand on fragile paper in a single manuscript.

Omar ibn Said begins his *Life* with a surprising demurral: "I cannot write my life, I have forgotten much of my talk as well as the talk of the Maghreb."[15] His apology deceptively echoes the rhetorical claim that the author is not up to the task, a de rigueur flourish that accompanies many a literary preface. Yet, the knowledge of Arabic the narrative reveals sets Omar apart from other early African American writers of slave narratives in that Omar had the language—was literate—*before* being captured, and wrote in a language that most of his enslavers could not read. Unlike Olaudah Equiano, author in 1789 of the first slave narrative by an African, or Frederick Douglass, whose autobiography stages his learning to read and write as a primal scene ironically related to his slavery, Omar did not learn the language in which he wrote his autobiography during his captivity.[16] Furthermore, his 1831 North Carolina autobiography exposes these conventions' regional and historical specificity by not subscribing to the implicit codes of African American first-person narratives written in the North.

The *Life*'s manuscript consists of twenty-three pages of quarto paper, of which pages six to thirteen are blank. Its content falls into two parts: first, a chapter from the Qur'an, *Surat al-Mulk*, followed by Omar's autobiography, which opens with his aforementioned apology to a "Sheikh Hunter," who had presumably asked Omar to write an account of his life. The narrative relates Omar's previous life in West Africa: "My name is Omar ibn Said; my birthplace is *Fut Tur*, between the two rivers," the Senegal and the Gambia (*Life*, 61). Omar describes his education, which lasted for twenty-five years under three Muslim sheiks, and the grisly circumstances of his capture in 1807: "Then there came to our country a big army. It killed many people. It took me and walked me to the big sea, and sold me into the hands of a Christian man" (*Life*, 61).[17] The text is silent on the horrors of the notorious Middle Passage; the author mentions only that it lasted a month and a half.

Landing in Charleston, Omar is sold to his first American owner. Although he is laconic when he describes the progress of his slavery, Omar's poignant awareness of his linguistic alienation and subjection marks his memories: "In a Christian language," he writes, "they sold me" (*Life*, 63). The "evil" Johnson, Omar's first owner, puts him to work in the fields despite the fact that Omar is a "small man who cannot do hard work" (*Life*, 63).

Omar escapes, walking north and hiding for about a month. He enters what he calls "houses" to pray, though it is not clear what he means by this term. Were they buildings, churches, or homes of sympathetic Southerners that served the

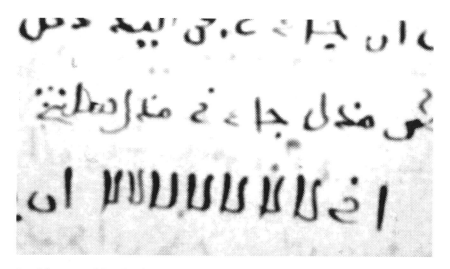

Detail from page of Omar's *Life*, page 64 in this volume (courtesy of Mr. Derrick Beard)

Underground Railroad? Omar is soon spotted by a young man on horseback, who denounces him to his father. A posse eventually captures Omar, walks him to Fayetteville, North Carolina, and imprisons him in the Cumberland County jail for "sixteen days and nights" (*Life*, 63). He is eventually sold to Jim Owen, the brother of a future governor of North Carolina, but, before that, "a man called Mitchell" tries to buy Omar and asks him if he wants to "walk to a place called Charleston," scene of his earlier suffering. The question terrifies Omar; his horror, and the enduring memory of his first owner's cruelty, are reflected in his unequivocal refusal: "No, no, no, no, no, no, no" (*Life*, 65).

Omar concludes his autobiography with an encomium to his owner: "I continue in the hands of Jim Owen, who does not beat me, nor calls me bad names . . . During the last twenty years I have not seen any harm at the hands of Jim Owen" (*Life*, 79). He also extols Owen's progeny: "This is a good generation. Tom Owen and Nell Owen had two sons and one daughter . . . This generation is a very good generation . . . O, people of America, do you have . . . such a good generation that fears Allah so much?" Reading Omar's praise, as well as other contemporary reports of how they treated their slave, it appears that the Owens were kind masters. Yet, Omar was never freed; and any statements regarding his masters must remain under this shadow.[18]

Omar ibn Said's *Life* is short. He did not raise a family in the United States, perhaps too aware that masters usually disregarded slaves' familial ties and often separated children and spouses. His *Life* does not elaborate on his family life in Africa, neither further describing his birthplace after he mentions his kidnapping, nor openly condemning slavery or graphically dwelling on his own tribulations. Yet in this introduction, I will argue that, though unsatisfying in its autobiographical desiderata, short on what we have come to expect of both a slave narrative and a self-fashioning confession, Omar's autobiography is richly rewarding when one attends to its two semantic mines. First, it is a text written by a captive under conditions of persecution, which, in the words of a recently influential American political philosopher, "gives rise to a peculiar technique of writing . . . in which the truth about all crucial things is presented exclusively between the lines."[19] Second, Omar's manuscript and other contemporary accounts refer to readers, connections, and networks of transmission that ought to influence our view of how Omar's contemporaries "read" his text. These sources sketch a map of individuals who not only struggled with the legacy of the slavery they had imposed on Omar and his kin, but whose writings, both earnest and blinkered, sincere and cynical, underscore the multiple facets of Omar's identity: an Arabic speaker, a Muslim, a Fulbe, a West African informant, an American slave, an anti-Colonizationist. Their texts limn a man whose autobiography is tied to Liberia, to North Carolina, to Lebanon—a part of the master narrative of American slavery but also informing the less well-known master narrative of early nineteenth-century Arab *Nahdah*, or renaissance, in Ottoman Syria.

Who asked Omar to write his life story; and what was the purpose of an autobiography that almost no American could read? Languages make communities, but which kind? Some thinkers still live with the Romantic notion of an organic bond between subjectivity and a mother language, tying tribe and tongue. The American notion of multiculturalism has, if anything, given a twist to this belief, implicitly assuring us that "respect" for the many ethnic and racial cultures that compose the United States is compatible with English monolingualism and linguistic assimilation.[20] What "multiculturalism apparently did not do," asserts Margaret Talbot in a recent issue of *The New York Times Magazine*, "was promote the study of other languages, or indeed of other cultures."[21] But the writing and reading of Omar's *Life*—as well as the production of other non-English literary texts in the United States—demonstrate that more interesting and vital than the Herderian *Volk* of native speakers is that group of persons who find themselves connected through their often imperfect knowledge of a second language, one which they learn with effort and for a purpose. The existence of this linguistic community underscores another facet of the story of Omar's manuscript. It points to a second-order narrative not of the content and Arabic textual analysis of

Omar's *Life*, but of the community of men who "read" Omar's *Life*, each in his own manner. In order to read Omar's text, we ought to take into account Roger Chartier's seminal examination of the "history of the book," which stresses the commonalities and mysteries of how readers in other times have read the same set of words we might be reading today.

Omar's manuscript includes a title page that offers clues to its "readership," pointing to a network of correspondents who performed "work" on his text, translating and circulating it, marveling at its strange but "noble" language; and who occasionally were even able to read it themselves, but most often heard about it from others. This title page, written in English in a different hand and probably a later addition, identifies the author as "Omar ben Saeed, called Morro, a Fullah slave, in Fayetteville, N.C., owned by Governor Owen." The narrative, continues the inscription, was "Written by himself in 1831 & sent to Old Paul, or Lahmen Kebby, in New York, in 1836, Presented to Theodore Dwight by Paul in 1836, Translated by Hon. (Alexander) Cotheal, Esq., 1848." Theodore Dwight (1796–1866), who graduated from Yale in 1814, studying "under his uncle Timothy, whose memory he revered," was a Free-Soiler opposed to the spread of slavery.[22] According to J. Franklin Jameson, a founder of the American Historical Association, who wrote the introduction to the first published translation of Omar's manuscript in 1925, reproduced in this volume, "Dwight was deeply interested in West Africa, and made special efforts to obtain information from or respecting Mohammedan slaves in the United States."[23]

Jameson presented a translation made by the Reverend Isaac Bird (1793–1835)—"who had been for a dozen years (1823–1835) a missionary in Syria"—with whom Dwight corresponded. Bird's translation was revised, added Jameson, "through the kindness of Dr. F. M. Moussa, secretary of the Egyptian Legation in Washington."[24] A Yale and Andover Seminary graduate and one of the so-called Seven Pioneers, who were early New England missionary envoys of the American Board of Commissioners for Foreign Missions (ABCFM) to Ottoman Syria, Bird carried out what he called "Bible Work in Bible Lands." But not only New Englanders influenced the "reading" of Omar's narrative. The manuscript title page does not mention the Georgia-born Orientalist William B. Hodgson, who traveled in West Africa and studied the local vernaculars' relation to Arabic.[25] Bird's and Hodgson's writings shaped the views of Dwight, who had orchestrated the commissioning and circulation of several Arabic texts in the United States.

My essay takes up some of these extra-textual meanings of Omar's narrative. Omar ibn Said's *Life*, as thin a confession and record of self-making as it might appear to a contemporary reader, is actually a thick text linking Arabic speakers and readers in distinct locales, language "workers" who performed different tasks

Daguerreotype of Isaac Bird (Isaac Bird Papers, Manuscripts and Archives, Yale University Library)

Isaac Bird's 1822 certification by the American Board of Commissioners for Foreign Missions as an "approved missionary . . . sent forth to communicate the blessings of the gospel to the ignorant and destitute" (Isaac Bird Papers, Manuscripts and Archives, Yale University Library) with Arabic. I would like to introduce the term "Arabic work" here, taking my cue from the title of Isaac Bird's book, to underscore that these men, including Omar, were non-native users of Arabic and to highlight the global role of Arabic: as an African language and an American language and, of course, as the language of the Arabs, Muslim and Christian.

Although no autobiography is a transparent account of its writer's life—for the literary act of emplotment simultaneously separates and ties lived experience and artful narration—slave narratives were multiply mediated. Slaves had no direct access to printers and publishers; they wrote because they were persuaded to by white "editors," who often co-wrote the slaves' autobiographies and had them published with one or more prefaces written by the editors. As John Blassingame asserts in relation to the historical value of the testimony of former slaves: "Since the antebellum narratives were frequently dictated to and written by whites, any study of such sources must begin with an assessment of the editors."[26] Literary analysts, of course, do not regard these writings as evidence to be sifted, but our definition of the slave narrative genre must still incorporate the roles of its editor(s) and readers. Insightful interpreters of African American first-person narratives have recently drawn our attention to the strenuous conditions of authorship under which the ex-slave authors labored. It would seem that, when it came to telling their stories to white audiences in the North, the authors' troubles began *after* their escape. Scandals impugning the authenticity of two narratives of escaped slaves published in the North in the 1830s had threatened "the continuing viability of the slave autobiographies."[27] Northern emancipators and editors of slave narratives became fixated on ensuring that they directed, edited, and circulated "true" stories. Having good intentions, they cherished the power of slave narratives to aid them in the battle for emancipation, but having a racially tainted moral view of blacks, they saw the free slaves as potential liars, whose published writings or speech ought to be protected for the cause from the slaves' own exaggeration and trickery. In a letter to the *Emancipator*, a leader of the American Anti-Slavery Society warned Northern readers that "Simple-hearted and truthful, as these fugitives appeared to be, you must recollect that they are slaves—and that the slave, as a general thing, is a liar, as well as a drunkard and a thief."[28]

Ann Fabian has observed how the editor of James Williams's *Life*, for instance, sought to convince his readers of the ex-slave's reliability by employing "one of the key devices of authenticity: he assured readers that Williams had successfully repeated the events of his life on several occasions, and he listed in a footnote the names of 'gentlemen, who have heard the whole, or part of his story, from his own lips.'"[29] Fabian stresses that the slave narratives "did not always end with the narrators' incorporation into a free society; they ended with narrators on the lecture circuit—no longer enslaved, to be sure, but suspended somewhere between slavery and freedom."[30] The "unfinished" form of the ex-slaves' narratives invited audiences to participate with probing questions. The ex-slave had to prove that he recognized "the difference between truth and lies . . . between experience and invention," often authenticating his suffering by displaying his scarred body. These displays were negative rituals, seeking to reduce the slave's narrative to a mold that "guaranteed" its truth, not to elaborate on his or her captivity, an elaboration that no doubt would vary with the ex-slave's historical and cultural background.

Such ceremonial strategies of authentication—repeating the same sequence of events, sticking to the facts of slavery, attestations by Southern whites—sought, critics now emphasize, to overcome these narratives' most authentic truth: the fact, unknown to these white editors, that "absolute, 'perfect' truth, could not be used to measure the value of Afro-American autobiography since the demands of truthfulness and self-preservation were often at odds in the experience of blacks in America."[31] Although, as William Andrews states, "experienced abolitionists recognized that first-person narration, with its promise of intimate glimpses into the mind and heart of an escaped slave[,] would be much more compelling to the uncommitted mass of readers than the oratory and polemics of the anti-slavery press," these editors and handlers steered the ex-slave toward rhetorical strategies that obscured him or her "behind the universally applicable facts of slavery."[32]

One is struck, then, by the fact that, but for the literary evolution of the Black memorialists themselves and their growing consciousness of the moral and rhetorical worth of their particular experiences, slave narratives would have continued to privilege the editors' attestations of the slave's veracity—what Robert Stepto has called an "authenticating machinery"—over the slave's own words.[33] These authenticating strategies and documents were elements in a developing literary template from which the ex-slaves were discouraged to deviate. The editors lacked interest in and regard for their charges' various histories and backgrounds. A "truthful" slave narrative was an account that stuck to the "facts," eschewing subjective judgments or feelings. As both Stepto and Andrews show, however, African American writers resisted, often quietly, but occasionally openly and explicitly, such a depreciation of their particular experiences: the "two alienating alternatives" of impersonal objectivity or unreliable subjectivity."[34]

Omar's narrative is a product of its context; and in order to understand its nuances, we must avoid a Whig history of American slavery that divides the United States before the Civil War into abolitionists and slaveholders. As Thomas Hietala insists, "[T]he concern with slavery must also be seen as part of a far more pervasive national concern with determining the future of the black man in a predominantly white society."[35] Many Americans accepted that slavery was a doomed institution but did not support emancipation. In 1817 some of them founded the American Colonization Society (ACS), an organization dedicated to solving both the slavery problem and the "problem" of the incompatibility of the races by encouraging free blacks to emigrate to and colonize what is today Liberia.[36] Rejecting or eschewing a condemnation of the institution of slavery itself or calls for the immediate emancipation of all slaves, these intellectual reformers—missionaries, politicians, and journalists—sought to prove the intellectual and moral worth of particular slaves, a worth that they argued made them unfit for slavery. When it came to Omar ibn Said and other Muslim slaves, the ACS intellectuals, influenced by their ethnographic interests, saw that value in these slaves' literacy, education, and, surprisingly, in their Islamic religion.

In ironic contradistinction to the Northern abolitionists' benevolent but tepid autobiographical templates, these Southern Colonizationists, racialist as their emigration endeavors were, attempted to win masters to their cause and more manumitted slaves for Liberia by interviewing slaves, and collecting, and publishing slaves' distinctive experiences or particular histories. Their fascination with certain distinguished blacks, free or slave, often led these Colonizationists to solicit, circulate, and publicize their biographies and histories.[37] Although this valuing of literacy echoes the beliefs about the escaped slaves in the North—that "the slave's acquisition of [his] voice is quite possibly his only permanent achievement once he escapes"—the differences between abolitionists' and Colonizationists' viewpoints are significant.[38] That Omar and other Arabic-writing slaves were masters of alphabets and words that their masters ignored, or admired and marveled at, endowed them with more independent and impressive cultural glamour. It also tied them to a nascent American ethnographic interest in Africa, its states, culture, and politics, which provided a counterbalance to the familiar racist notion of the continent as a land of undifferentiated "darkness." These conditions also meant that their writings were read and circulated in a manner different from English-language slave writings in the abolitionist North.

It is to the writings of Theodore Dwight, a member of the New York Colonization Society and a founder of the American Ethnological Society, that we must turn to appreciate how Omar's narrative bolstered an increasingly influential argument linking literacy, Islam, and manumission. In his 1864 "Condition and Character of Negroes in Africa," Dwight chastises his countrymen: "The people of the United States are doubly blamable for their false views [of the condition of the Negro race in Africa] because we owe debts to that portion of our fellowmen for ages of wrongs inflected on them . . . and because we continue to deny them intellectual faculties and moral qualities which the Creator has bestowed on the entire human family."[39] As Dwight saw it, however, Africans varied in their degree of progress and civilization. Although "millions of pagan negroes, in different parts of that continent, have been for ages in practice of some of the most important arts of life, dwelling in comfort and generally at peace," we "find between the tenth and twentieth degree of latitude, five or six kingdoms, most of which have been in existence several centuries . . . mostly under the influence of Mohammedan institutions, [that enjoy] fixed laws, customs, arts, and learning; and, although abound[ing] in errors and evils on the one side, [they] embrace benefits on the other which are not enjoyed by such portions of the negro race as remain in paganism." Dwight posits an ambiguous relation between Islam in West Africa and Christianity: although the two religions are antagonistic, Islam is laying the ground for wide-scale Christian missionary work and conversions. For, on the one hand, Islam is not foreign to the "true religion." "The Koran," asserts Dwight, invoking an argument then gaining force in African missionary circles, "has copied from the Hebrew scriptures many of the attributes of God and the doctrines of morality, with certain just views of the nature, capacities, and duties, and destiny of man." The literacy that Muslims propagate, on the other hand, and the fact that many formerly strictly oral African languages have been "reduced to writing books that have been translated from the Arabic" provide missionaries with an unexpected gift: an alphabet for local languages into which the Bible might be translated and disseminated.[40] "The truth . . . hitherto unknown . . . [is] that large portions of the African Continent lie open to the access of Christian influences through channels thus prepared by education."[41]

This advanced literate culture, Dwight argues, ought to influence Americans' views of blacks and slavery. "It certainly will bring more compunction to the hearts of the humane among us," Dwight moralizes, "to learn that the race which we have been accustomed to despise, as well as to ill-treat, still lie under a load of evils perpetuated by the prejudices prevailing among many of the most enlightened Christians." Dwight's next sentence neatly encapsulates the Colonizationists' rhetorical strategy: "It will be surprising to be told that among the victims of the slave-trade among us have been men of learning and pure and exalted characters, who have been treated like beasts of the field by those who claimed a purer religion."[42] As I stated above, the American Colonization Society (ACS) highlighted slaves' learning in order to support manumission and emigration.

In his *Methodist Quarterly* essay, published almost twenty-seven years after he had received Omar ibn Said's *Life*, Dwight perhaps explains the mystery of the *Life*'s moment of writing: "The writer [Dwight] has found a few native Africans in the North, of whom only three were able to write . . . from 'Morro,' or

'Omar-ben-Sayeed,' long living in Fayetteville, N.C., he procured a sketch of his life in Arabic."[43] The ACS may have commissioned and certainly disseminated Omar's *Life*, an autobiography that though "unfiltered by abolitionist rhetoric," as Sollors has written, nevertheless rhetorically supported what its readers saw as the preferred solution to slavery.[44] The journey of Omar ibn Said's manuscript demonstrates that he was fairly famous, a testament to the fact that, as Lamin Sanneh points out, "the colonization movement had availed itself of the most sophisticated techniques of mass propaganda, of a web of interlocking local agents fanning out and cohering in one active, coordinating site, with an uncanny ability to pick on the right subject for maximum public effect."[45] Several evangelists and members of the ACS, including Ralph Gurley, its influential secretary, met Omar and wrote about him. Their accounts debated his conversion to Christianity. Although I could not identify the "Sheikh Hunter" who had presumably asked Omar to write his story, Dwight, a member of the New York Colonizationist Society and the ACS, approached Omar and/or his masters and requested his writings. As the title page of Omar's narrative makes clear, his *Life* was sent to Dwight, via "Old Paul," the slave name of Lahmen Kebby, or Lamine Kebe, a former slave who was manumitted in 1835 after being in bondage for about forty years.

In addition to his ethnographic and Colonizationist interest in an educated, Arabic-speaking slave, Dwight—and the ACS—kept contemporary events in mind. It seems significant that Omar was asked to pen his narrative in 1831, for this was the year of the fiery rebellion of Nat Turner—in the words of William Styron, "the only effective, sustained revolt in the annals of American Negro slavery"—which shook Virginia and the slave-owning South in general.[46] It was the quiet before the storm that unnerved slave owners: "It will thus appear, that whilst every thing upon the surface of society wore a calm and peaceful aspect; whilst not one note of preparation was heard to warn the devoted inhabitants of woe and death," marveled magistrate T. R. Gray, who recorded Turner's confession, "a gloomy fanatic was revolting in the recesses of his own dark, bewildered and overwrought mind schemes of indiscriminate massacre to the whites."[47]

As terror swept the South in the wake of "the Turner Cataclysm," were Southern Colonizationists and sympathetic slave owners looking for a "good" slave narrative to counter the effects of Turner's dangerous example?[48] The results of Turner's rebellion were striking. Scores of blacks were murdered by vengeful vigilantes; decisions were made to "bar black preachers and to forbid public funerals without a white man present to officiate." More telling reactions included "laws against teaching slaves to read and write," as well as increased attention to the religion of slaves and "encouragement of oral instruction of slaves in the Christian faith."[49] It is difficult to believe that, in this charged atmosphere, "Sheikh Hunter's" request was unrelated to the repercussions of the rebellion.

Omar's narrative may have been related directly to the violent events of August 1831. It is possible that Omar's relatively kind owners wanted to dissuade more hard-line masters from further acts of cruelty. An autobiography by a "good" slave might prove that not all (literate) slaves were contemplating murder, that Turner's was an isolated example. Another possibility, not unrelated to my first speculation, emphasizes the Kebe connection.[50] The Arabic manuscript was sent to Kebe a year before the latter emigrated to Liberia, supported by the American Colonization Society. It is conceivable that the ACS wanted to capitalize on the Turner aftermath to support its policy of encouraging former slaves to emigrate. The ACS received some support in the Upper South; were its members collecting information from Southern plantations with sympathetic owners? As mentioned above, the Reverend Ralph Gurley, a prominent member of the ACS, met and interviewed Omar in 1837, six years after he wrote his narrative. Earlier connections are likely. Perhaps the "Sheikh Hunter" who asked Omar to write his "life" was a member of the ACS, who had heard of Omar through Kebe, and traveled to North Carolina to meet him. (Indeed, based on recent evidence, it seems possible that "Sheikh Hunter" was the "Reverend Eli Hunter, from New York, who is known to have toured North Carolina for the ACS in 1839." It is possible that he had met Omar earlier.)[51] Hunter might have been sent by Dwight or later informed Dwight of the existence of an Arabic-writing slave. Other ACS members spoke of Omar emigrating to Africa much earlier than 1831. Omar's two-page 1819 manuscript mentioned above was sent by sitting Chief Justice of the North Carolina Supreme Court John Louis Taylor to Francis Scott Key, of "Star-Spangled Banner" fame and a prominent Colonizationist, accompanied by a letter in which Taylor informed Key that Omar might not mind being sent back to Africa.[52] Key, the chief agent of the ACS auxiliary in Baltimore, painted bright tableaus of Africa for the Colonization movement, speaking of "spires of temples glittering in the sun . . . harbors shaded by the snowy wings of departing and returning commerce." "Africans," he prophesied, "would point to the star-spangled banner in deepest gratitude for the blessings of civilization."[53]

However, I believe that only if one stays on the surface of Omar's autobiography can one think of Omar's text as a "safe" pro-slavery story, praising his good life in America. In what follows, I will argue that Omar's *Life* is replete with concealed utterances that not only hide his views from potentially dangerous readers, but also test the readers, sifting them into those who can interpret the utterances and are, therefore, within Omar's circle—his community—and those who cannot decipher them, and are outside it. Before beginning his own life story, Omar interpolates a chapter from the Qur'an, choosing *Surat al-Mulk* as a kind of prologue. Omar's choice of this *sura*, or Qur'anic chapter, seems deliberate and highly significant in the context of a slave narrative. The first two *ayas*, or verses, in *Surat al-Mulk* read:

> Blessed be He in whose hand is the *mulk* and who has power over all things. He created death and life that He might put you to the proof and find out which of you had the best work; He is the most Mighty, the Forgiving One. (*Life*, 51)

The noun *al-mulk* comes from the tripartite Arabic root *malaka*, meaning both "to own" and "to have dominion."[54] The title of the *sura* is, therefore, the perfect allusion to slavery: absolute power through ownership. The verb and the noun conflate persons and things. The *sura* contends that it is God who is the owner of all and everything; through his choice of *Surat al-Mulk*, Omar seems to refute the right of his owners over him, since only God has the *mulk*, the power and the ownership.

There is a striking similarity between Omar's counter-argument from divine possession and the anti-slavery language employed in David Walker's *Appeal in Four Articles; Together with a Preamble, to the Coloured Citizens of the World* (1829). Walker, suggestively modeling his appeal on the American Constitution, analyzes slavery and concludes that modern American bondage is far crueler than that of the Greeks and the Romans. Jeremiah-like, he asks for divine punishment "in behalf of the oppressed."[55] In the *Appeal*'s preamble, Walker, "displaying a vehemence and outrage unprecedented among contemporary African American authors," challenges the right of whites to hold slaves because "[a]ll persons who are acquainted with history, and particularly the Bible . . . who are willing to admit that God made man to serve Him *alone*, and that man should have no other Lord or Lords but Himself—[would also agree] that God Almighty is the *sole proprietor* or *master* of the WHOLE human family."[56] This argument against slavery is very similar to the one Omar esoterically presents when he cites the aforementioned *sura*.

Walker published his *Appeal* in 1829; its power and popularity made him a hated man in the South. By the end of December 1829, "new laws had been passed quarantining all black sailors entering Georgia ports and punishing severely anyone introducing seditious literature into the state. . . . In late March 1830, a number of copies were distributed to several black longshoremen in Charleston by [a] white seaman. . . . In the same month, four blacks were arrested for circulating numerous copies in New Orleans. . . . By early 1830, the coastal South was in an uproar over the circulation of the *Appeal*."[57] There were efforts in Virginia to bar black ministers from preaching to their own people because slaveholders feared some would use the *Appeal* as their text. Walker himself worked feverishly to distribute his book; in a letter to a Mr. Thomas Lewis in Virginia, for instance, he advises that "The price of these Books is Twelve cents pr Book,—to those who can pay for them,—and if there are any who, cannot pay for a Book give them Books for nothing."[58]

Remarkably, Omar might well have known of the *Appeal*'s existence. The book was distributed widely in North Carolina, Walker's native state. Walker sent two hundred copies to a Wilmington slave, who was "allowed to keep a little tavern, which he then secretly used to circulate the *Appeal*," until he was denounced and arrested. On August 7, 1830, John Owen, Governor of North Carolina and brother of Omar's master, received a letter from a police agent informing him of

> a pamphlet published by one David Walker of Boston, treating in most inflammatory terms of the conditions of the slaves in the Southern states, exaggerating their sufferings . . . and underrating the power of the whites . . . and inculcating principles wholly at variance with the existing relation between the two colors of our Southern population. An investigation of the affair has shewn [*sic*] that the author had an Agent in this place [a slave] who had received this book with instructions to distribute them throughout the State particularly in Newbern, Fayette, & Elizabeth. The agent for the distribution of this seditious book is now in Jail [but] keeps us ignorant of the extent to which the books may have circulated.[59]

Omar ibn Said could not have read Walker's book; he never learnt to read English.[60] Walker, however, was aware of his potential audience's limitations and asked his educated readers to "cast your eyes upon the wretchedness of your brethren" and to read the book to unlettered blacks.[61] The *Appeal*'s oratorical vigor and repetitions indicate that Walker "expected the book would be read aloud to large groups of illiterate blacks far more often than read silently."[62] It is possible that Omar, knowing of the book's existence, might have had parts of the *Appeal* read and explained to him and have been influenced by Walker's reasoning to preface his own *Life*, written two years after the *Appeal* was published, with that Qur'anic *sura* he certainly knew.[63] Yet, a contrary interpretation is possible. For what if a particularly Muslim argument against slavery, which finds its expression in *Surat al-Mulk*, has spread orally and was incorporated by Walker in his *Appeal*? It is noteworthy that Walker interpolates several verses from the Bible into his tract and draws the reader's attention to the appropriate chapter and verse. However, when he mentions that "God Almighty is the *sole proprietor*," Walker does not refer to the Bible. Was this, then, an argument that he coined or a borrowing from *Surat al-Mulk*? Could Walker, an indefatigable anti-slavery polemicist, have met any Muslims from whom he might have learnt a new anti-slavery argument?[64]

David Walker's connections with Muslim slaves are more than possible, it turns out; they are documented. Although Walker, a prominent community activist in Black Boston, never met Omar, he toasted another famous Muslim ex-slave who wrote in Arabic. In 1828, newly freed, the sixty-five-year-old Abd al-Rahman Jallo, of Natchez, Mississippi, set out on an exuberant farewell journey, "conducted on steamboats and stage coaches . . . through three New England states," passing through New York City, and, eventually by boat, to Norfolk, Virginia, and then to Liberia. He had by now embraced the legend that made a "Prince" out of him, traveling in an opulent costume. Like Omar, he was interviewed by ACS members Francis Scott Key and Ralph Gurley; and like Omar, he seems to have equivocated with the ACS. In hopes of helping his family, as Austin observes, "[Abd al-Rahman] promised ministers he would preach Christianity, promised merchants he would promote trade, and showed promise of being very helpful to the American Colonization Society (ACS) in its goal of exporting freed black people to Liberia."[65] Yet, to his credit, he also joined the African American opposition to the ACS in fêtes arranged by black leaders in Boston, New York, and Philadelphia. Both Northern and Southern newspapers followed his American travels. *The American Traveller* reported in October 1828 that "the colored inhabitants of the city [Boston] gave a public dinner to their fellow countryman the Prince Abdul Rahman."[66]

Walker, Second Marshal of the Boston gala, whose later *Appeal* shows him an inveterate enemy of Colonization, toasted Abd al-Rahman in words that anticipate the relation between God and justice that he eloquently stresses in his *Appeal*: "Our worthy Guest, who was by the African's natural enemies torn from his country, religion and friends; and in the very midst of Christians, doomed to perpetual though unlawful bondage, may God enable him to obtain so much of the reward of his labor, as may purchase the freedom of his offspring."[67] In his *Appeal*, Walker decried the chasm between Christianity as precepts and as a historical institution that supported slavery and upheld oppressive states.[68] He observed how ecclesiastical authority has buttressed evil practice: "The wicked and the ungodly, seeing their preachers treat us with so much cruelty, they say: our preachers, who must be right, if any body are, treat them like brutes, and why cannot we?"[69] He also approached religion comparatively, emphasizing ethical practice over theology. "The Pagans, Jews, and Mahometans," he noted, "try to make proselytes to their religion, and whatever human beings adopt their religions they extend to them their protection. But Christian Americans not only hinder their fellow creatures, but thousands of them *will absolutely beat a colored person nearly to death, if they catch him on his knees, supplicating the throne of grace.*"[70] It is not unlikely that Walker would have engaged Abd al-Rahman in conversation regarding anti-slavery arguments. If there were one Qur'anic text that Abd al-Rahman would have remembered as refuting the rights of slave owners, it would have been *Surat al-Mulk*. In addition to conversations, Walker, a voracious reader, might also have had access to George Sale's 1734 English translation of the Qur'an.[71]

Literary resistance is more difficult than just writing fighting words. When it came to slave writing, "changing the joke and slipping the yoke" was not easy, for to begin to write is often to follow a literary model. But "[w]hat terms for order were available to [early slaves] as they looked upon chaos?" wonders Houston Baker.[72] It is ironic, though not surprising, that, as Baker argues, the earliest slave poets imitated the Calvinist literary forms of their enslavers, casting their experiences as spiritual autobiographies. These models were not always felicitous. In search of salvation, the slave poet Jupiter Hammon, for instance, "spent so much time in heaven that he scarcely had time to think of the demands of the tangible world in which he lived."[73] His spiritual imitations ignored the crucial struggle in the here and now that lent enormous energy to the Puritans' quest for heavenly election. Walker's great text, however, subverted a model even as it adopted it. As William Andrews argues, "David Walker's *Appeal* represents a signal act of Afro-American misreading of [a] quasi-sacred American text, the US Constitution. . . . Thus as black autobiography necessarily establishes its relationship to the essential texts of oppressive American culture, it also becomes a revisionistic instrument in the hands of its greatest practitioners."[74] It is intriguing to reflect that Walker might in fact have used the Qur'an, a sacred text seemingly extraneous to America, to misread the central sacred text of America. But whether or not the anti-slavery argument from possession that Walker employs is in fact related to Omar's, both Arabic-speaking slave and free anti-slavery activist enlisted the contradictory powers of sacred texts: their aura that places them above dispute, but also their eloquence that elicits, even compels, mimicry and identification.

In a rare instance, on the penultimate page of his *Life*, Omar explicitly condemns the injury done to him: "I reside in our country here because of the great harm" (*Life*, 77). Throughout the autobiography, however, Omar's views are most often expressed esoterically; that is, they are intended for a group of readers within a circle.[75] In introducing the 1925 translation, included here, Jameson writes, "The earlier pages of the manuscript are occupied with quotations from the Koran which Omar remembered, and these might be omitted as not auto-biographical . . . but it has been thought best to print the whole."[76] I disagree with the judgment that these quotations are not autobiographical, as is made evident by my preceding analysis of the concealed purpose of the *sura*'s incorporation and its possible connection to Walker's anti-slavery argument. Jameson's view is predicated on the assumption that the writer is free to deliver his message directly. Such freedom is denied the slave, for revolt, even in the eyes of the most benign of masters, is an unpardonable offense.

How does Omar openly address his enslavers? There are in his narrative two moments of his encounter with the Other's language that seem to me to function as polar opposites. The first occurs when he describes the earliest moments of his capture. "In a Christian language," he writes, "they sold me." At that moment perhaps the entire crime is encapsulated in the foreignness of that incomprehensible language that turns a man into chattel in America. Later, however, Omar addresses his audience: not only the Sheikh Hunter who asked him to compose the narrative, but indeed the "people of America, all of you" (*Life*, 67). This is a moment of reaching out. Between these two instances, however, Omar's language is rich in hidden meanings, with nuances that seem to separate him from the white community of his owners, to guard his identity even as a slave.[77] As James Scott asserts, "Most of the political life of subordinate groups is to be found neither in overt collective defiance of powerholders nor in complete hegemonic compliance, but in the vast territory between these two polar opposites. . . . By the subtle use of codes one can insinuate into a ritual, a pattern of dress, a song, a story, meanings that are accessible to one intended audience and opaque to another audience the actors wish to exclude."[78] These double utterances—such as his use of *Surat al-Mulk*—do more than enable Omar to conceal his deeper message; they permit him to reconstruct a community that is not the one circumscribed by slavery. Similarly, other forms of slaves' literary production, for example, Negro spirituals, "became an almost secretive code for the slave's critique of the plantation system, and his search for freedom in this world."[79]

Omar uses *Surat al-Mulk* not only to argue against slavery, but also to cast a symbolic role for himself in that resistance. Prominent in that *sura* is a verse that describes the suffering and torture in hell (in Arabic, *juhanam*) of those who did not accept the message of the prophet Muhammad:

> When they are flung into its flames, they shall hear it roaring and seething, as though bursting with rage. And every time a multitude is thrown therein, its keepers will say to them: "Did no one come to warn you?" "Yes," they will reply, "he did come, but we rejected him (as a liar) and said: 'God has revealed nothing: you are in grave error.'" And they will say: "If only we had listened and understood, we should not now be among the heirs of the Fire." (*Life*, 51–53)

Who is the "one" who came—in the original Arabic, *natheer*, "he who warns"? On the surface, it is Muhammad who brought Islam as the warning to the *Kuffar*, the infidels, who denied him. Islam, however, like Christianity, is a proselytizing religion. Theoretically, it is the duty of Muslims to call others to Islam, to warn them of the consequences of not believing. Therefore, in the hidden meaning, Omar ibn Said is the one who brought the message, suffered for it, and was denied. And those who will confess their errors and suffer judgment are not only the unbelievers among Muhammad's tribe of *Quraish* in Mecca—for whom the original *sura* was intended—but also Omar's unbelieving owners.

That Omar did not choose this particular *sura* at random, but, as I have argued, to fit the context of his life, is supported by evidence from his other writings. Although Omar wrote *Surat al-Mulk* more than once—for example, earlier in the 1819 letter sent to Francis Scott Key—he inscribed other Qur'anic *suras* to suit other occasions. Remarkably, his last known writing, in 1857, is *Surat al-Nasr*, the Victory:

> When God's help and Victory come, and you see people embrace God's faith in multitudes, give glory to your Lord and seek His pardon. He is ever disposed to mercy.[80]

This *sura* can be interpreted as an invocation to God: a wish for victory, for liberation from slavery, which calls into question Omar's seeming contentment in the hands of the Owens. Yet, what is fascinating is the occasion of the delivery of this *sura* to Muhammad, namely the prophet's victory over his own tribe and his triumphant, and merciful, entry into Mecca in 630 AD. Muhammad's victory and return to Mecca, the native city from which he had escaped eight years earlier under cover of night to flee death, was vital to the survival and spread of Islam. Again, Omar analogically links himself with Muhammad, setting his own hoped-for vindication in parallel with Muhammad's actual victory.

Omar's education in an Islamic *madrasa*, or religious school, would have comprised not only the study of Qur'anic exegesis, but also the memorization of large tracts of the Qur'an, if not the whole text. Omar says that he "sought knowledge" under the direction of various Sheiks for twenty-five years. Therefore, it is not unlikely, even after twenty-four years in America, for him to remember much of the Qur'an in the original words, which he had undoubtedly recited many times. Most of *Surat al-Mulk*, which Omar interpolates in his *Life*, is perfect in its reproduction of the Arabic Qur'anic text. I have relied on it as a Rosetta stone to resolve certain problems inherent in reading Omar's idiosyncratic orthography. Yet, as I remark in my translation of Omar's *Life*, there are some errors in Omar's *sura*. This is proof, I think, that Omar was writing from memory and not copying.

Omar's latest known extant writing: a copy of *Surat al-Nasr* (but with a spurious emendation), 1857 (North Carolina Collection, University of North Carolina at Chapel Hill)

Such a judgment is supported by contemporary witnesses' observation that Omar owned a copy of an English Qur'an, not an Arabic one.[81]

To sum up, Omar's deliberate choice of the two *suras* above—*al-Mulk* and *al-Nasr*—and the fact that he remembered them, can best be understood as occasional: Omar writes from memory the *suras* that fit the context within his *Life*. My interpretation of the double significance of the Qur'anic fragments that Omar often inscribed into his writings constitutes the first attempt to link these fragments to the context of their utterance in Omar's life.[82] Just as he analogically figures Muhammad's suffering or victory to stand for his own experiences, Omar reenacts the occasional nature of the delivery of the Qur'an to Muhammad. For, as Muslims believe, the Qur'an was not delivered to the prophet in one installment. Nor was it, like the New Testament, a compilation of various accounts of Muhammad's life and words. Instead, as the example of *Surat al-Nasr* demonstrates, the *suras* that Muhammad received from God addressed the specific contexts and occasions of their delivery.

In regard to questions of conversion, it is well to keep in mind that resistance to slavery did not always entail rejecting the master's religion. It could frequently mean, as is vividly manifested in the case of Nat Turner, interpreting the master's religion in a manner he did not like. Omar's use of the Qur'anic chapters in occasional contexts raises fundamental issues regarding his resistance to slavery and changes the terms in which the matter of his conversion should be cast. Did Omar, as some of his contemporaries claimed, convert to Christianity, or did he, as others suspected, remain a Muslim? In addition to *Surat al-Mulk* cited in his *Life* and *Surat al-Nasr* later, other evidence supports the belief that Omar did not abandon the "blood-stained Koran" to worship "at the feet of the Prince of Peace."[83]

Another example of Omar's persistence in his Islamic beliefs comes after he has praised his masters because "They are good men for whatever they eat, I eat; and whatever they wear they give me to wear." He writes:

> Before I came to the Christian country, my religion *was* [emphasis added] the religion of Muhammad, the prophet of Allah, may Allah bless him and grant him peace. I used to walk to the mosque [*masjid*] before dawn, and to wash my face, head, hands, feet. I used to hold the noon prayers, the after-noon prayers, the sunset prayers, the night prayers. I used to give alms [*zakat*] every year in gold, silver, harvest, cattle, sheep, goats, rice, wheat and barley—all I used to give in alms. I used to join the *Jihad* every year against the infidels [*Kuffar*]. I used to walk to Mecca and Medinah as did those who were able. (*Life*, 67–69)

The message of the passage is ambiguous, however, for two reasons. Omar does not use the Arabic past construction (*kana*) to render the past state of his religion (the italicized "was"), matching the time of the adverb "before." The literal translation into English would thus read: "Before . . . my religion is the religion of Muhammad." So either this is a grammatical error or an indication that indeed his religion was, and is, that of Muhammad.

Furthermore, it may seem on the surface that Omar is relating what he used to practice back in Africa, before converting to Christianity. It is more probable, however, that he is enumerating some of the tenets and duties, or *arkan* and *furod*, respectively, of Islam, rather than asserting what he had done. It is unlikely that he "used to walk to Mecca and Medinah," or that he gave alms in all of nine different products. Maybe he performed the pilgrimage once; he probably gave alms of money and livestock. However, the language he employs echoes that of an instructional book. I think Omar is mixing a description of his particular deeds, such as praying five times a day, with catechizing, such as "one should go to Mecca and Medinah if able." It is courageous for a slave to catechize his native religion where, on the surface, he is supposed to be extolling his conversion.

Omar probably did not convert in the sense that Gurley (and probably the Owens) believed. He retained the faith that he brought with him from Africa. Yet, as Genovese acutely observes: "From the moment the Africans lost the social basis of their religious community life, their religion itself had to disintegrate as a coherent system of belief. From the moment they arrived in America and began to toil as slaves, they could not help absorbing the religion of the master class."[84] Omar may, I believe, have escaped losing his religion because his Islam allowed him some leeway in dealing with Christian efforts to convert him. A Muslim believes that Christians and Jews are people of the book, that Moses and Jesus were precursors of Muhammad. Omar, in fact, copied out various Christian pieces, such as the Lord's Prayer—which he includes in his *Life* and interjects on other occasions— and the Twenty-third Psalm, "The Lord is my Shepherd." Neither of these pieces, however, contradicts Islamic beliefs. Omar never, for example, alludes to the godhead of Jesus or to his crucifixion, which Islam rejects. He also, I think, was able to improvise with his knowledge of Islamic and Christian texts. I have puzzled over the part of his *Life* in which Omar lauds his masters by enumerating their progeny. Does he intend to praise them by referring to their lives using the conventions of an Arabic-Islamic autobiographical subgenre, the Islamic *Sira*—an exemplary life narrative—which "document[ed] the subject's career from birth to death using eye-witness testimony and lists of teachers, students, family members, and works composed"?[85] Or, should we, recalling Omar's assertion that his masters read the Bible to him "a lot," rather believe that he here imitates the Biblical style of chapter 5 of Genesis, "the book of the generations of Adam" or chapter 10 in which we read, for instance, that "The children of Shem; Elam and Asshur, and Arphaxad, and

Lud, and Aram . . . These are the families of the children of Noah, after their generations"? Omar had met an Arabic scholar and missionary, Jonas King, a colleague of Isaac Bird, years before he wrote his *Life*. It is possible that King translated the word "generation" to him in this Genesis verse, as *jeel*, the word that Omar uses above (*Life*, 71). Both of these answers are perhaps partial. Most likely, Omar utilized all the religious texts and traditions available to him to survive slavery.

Abducted in the waning days of the Atlantic slave trade, Omar—whose English remained elementary—may have held aloof from American-born African American slaves, or he may have been snubbed by a Creole black population now thoroughly in control of the New World's language and customs. In reading his Arabic Bible and going to church, Omar may have sought out spiritual Christians to make up for the loss of community inevitable for a slave, as Genovese asserts. Yet, it is also likely that his religion did not disintegrate because he used it as a resistance mechanism. That Omar narrates his tale of slavery gives the reader a rare glimpse of a slave's agency, an account largely missing from the historical record. That Omar wrote in Arabic complicates the view that all literate slaves in the United States owed their literacy to their masters. It also places Arabic in the linguistic map of America, making it an "American" language.[86]

As I argue above, translating Omar's narrative also entails recovering both the context of its writing and that of its multiple "readings." Theodore Dwight's aforementioned 1864 *Methodist Quarterly* essay exhibits the many African writings in Arabic he collected and had translated by his friends and colleagues, giving clues concerning the network of texts to which Dwight considered Omar's *Life* to have belonged. Incorporating lengthy English translations by Isaac Bird of several Arabic manuscripts "written in Monrovia, by a negro from the interior at the request of President Benson of Liberia," the essay ends with an interpolated translation of Omar's text, "extracts from a letter sent to 'Old Paul' by a venerable old slave, long known at Fayetteville, N. C., and there called 'Morro,' in reply to one addressed to him."[87] Dwight includes most of Alexander Cotheal's translation of Omar's autobiographical narrative—the translation mentioned on the manuscript's title page. Dwight knew Kebe ("Old Paul"), a Muslim who hailed from Omar's province, as well as other blacks who wrote in Arabic. Thus, although Omar himself might not have known other Muslims besides Kebe (Dwight calls him Kibby), the whites who solicited these Arabic texts corresponded with and often knew one another. In other words, one ought to investigate these Arabic texts' relations not directly, but by studying the purposes and reflections of those agents who requested and circulated them for related political and cultural reasons. Omar's text is exemplary in this regard, "commissioned" as it was both to assuage slaveholders' fears in 1831 and to investigate and broadcast Omar's education and African background. Cotheal's esteem of Omar, whose narrative "affords an idea of the degree of education among Moslem blacks, when we see a man like this able to read and write a language so different from his own native tongue," echoes Dwight's linking of culture and multilingualism above.[88] That this ethnological argument is also one for cultural equality—and a veiled call for manumission—is also asserted by Omar's first translator: "Where is the youth, or even the adult, among the mass of our people who is able to do the same in Greek or Latin?"[89]

Although Dwight was a travel writer—who once recounted his journeys in Italy—he did not travel in Africa. His position as a member of the New York Colonization Society and a founding member of the American Ethnographic Society (AES), however, put him at the center of a network of what I earlier called "Arabic workers," a community of professional and amateur scholars who either knew Arabic or performed "metareadings" in which they interpreted Arabic texts and speculated on the political, cultural, and moral significance of literacy in Arabic and other African languages in the United States and abroad. We saw how Omar's narrative found its way to Dwight and how he in turn sent it out to be translated, first to Alexander Cotheal and later to Isaac Bird (Appendix 2). It is important to stress, however, that Dwight's central concern was not slave autobiographies in our modern sense of the genre—the unfolding of singular experiences and the slaves' or ex-slaves' subjective interpretation of these experiences—but rather these black men's particular educations. Dwight's interest perhaps explains why Omar opens his *Life* with an account of his teachers and Qur'anic education. It is also why Dwight devotes the bulk of his discussion of the three literate slaves he mentions in his essay to Lahmen Kibby, Old Paul, whom Dwight interviewed and saw as an exemplar of a highly developed, but, for Americans, unknown African educational system.[90]

That Dwight was a member of the American Ethnographic Society, dedicated to inquiring "into the origin, progress, and characteristics of the various races of man," intimates that he probably saw Omar's text as both a linguistic and an ethnographic object. The AES's records show that members discussed but did not always print their papers. In volume 2 of the *Transactions of the American Ethnographic Society*, Dwight published expositions and summaries of the philological and ethnographic writings of other travelers.[91] His ethnographic opinions of Africa and Africans are likewise a digest of the consensus of the AES at this time. The linguistic twist in Dwight's opinions on West Africa discussed above echoes the lectures and books of another member of the AES, the Orientalist William B. Hodgson, who also described the Fulbes' culture, emphasizing their education, Islamic religion, and Arabic literacy. Dwight's *Methodist Quarterly* essay in fact refers to Hodgson, "a gentleman who made exertions in the South [to collect Arabic texts written in America] but was compelled to abandon the undertaking in despair, although he had resided in Africa, and had both the taste and the ability necessary to success."[92] Hodgson seems to have acted as a link in that network of ACS and AES correspondents who attempted to collect texts by blacks in the South.

After his return to the United States, Hodgson—who served as Consul of the United States in Tunis—published in 1844 *Notes on Northern Africa, the Sahara, and Soudan*, which clearly influenced Dwight's 1864 essay. One essay in Hodgson's text, "Nations of Soudan: Fellatahs or Foulahs" highlights—in more starkly racist terms—the cultural differences between African tribes, correlating skin color with signs of progress and civilization. According to him, "The Foulahs [Omar's and Kebe's tribe] are *not* negroes. . . . All travellers concur in representing them as a distinct race, in moral as in physical traits."[93] Hodgson, like Dwight, ties the Fulbes' Islam to both their literacy and their higher level of civilization: "In Central Africa, education and religious instruction are entirely in the hands of the Mohammedans. The Koran has introduced its letters, where it has been adopted, as the Bible from Rome, has substituted its letters, for the alphabets of Europe. Let not the humanizing influence of the Koran, upon the fetishes, greegrees, and human sacrifices of pagan, homicidal Africa, be depreciated."[94]

Hodgson's book is a curious amalgam of ethnographic and sociological observations, speculations on the origin and progress of races and their relations, and accounts of missionary activities in Africa, all subordinated to philological analyses of several African languages and their dialects. (It also includes several lists of words and their translations.) Hodgson mapped "races" and their geographic movements linguistically. Thus the great migrations that slavery imposed on African men and women are visible in his writings—unlike in those of the universalist Northern abolitionists. Analyzing a tablet—under the provocative title "A Numidian Inscription in America?"—found with an ivory-bejeweled skeleton in the Ohio river, Hodgson wonders: "Who was the gorgeous chieftain whose engraved signet was found by his side? Did he come from the Canary Islands, where the Numidian language and characters prevailed? Could any of the Carthegenian or African vessels, which usually visited the Fortunate or the Canary Islands, have been carried by accident to the New World?" Despite these uncertainties, Hodgson anchors his speculations in the archaeological-linguistic evidence, tying a "foreign" language and his "native" country: "The peopling of America is quite as likely to be due to Africa and Europe, as to Asia."[95] This unlikely survival of languages in America occupies him in his essay on the "Fullahs" as well.

To that essay, "*Fellatahs or Foulahs,*" in *Notes*, Hodgson appended a letter that he had received from James Hamilton Couper, a plantation owner in Georgia, of whom Hodgson had first heard through an account of a fossil discovery on the latter's land. Couper's interests, it seems, combined zoological and human artifacts.[96] His letter, which Hodgson read to the membership of the American Ethnographic Society, describes the native country as well as the education of one of his slaves, "Tom, whose African name was Sali-bul-Ali [and who] was purchased about the year 1800, by my father, from the Bahama islands." Couper reports that Tom was a native Foulah, to whom "Timbucto, Jenne and Sego, are familiar as household words."[97] He "possesses great veracity and honesty. He is a strict Mohametan; abstains from spirituous liquors, and keeps the various fasts, particularly that of Rhamadan. . . . He reads Arabic, and has a Koran in that language, but does not write it." Couper echoes Hodgson's and Dwight's praise for the effect of Islam on character, adding that "Tom was promoted to head-driver of this plantation in 1816; now has under him about four hundred and fifty negroes." Tom's literacy is also due to his religion, as "All the children are taught to read and write Arabic by the priests (Maalims). They repeat from the Koran and write on board, which when filled, is washed off."[98]

Couper's narrative supports Hodgson's conjectures; but beginning as it does with Tom's purchase and aspiring to scientific objectivity regarding the writer's declared property, it ought to remind us of the curious context in which American ethnography developed. Couper's account is nevertheless valuable because it shows that the AES's views regarding Islam seem to have been held by sedentary plantation owners and not only by traveling ethnographers and missionaries. It also demonstrates that slave owners paid attention to their slaves' "native" languages. But Hodgson and Couper, unlike Omar's masters, had a subtler understanding of Bul-Ali's language, realizing that despite his Arabic, his native tongue was a Foulah language, and appending a glossary of "the vocabulary of the language of Massina, in Soudan, as taken from driver Tom." Imitating Hodgson, Couper in this letter provides the "expert" with an example in which the "peopling of America" might be unearthed linguistically. If geology tied Georgia's current rocks to their ancient progenitors, philology operated spatially, tying local and distant languages, unearthing human connections that compelled apologetic defenses of slavery, and revealing a global—not always unambiguous—set of conflicts that slavery imported to the United States. Bul-Ali's contempt for his "infidel" co-slaves echoes the unfortunate prejudice that Islam, a remarkably egalitarian religion, paradoxically created in West Africa.[99]

But, despite Hodgson's prolific writings—as well as the energetic pronouncements of the AES and related groups, such as the American Philological Society—American investigations at this time were subordinate to European studies, Europe having the advantage of its centuries of imperial philological scholarship and linguistic expertise. Hodgson, for instance, discusses the Berber dialects and acknowledges the "Berbero-Arabic dictionary" published by the Geographic Society of Paris and mentions that another "dictionary of this language has just been published by order of the minister of war, [. . .] France having conquered the extensive territory of Algeria [and] is now pushing forward her victorious legions."[100] This American marginality in contemporary foreign affairs, and the fact that American travelers and anthropologists lacked the military and political muscle that backed their European counterparts, provided— consciously or unconsciously—a convenient alibi: the South was the passive recipient of its current "race problem." Hodgson shared with AES members a lack of interest in analyzing contemporary American events' influence on "races" and their current state of affairs. This anthropological point of view, concerned with analyzing and describing the status quo, was a "scientific" counterpart of the ACS's slavery rhetoric: the Colonizationists condemned slavery in moral terms, but rather than discussing the South's specific historical agency, they moralized that the South was a victim to the "problem of slavery." The Colonizationists' remedy, emigration, was less altruistic than they allowed, however. Several years before Hodgson's text appeared, Tocqueville's astute eyes had recognized the truth: "In the US people abolish slavery for the sake not of the Negroes but of the white men."[101]

In his essay on the Fulbe cited above, Hodgson notes the remarkable extent of the Fullahs' power and unity in Africa, the fact that, although they comprise four independent political states, these states are related by their religion, culture, and language. He also presents a brief history of Christian missions to Fullahs. Echoing the ACS's hopes for emigrants' potential to spread Christianity and civilization in Africa—expressed in the magniloquent and somewhat self-serving words of Francis Scott Key we read above—Hodgson ties that proselytizing effort to Arabic literacy but paints the conflict with Islam in more militant terms than Dwight does. His global view of the relation of literacy to religious influence bears quoting in full:

> In Africa . . . the Gospel now stands face to face with the Koran. There, the two confluent tides of religious instruction from the West and the East meet. From the Senegambia to the Equator, along this vast extent of the coast, Christianity has her stations; and she opposes by *her Book*, the further advance of the *Moslem's Book*. The colony of Liberia is an advanced post of Christianity. The Arabic Bible is eagerly sought and gratefully received by the tribes; and it has been brought to the Western coast, by merchants and pilgrims from Egypt across the whole breadth of that

continent. *Let, therefore, the Gospel be disseminated in Arabic characters,
into whatever languages the pious zeal of missionaries may be able to translate
it*, since Arabic letters have, for centuries, been introduced into Africa.[102]
(emphasis added)

Hodgson here forcefully provides the critical terms that Dwight draws upon
twenty years later: the advantage of Arabic literacy and its alphabet to Christian
evangelization and the fact that Islam is not wholly benighted, sharing as it does
with Christianity "the names of Abraham and Moses . . . and an abhorrence of the
bloody rites and sacrifices of the Pagans." In fact, the Fullahs would support one of
the key roles that missionaries and Colonizationists saw for Liberia: "If Sultan
Bello should be induced to abolish the slave trade, the most efficient means will
have been discovered for its entire suppression. . . . To a certain extent, the
Mohammedans go along with us. Their civil code, contained in the Koran, forbids
the *enslaving of a man born of free parents, and professing the Mussulman religion;*
nor can a Mussulman be reduced to slavery in *any case.*"[103]

Hodgson's, and later Dwight's, racialist "scientific" belief in the superiority of
"non-black" to "black" civilization and practices is a "high culture" counterpart of
what shapers of popular culture—journalists and itinerant Colonizationists and
community leaders—expressed using the familiar commonplaces of romance.
They portrayed Omar and other distinguished captives or slaves in the United
States and elsewhere as "Arabs," "princes," and the like, wreaking havoc with
ethnography and history. An 1825 article in the *Christian Advocate*, for instance,
speculated that "[Moro] was a prince in his own country . . . [and] his intercourse
with the Arabs has enabled him to write and speak their language with the most
perfect ease."[104] *The Wilmington Chronicle* reported in 1847 that "Monroe, the
servant of General Owen . . . belonged to the Foulah [Fulbe] tribe in Africa [who]
are known as the descendants of the Arabian Mahomedans who migrated to
Africa. . . . Monroe is an Arab by birth, of royal blood."[105] Other exposés stressed
Omar's Arabic language skills rather than, or in addition to, his alleged "Arabian"
origins. In fact, more than any other Arabic-speaking slave, Omar was the subject
of several reports that emphasized, even fetishized, his Arabic knowledge. Thus,
an 1854 article in the *North Carolina University Magazine* reported that "Finding
some coals in the ashes, [Uncle Moreau] filled the walls of his room with piteous
petitions to be released, all written in the Arabic language. The strange characters,
so elegantly and correctly written by a runaway slave, soon attracted attention,
and many of the citizens of the town visited the jail to see him."[106]

Omar, a literate but pious and peaceful man, might have become important
to the American Colonization Society—as I speculated earlier—to counter the

influence of Nat Turner's 1831 rebellion on slavers' views of manumission. Several prominent Colonizationists, including Francis Scott Key, an early advocate of the cause, and Ralph Gurley, the Secretary of the ACS, visited and wrote about him. In his report to the board in 1837, Gurley gave a summary of the progress of various auxiliary Colonization societies in the South, including Virginia (the scene of Turner's uprising) and North and South Carolina. Gurley's analysis shows that he did not advocate emancipation on universalist grounds, but rather made the case that "numerous free colored persons of respectable intelligence and moral character . . . after careful reflection . . . have resolved to remove to Africa." According to him, these future emigrants will abet the "awakening of a new and extended interest throughout a large portion of the State in the prosperity of the African Colonies and in the diffusion, through them, far over the barbarous territories of Africa, of knowledge, civilization, and the inestimable blessing of the Religion of Christ."[107]

Proselytizing for emigration meant that the more religiously-minded Colonizationists, unlike the ethnographers described above, were less exacting in reporting the black men's words, often co-opting their voices into a collective missionary discourse extolling key Christian messages. Thus, although one reporter mentions Omar's rudimentary English, the Secretary of the ACS ventriloquizes a passionate, and fluent, exhortation in English by Omar to his countryman "Paul," encouraging Colonization:

> Moro is much interested in the plans and progress of the American Colonization Society. . . . His prayer is that the Foulahs and all other Mohamedans may receive the Gospel. When, more than a year ago, a man by the name of Paul, of the Foulah nation and able like himself to understand Arabic, was preparing to embark at New York for Liberia, Moro corresponded with him and presented him with one of his two copies of the Bible in that language. Extracts from Moro's letters are before me. In one of them he says "I hear you wish to go back to Africa; if you do go, hold fast to Jesus Christ's law, and tell all the Brethren that they may turn to Jesus before it is too late. . . . I have been in Africa; it is a dark part. I was a follower of Mahomet, went to church, prayed five times a day. . . . The Lord put religion in my heart about ten years ago. . . . I turned away from Mahomet to follow Christ. . . . I loved and served the world a long time, but this did not make me happy.[108]

Omar's letters to Paul have not been found. Did they exist at all? Even if they did—and Gurley is the only witness—they would have been written in Arabic, which Gurley did not read. Gurley's "translation" reads less like the words of a real convert—"I loved and served the world a long time"—and more like a universal spiritual autobiography ascribed to a convert. Omar's actions, however, matter more than his words. The aforementioned *North Carolina University Magazine*, in fact, reports that "When Dr. Jonas King, now of Greece, returned to this country from the East, he was introduced in Fayetteville to Moreau. Gen. Owen observed an evident reluctance on the part of the old man to converse with Dr. King. After some time he ascertained that the only reason of his reluctance was his fear that one who talked so well in Arabic might have been sent by his own countrymen to reclaim him, and carry him again over the sea. After his fears were removed, he conversed with Dr. King with great readiness and delight."[109] Further, despite his "interest," Omar told Gurley that "He thinks his age and infirmities forbid his return to his own country." Omar's real or cagey illness is one instance of a major problem the Colonizationists faced. It seems that, Gurley's sugarcoating of Liberian emigration not withstanding, Omar, like many others, hated the idea. He might have been quite relieved that it was "Paul" who emigrated and that his own support of the "progress" of the ACS cost him no more than one Arabic Bible.

If the Colonizationists imagined a voluntary mass emigration of black men and women to their "home" in Africa that would undo the damage of forced immigration, they were frustrated. ACS members and supporters had many explanations for the lukewarm interest of black men and women, including the fact that many slaves, such as Omar, liked their masters and refused to leave.[110] Nor did their emigration scheme find the support of the Federal government. Soon, the United States was to face the enormous challenge of Western expansion, which changed the face of slavery in the United States. Even as the May 1845 meeting of the New England Anti-slavery Society welcomed Douglass's *Narrative* as "The New Anti-Slavery lecturer," the annexation of Texas into the United States had been settled: two consecutive American presidents, John Tyler (1841–45) and James K. Polk (1845–49), had ardently advocated it. Expansion bolstered slavery. Northern and Southern supporters of annexation "embraced it as a means for easing the tension over slavery while simultaneously providing a method for the ultimate removal of the entire black population from the United States. Texas, they argued, would attract free blacks and slaves, and its location would facilitate the eventual exodus of all blacks to Central and South America."[111] A new slave state answered the "Negro question," providing an alternative to abolitionism and Colonization.

But perhaps what most doomed the latter is the fact that the American Colonization Society was powerfully denounced and opposed by Northern abolitionists. The year Omar wrote his *Life*, 1831, was also the year in which William Lloyd Garrison issued his manifesto demanding total and immediate emancipation. Today most Americans are more familiar with the great emancipator and his views than with the American Colonization Society, several of whose members we have already met. Yet the 1830s witnessed an important struggle between Garrison and those intellectuals, mostly from the middle Southern states, who sought an end to slavery but believed that a large number of free blacks would threaten society. Consonant with Tocqueville's astute observations, Henry Clay, the "Compromiser," questioned the effect of emancipation: "What is the true nature of the evil of the existence of a portion of the African race in our population?" he asked. "It is not that there are *some*, but that there are so many among us of a different caste, of a different physical, if not moral constitution, who never could amalgamate with the great body of our population."[112] In his study of the relation of American colonization to Liberia, Lamin Sanneh reports that a founding member of the ACS thought that "colonization would offer a route by which free blacks could be taken away, and with them a source of insecurity for slave owners who feared that free blacks fomented trouble among slaves by running errands, circulating rumors, aiding and abetting runaway slaves, and acting as 'depositories of stolen goods.'"[113]

"Colonization," as Eric Burin stresses, "lurked behind the era's great debates."[114] As I have argued, the ACS carved a significant middle place between abolition and slavery. The historian Early Lee Fox makes the important case that "[i]t was a great struggle between the Garrisonians and the Colonizationists. . . . It was the first American civil war on the subject of slavery. . . . In the New England section, it was the Abolition sentiment; in the Middle Section, it was the Colonization sentiment; in the Southern section, it was the positive pro-slavery sentiment. The outcome of that struggle is of deep significance; for when the end of it had come, the middle section had disappeared, as far as its importance as a 'buffer state' of public sentiment is concerned. Henceforth there was to be North and South."[115] Although Fox is an apologist for Colonization, his book fleshes out the struggles, sometimes righteous, often morally suspect, of a number of Southern intellectuals who generally believed that "a general, immediate, and unconditional emancipation of all the slaves in the Union was impracticable and undesirable."[116] As it sought a compromise between immediate abolition and slavery, the ACS, however, ultimately found itself between a rock and a hard place: "The bitterest opposition Colonization ever encountered came from the Abolitionists of William Lloyd Garrison's school. Next to these, its fiercest enemies were the slaveholders of the Southeastern States."[117] Its adherents finally gave up their effort to influence American slavery in favor of concentrating on Liberia and its anticipated role in stopping the slave trade. But short-lived as the ACS's heyday might have been, and alien as Fox's regret is that "It's a pity Garrison could not realize that there were actually anti-slavery slaveholders in the South," the ACS's middle strategy was fundamental to the interest we saw above in black writing and culture.

It is this literacy and culture that Colonizationists desired for their Liberian colonists. And it is within this constellation of Arabic writings and Islamic cultural achievements that they placed Omar's narrative, tying together poetics and politics.[118] Omar's Islam and knowledge of Arabic ennobled him in the eyes of Dwight, Hodgson, Bird, Cotheal, and others: the beliefs of these scholars and Colonizationists are important to a fuller understanding of Omar ibn Said's autobiography's place in the corpus of American slave literature. For, whereas English-language slave narratives were co-written and circulated by abolitionists, most of the men who read and wrote about Omar's *Life* were partisans of Colonization.[119] The latter, however, were obviously familiar with the slave narrative genre. When "Sheikh Hunter" asked Omar to write his narrative, he translated this genre's name, "life," to the Arabic literal equivalent, *Hayat*, as Omar's response makes clear.[120] Omar, and his interlocutor, do not use the Arabic generic name for autobiographical narratives, *sira* or *tarjama*. Yet, in recounting his "name and ancestry . . . a catalog of teachers . . . travel and pilgrimage accounts, and collections of entertaining or illuminating anecdotes," Omar seems to follow the conventions of an Arabic *tarjama*, as Dwight Reynolds enumerates them.[121] His Arabic slave narrative, furthermore, illuminates the international reach of slavery and the manner in which opinions regarding literacy and Islam in Africa influenced how Americans saw the mental capacities of slaves and the conditions under which they lived in the United States.

Omar's *Life* remaps English-language slave narratives because it brings to light the unfamiliar expectations and interpretations of a different set of readers and also because, in recording Omar's reflections on his identity, his open praise of his masters, and his hidden resistance, it performs different rhetorical gestures and autobiographical symbolic actions that highlight his African education and his lingual alienation. The *Life*'s English title page clearly demarcates his editors' words from the Arabic narrative that follows. James Olney, in contrast, alerts us to the many instances (such as the "true" narratives of William Wells Brown and Solomon Bayley) in which "the style of the abolitionist introducer carries over into a narrative that is certified as 'Written by Himself.'"[122] More importantly, if mere episodic narration becomes autobiography when memory not only recalls past events but also recasts them into a significant pattern, as Olney argues, then literacy has distinctive symbolic meanings in Omar's construction of his life's story. Omar's education and his religion are intertwined. His learning is both an individual achievement and a quality of his African society: When he describes his Islamic education, Omar inscribes the names of his African teachers in his narrative (*Life*, 61). In contrast, Frederick Douglass famously paints his literacy as first a gift of his mistress, who begins teaching him his "A, B, C," and later, after his master forbids her, a reaction to his master: "What he most dreaded, I most desired."[123] Literacy is a mystical discovery, "explaining dark and mysterious things." As Sollors puts it, Douglass represents "the drama of his struggle against slavery in metaphors of Christian rebirth."[124] Omar's narrative has no such triumphant plot or primal scene, yet the fact that he wrote in Arabic complicates the path that American slave narratives trace between a slave's literacy and his identity. Still, these autobiographies are both valuable instances of "the expression in words of the tragic experiences of the Negro race," which, W. E. B. Du Bois insisted, "is to be found in various places."[125]

All scholars contributing to this volume have in their published writings treated slavery in its international context; their essays here investigate the multiple facets of Omar's *Life*. Allan Austin, whose two earlier books have provided a rich record of the lives and writings of several enslaved African Muslims in antebellum North America, comments on Omar's possible interactions with other Muslim slaves and describes the available writings and their provenance. He makes the case that these Arabic and English texts are diverse, encompassing memoirs, historical narratives, and accounts of African education. Austin discusses the "diary" of Bilali, a Muslim slave on Sapelo Island, Georgia, which, until the rediscovery of Omar's *Life*, was perhaps the most intriguing example of Arabic writing by a slave preserved in the United States. Austin's essay finally adumbrates several other shorter Arabic writings of Omar ibn Said.

Sylviane A. Diouf has stressed elsewhere that "America may have demanded generic African laborers, but Africans did not sell other Africans indiscriminately. Specific events led to the deportation of specific peoples, either as individuals or as groups."[126] In her essay here, she examines the West African political and military context of slavery and brings to light the historical genealogy of the various Islamic reform movements in West Africa, emphasizing the resistance of Muslim African political leaders to the Atlantic slave trade. Although Islam did not allow the enslavement of Muslims by other Muslims, as Diouf states, this precept was frequently violated, with prisoners of war supplying the Atlantic slave trade. Diouf theorizes that Omar's sale into "the big ship on the big sea" was the result of such a conflict. Her essay also reminds American scholars of slavery of the importance of French scholarly sources, especially in regions like Senegambia in which the French led the slave trade.[127] The imperial states' future power not withstanding, Diouf's essay shows that French and British slave purchases were constrained, sometimes controlled, by the Muslim leaders' policies.

Robert Allison's essay analyzes the United States' political and diplomatic "macro" relations with Muslim North African states. Examining both literary and historical sources, Allison contends that even though victorious against the North African "piratical" states of Algiers and Tripoli in the early nineteenth century, Americans confronted uncomfortable parallels between Barbary Coast slavery and their own. He describes a fascinating satire by Benjamin Franklin in which America's great Enlightenment man mocked pro-slavery congressmen, praising them using a speech that North African kidnappers of Americans had used to justify slavery. Allison draws on a wealth of fictional, diplomatic, and autobiographic texts to illustrate how writers dramatized the lessons that Americans learnt from captivity's "inverted world." His essay also highlights how the early "globalist" take on slavery that was tending to its abolition was overwhelmed with a strictly isolationist, Southern-oriented view after the invention of the cotton gin.

Arguing that "the dawn of Islam in the Americas and its association with Africans have yet to receive the scholarly attention that is merited," Michael Gomez's seminal "Muslims in Early America," reprinted here, makes a strong case for the presence of a large number of Muslims in America by analyzing historical records on both sides of the Atlantic. Gomez examines the "ethnic and cultural make-up of the African supply zones, the appearance of Muslim names in the ledgers of slave owners and in the runaway slave advertisements in the newspapers, references to Muslim ancestry in interviews with ex-slaves" as well as slave holders' "preferences for certain 'types' of Africans." His essay also discusses the extent to which Muslims in early America were able to practice their faith and to pass their Muslim traditions to their progeny. Gomez gives intriguing examples of slaves who gave their children Muslim names even though their own names were the likes of "Venus" and "Nelson."

Ghada Osman's and Camille Forbes's essay provides further literary analysis of Omar's narrative, paying special attention to his use of the Qur'an. Arabic, they note, "was associated with his freedom of expression." They also focus on the matter of Omar's conversion and the "striking ways in which some Africans identified themselves in the new American context."

Why did some slaves' Muslim religion and knowledge of Arabic ennoble them in the eyes of Dwight, Hodgson, Bird, and others? And, why are these scholars' and Colonizationists' beliefs important to a fuller understanding of Omar ibn Said's autobiography's place in the corpus of American slave literature?[128] "In slave societies," M. I. Finley exquisitely observes, "everyone, free and slave alike, accepted the ambiguity inherent in a property with a soul."[129] That ambiguity hid under rhetorical masks, metaphors with which masters concealed the hateful and inhuman aspects of treating other human beings as chattel. Most often in the slave-holding South, that literary mask took the form of the patriarchal metaphor, the fiction that the master was a benevolent father, whose occasional cruelty was necessitated by the need to control and guide his benighted, child-like charges.[130] Faced with slaves who were not only literate, but whose foreign languages excited admiration and curiosity, ethnographers and Colonizationists abandoned the patriarchal metaphor in favor of one that emphasized shared values but incomplete acculturation by the slaves—they still lacked the true religion. Yet Omar's literary intentions and achievement, his "Arabic work" of resistance and his double utterances, remained opaque to these readers.

NOTES

1. All references to Omar ibn Said's slave narrative are to my translation in this volume. Henceforth, this text will be referred to as *Life*.

2. See A. D. H. Bivar, "The Arabic Calligraphy of West Africa," *African Language Review* (London) 7 (1968): 3–15. Bivar observes that the "Maghribi characteristics" of this script are derivable "from varieties of the monumental Kufic script used in the Far West by the [Islamic dynasty] Almoravids during the fifth century of the Hijra (AD 1009–1106)."

3. For other slave writings in Arabic, see both Allan D. Austin, *African Muslims in Antebellum America: A Sourcebook* (New York: Garland, 1984), and Austin, *African Muslims in Antebellum America: Transatlantic Stories and Spiritual Struggles* (New York: Routledge, 1997).

4. João José Reis, *Slave Rebellion in Brazil: The Muslim Uprising of 1835 in Bahia*, trans. Arthur Brakel (Baltimore: Johns Hopkins University Press, 1993), 93. Michael A. Gomez states that "the first collective insurrection of Africans in the Americas," in Hispaniola in 1522, was "a movement largely composed of Senegambians, a significant proportion of whom were probably Muslim." *Black Crescent: The Experience and Legacy of African Muslims in the Americas* (Cambridge: Cambridge University Press, 2005), 3.

5. For more on the possible circumstances of Omar's capture, see Sylviane Diouf's essay in this volume.

6. Thomas Parramore, "Said, Omar Ibn," *Dictionary of North Carolina Biography*, ed. William S. Powell (Chapel Hill: University of North Carolina Press, 1994), 5:278.

7. "Uncle Moreau," *North Carolina University Magazine* 3, no. 7 (September 1854) [reproduced here, 207–11].

8. "Prince Moro," *Christian Advocate*, July 1825.

9. Austin, *African Muslims in Antebellum America: A Sourcebook*, 447. Austin points out in his essay here that his writings "were not always these two pieces."

10. Quoted in Austin, *African Muslims in Antebellum America: Transatlantic Stories and Spiritual Struggles*, 137. See John Hunwick, "'I Wish to Be Seen in Our Land Called Afrika': 'Umar b. Sayyid's Appeal to Be Released from Slavery (1819)," *Journal of Arabic and Islamic Studies* 5 (2003): 62–77. Appendix 1 includes Hunwick's translation of this text.

11. Rev. William S. Plumer, "Meroh, a Native African," New York *Observer* (January 8, 1863). Quoted in J. Franklin Jameson, ed., "Autobiography of Omar Ibn Said, Slave in North Carolina, 1831," *American Historical Review* 30, no. 4 (July 1925), 789 [reproduced here, 81–92]. These accounts of Omar contradicted one another on many issues, including his name. As Plumer remarked, "I write his name Meroh. It was originally Umeroh. Some write it Moro; and some put it in the French form Moreau."

12. Werner Sollors, "Ethnic Modernism," *The Cambridge History of American Literature*, ed. Sacvan Bercovitch (Cambridge: Cambridge University Press, 1994–96), 6:430.

13. Beginning at a conference at Houghton Library, Harvard University, in May 1998. Mr. Derrick Beard lent it to the library for the occasion and continues to make it available.

14. Examples include Ellen Barry, "Owning Omar," *Boston Phoenix*, July 6, 1998; an interview with Gustav Niebuhr that aired on National Public Radio on February 27, 2002; and Jonathan Curiel, "The Life of Omar Ibn Said," *Saudi Aramco World*, March/April 2010.

15. *The Life of Omar Ibn Said, Written by Himself*, trans. Ala Alryyes, page 59 in this volume. Unless otherwise noted, all following quotations refer to this translation.

16. Cf. Frederick Douglass's observation regarding his literacy that when his master "forbade Mrs. Auld to instruct me further, telling her . . . that 'Learning would spoil the best nigger in the world,' these words sank deep into my heart, stirred up sentiments within that lay slumbering. . . . From that moment, I understood the pathway from slavery to freedom." *Narrative of the Life of Frederick Douglass*, ed. John W. Blassingame (New Haven, CT: Yale University Press, 2001), 31–32.

17. Omar says that he wrote the narrative in 1831, and that he has "been residing in the Christian country for twenty four years" (*Life*, 69).

18. Cf. Ralph Gurley's statement that "Since his residence with General Owen [Moro] has worn no bonds but those of gratitude and affection . . . the garden has been to him a place of recreation rather than toil." "Secretary's Report," Ralph Gurley to the Board of Managers of the American Colonization Society, May 21, 1837, reprinted in *African Repository and Colonial Journal* 13, no. 7 (July 1837): 201–6 [reproduced here, 213–20].

19. Leo Strauss, *Persecution and the Art of Writing* (Westport, CT: Greenwood Press, 1952), 25.

20. As Gavin Jones writes, "Some [in the United States] find it surprising, even frustrating, that the Constitution is silent on the language question . . . [but] not only were non-English languages tolerated by the founding fathers: they were actively used to spread national principles." "Language Nation," *American Literary History* 13, no. 4 (2001): 776.

21. Margaret Talbot, "Other Woes," *New York Times Magazine*, November 18, 2001.

22. "Theodore Dwight," *Dictionary of American Biography*. Dwight was a polyglot who met and adulated Garibaldi. He is not to be confused with his father, Theodore Dwight (1764–1846), a "Connecticut Wit."

23. Jameson, "Autobiography of Omar Ibn Said," 788 [84].

24. Ibid., 789 [85].

25. For a catalogue of Hodgson's remarkable personal library, see *A Catalogue of Arabic, Turkish, and Persian Manuscripts: The Private Collection of WM. B. Hodgson* (Washington, 1830).

26. John Blassingame, "Using the Testimony of Ex-Slaves: Approaches and Problems," *The Slave's Narrative*, ed. Charles T. Davis and Henry Louis Gates, Jr. (Oxford: Oxford University Press, 1985), 79.

27. John Blassingame, introduction to *Narrative of the Life of Frederick Douglass*, xviii. In 1837, historian and abolitionist Richard Hildreth admitted that he had created the *Memoirs of Archie Moore* (1836) and disguised it as a genuine autobiography. The next year, the Executive Committee of the Massachusetts Anti-Slavery Society concluded that the details and statements of the *Narrative of James Williams* were "wholly false" and withdrew the book (ibid., xviii–xx).

28. Gerrit Smith, "Letter to the Editor of the Union Herald," *Emancipator*, January 3, 1839. Quoted in William L. Andrews, *To Tell a Free Story: The First Century of Afro-American Autobiography, 1760–1865* (Urbana: University of Illinois Press, 1988), 3.

29. Ann Fabian, *The Unvarnished Truth: Personal Narratives in Nineteenth-Century America* (Berkeley: University of California Press, 2000), 82.

30. Ibid., 85.

31. Andrews, *To Tell a Free Story*, 3.

32. Ibid., 6.

33. Robert Stepto, *From Behind the Veil: A Study of Afro-American Narrative* (Urbana: University of Illinois Press, 1979), 5. Stepto proposes a classification of black first-person narratives according to the degree of the writer's independence from the editorial apparatus, asserting that "autobiography" as a genre should be reserved for a later stage of more independent black self-narratives.

34. "Black narrators' prefaces and public pronouncements generally abide by the proposition that objective facts can be distinguished from subjective perception. However, their actual life stories often dispute, sometimes directly but more often covertly, the positivistic epistemology, dualistic morality, and diachronic framework in which antebellum America liked to evaluate autobiography as either history or falsehood." Andrews, *To Tell a Free Story*, 6.

35. Thomas Hietala, *Manifest Destiny: Anxious Aggrandizement in Late Jacksonian America* (Ithaca, NY: Cornell University Press, 1985), 11.

36. In 1822 the ACS established Monrovia (later Liberia, with Monrovia as its capital) on the west coast of Africa. Over the next forty years the Society settled some twelve thousand African Americans in that country. Although the Society existed until 1912, after 1860 it functioned primarily as the "caretaker" of the settlement in Liberia.

37. A particularly interesting example is that of Abd al-Rahman Jallo mentioned below. See other examples in Austin, *African Muslims in Antebellum America: A Sourcebook*.

38. Stepto, *From Behind the Veil*, 3. In this context, cf. Frederick Douglass's assertion that, had he not left his old master's plantation, "it is possible . . . that I should have to-day, instead of being here seated by my own table . . . writing this Narrative, been confined in the galling chains of slavery." *Narrative of the Life of Frederick Douglass*, 30.

39. Theodore Dwight, "Condition and Character of Negroes in Africa," *Methodist Quarterly Review* 46 (January 1864): 77–90. A case in point is an article on Omar, entitled "Uncle Moreau," in the *North Carolina University Magazine* (September 1854), which states that "the tribes living in eastern Africa are engaged almost incessantly in predatory warfare" (see Appendix 3 in this volume).

40. For an interesting more recent appraisal of vernacular literacy in West Africa, see Peter K. Mitchell, "A Note on the Distribution in Sierra Leone of Literacy in Arabic, Mende, and Temne," *African Language Review* (London) 7 (1968): 90–100.

41. Dwight, "Condition and Character of Negroes in Africa," 79.

42. Ibid., 80.

43. Ibid.

44. Werner Sollors, "The Blind Spot of Multiculturalism," *Chronicle of Higher Education*, October 30, 1998, B2.

45. Lamin Sanneh, *Abolitionists Abroad: American Blacks and the Making of Modern West Africa* (Cambridge: Harvard University Press, 1999), 199. As Austin points out, Omar's story was widely, if inaccurately, known.

46. Denmark Vesey's abortive revolt in 1822 was better organized, but it was betrayed, and he and his recruits were captured before they had even started.

47. T. R. Gray, "The Confessions of Nat Turner" (Richmond, 1832).

48. Herbert Aptheker, *American Negro Slave Revolts* (New York: Columbia University Press, 1943), 293.

49. Eugene D. Genovese, *Roll, Jordan, Roll: The World the Slaves Made* (New York: Vintage, 1972), 186–94.

50. Omar's narrative may also be linked to the aftermath of one of the most notorious judicial decisions concerning slavery. In 1829 a North Carolina court convicted a white man for battery on a female slave who resisted a whipping. The defendant, John Mann, then appealed. Though siding with Mann and reversing the lower court's decision, because "the power of the master must be absolute, to render the submission of the slave perfect," Thomas Ruffin, the North Carolina Supreme Court judge who wrote *State v. Mann* in 1830, famously complained that "the struggle, too, in the Judge's own breast between the feelings of the man, and the duty of the magistrate is a severe one." Judge Ruffin's ostensible humane feelings notwithstanding, one could not imagine a more committed defense of slavery than *State v. Mann*. Judge Ruffin's opinion codified a sentimental separation between official duty and private heart. His "rhetorical performance" was much admired by Harriett Beecher Stowe, who in *A Key to Uncle Tom's Cabin* "insisted that she had tried 'to separate carefully, as far as possible, the system from the men.'" See Mark V. Tushnet, *Slave Law in the American South:* State v. Mann *in History and Literature* (Lawrence: University Press of Kansas, 2003), 2–4.

51. Ansley Wegner, e-mail message to author, February 7, 2011.

52. Austin, *African Muslims in Antebellum America: Transatlantic Stories and Spiritual Struggles*, 131.

53. Francis Scott Key as quoted in P. J. Staudenraus, *The African Colonization Movement, 1816–1865* (New York: Columbia University Press, 1961), 38.

54. All Arabic words derive from a tripartite root, usually the third-person singular past tense of the related verb.

55. David Walker, *Walker's Appeal in Four Articles; Together with a Preamble, to the Coloured Citizens of the World*, in *The Norton Anthology of African American Literature*, ed. Henry Louis Gates Jr. and Nellie Y. McKay (New York: Norton, 1997). See the editors' introduction to Walker's text.

56. Walker, *Appeal*, 181.

57. Peter P. Hinks, *David Walker's Appeal to the Coloured Citizens of the World* (University Park: Pennsylvania State University Press, 2000), xxxix. I have benefited from Hinks's analysis. The following citations refer to this edition.

58. Walker, letter to Mr. Thomas Lewis, Richmond, Virginia, appended to Hinks, *Appeal*, 92.

59. Letter by James F. McKee, Mag. of Police, Wilmington, to His Excellency John Owen. Appended to Hinks, *Appeal*, 104–6.

60. One visitor to Omar said that he had never heard such bad "broken English."

61. Walker, *Appeal*, Article II, 30.

62. Hinks, *Appeal*, xxxviii.

63. *Surat al-Mulk* is a chapter of the Qur'an thought by many Muslims to have a talismanic protective power, and is recited frequently.

64. Walker's full sentence reads: "that God Almighty is the sole proprietor or master of the WHOLE human family, *and will not on any consideration admit of a colleague, being unwilling to divide his glory with another.*" *Appeal*, 181; emphasis added. The emphasized part supports my argument as it echoes Islam's strongly unitarian view.

65. Austin, *African Muslims in Antebellum America: Transatlantic Stories and Spiritual Struggles*, 68.

66. Quoted in Austin, *African Muslims in Antebellum America: A Sourcebook*, 163. For further reading on this meeting, see Keith Cartwright, *Reading Africa into American Literature: Epics, Fables, and Gothic Tales* (Lexington: University Press of Kentucky, 2002), chapter 7.

67. Walker's toast, as quoted in Austin, *African Muslims in Antebellum America: A Sourcebook*, 164.

68. "Indeed, the way in which religion was and is conducted by the Europeans and their descendants, one might believe it was a plan fabricated by themselves and the *devils* that oppress us. But hark! My master has taught me . . . that his gospel as it was preached by himself and his apostles remains the same." Walker, *Appeal*, Article III, 37.

69. Ibid., Article III, 40.

70. Ibid., 39.

71. George Sale, *The Koran: Commonly Called the Alcoran of Mohammed: Translated into English Immediately from the Original Arabic* (London, 1734). Sale was accused of blasphemy as a result of his translation.

72. Houston Baker, *The Journey Back: Issues in Black Literature and Criticism* (Chicago: University of Chicago Press, 1980), 3.

73. Ibid., 5.

74. Andrews, *To Tell a Free Story*, 14.

75. It is possible that, since the "great harm" had taken place twenty-four years earlier, Omar may have felt safe to condemn it explicitly.

76. Jameson, "Autobiography of Omar Ibn Said," 791 [87].

77. For an earlier treatment of Omar's double utterances, see Ala Alryyes, "'And in a Christian Language They Sold Me': Messages Concealed in a Slave's Arabic-Language Autobiographical Narrative," in *American Babel*, ed. Marc Shell, Harvard English Studies 20 (Cambridge: Harvard University Press, 2002), 46.

78. James Scott, *Domination and the Arts of Resistance: Hidden Transcripts* (New Haven, CT: Yale University Press, 1990), 158.

79. Melvin Dixon, "Singing Swords: The Literary Legacy of Slavery," in Davis and Gates, *The Slave's Narrative*, 298. See also Henry Louis Gates Jr., *The Signifying Monkey: A Theory of African-American Literary Criticism* (New York: Oxford University Press, 1988).

80. Omar's last writing in 1857 is preserved at the University of North Carolina at Chapel Hill.

81. It is worth noting that Omar's version of *Surat al-Nasr* (not the translation I have provided) intercalates an extraneous addition, a verse promising victory to Muslims. That it is *Surat al-Nasr* is beyond doubt, however.

82. For an earlier treatment of this argument, see my *The Life of Omar Ibn Said, Written by Himself*, in *The Multilingual Anthology of American Literature: A Reader of Original Texts with English Translations*, ed. Marc Shell and Werner Sollors (New York: New York University Press, 2000), 60.

83. For example, Ralph Gurley declared that Omar "had completely converted to Christianity," whereas Rev. Mathew B. Grier, "the minister of the church Omar last attended . . . expressed some doubt about the absoluteness of his conversion to Christianity." See Austin, *African Muslims in Antebellum America: Transatlantic Stories and Spiritual Struggles*, 131–32.

84. Genovese, *Roll, Jordan, Roll*, 184.

85. Dwight Reynolds, *Interpreting the Self: Autobiography in the Arabic Literary Tradition* (Berkeley: University of California Press, 2001), 39.

86. For further discussion of the United States' linguistic map, see *The Multilingual Anthology of American Literature: A Reader of Original Texts with English Translations*, ed. Marc Shell and Werner Sollors (New York: New York University Press, 2000); *American Babel*, ed. Marc Shell (Cambridge: Harvard University Press, 2002); Lawrence Rosenwald, *Multilingual America: Language and the Making of American Literature* (Cambridge: Cambridge University Press, 2008); Werner Sollors, ed., *Multilingual America: Transnationalism, Ethnicity, and the Languages of American Literature* (New York: New York University Press, 1998).

87. Dwight, "Condition and Character of Negroes in Africa," 85–88.

88. Ibid., 89.

89. Ibid., 90.

90. Dwight held many interviews with Kibby (Paul), "a venerable old man liberated in 1835 after being about forty years a slave in South Carolina [and] Alabama . . . and [who] spent about a year in New York, under the care of the Colonization Society, while waiting for a vessel to take him back to his native country," linking his education to his "ethnic" background. This essay is not the proper place to elaborate Kebe's remarkable life—Allan Austin devotes a chapter to him—but it is worth emphasizing that he perfectly illustrates the shared interests and dialogue of the ACS and the American Ethnological Society. Successfully sent to Liberia by the ACS, whose journal, *The African Repository*, described his plight, Kebe was also the subject of two published articles by Dwight extolling his education. "Paul's native country is Footah," writes Dwight, "a Mohammedan country," a "great advantage" of which "consists in the use of letters. . . . The books [used in free schools] were all in manuscript; and what has seemed difficult of belief, even by well-informed persons in our country, several native African languages were written in Arabic characters." Because the central text that "Paul's" culture studied and taught, the Qur'an, is written in a non-native language, Kebe describes a pedagogical system which—in the eighteenth century—is already remarkably attuned to the subtleties of bilingualism. Dwight records: "Lamen Kebe [Paul] has a high opinion of a certain process practised in some of the institutions of his native land, which he calls doubling . . . [in which] the meaning of the Arabic word is explained as well as translated. He inquires with some interest, whether the doubling or explaining [bilingual] system is properly cultivated in the United States."

91. The *Transactions* were published in three volumes from 1845 to 1852. Article II of the "Constitution" of the AES states that, "The objects of this Society shall comprise inquiries into the origin, progress, and characteristics of the various races of man" (vol. 1, p. iii).

92. Dwight, "Condition and Character of Negroes in Africa," 80.

93. William Hodgson, *Notes on Northern Africa, the Sahara, and the Soudan* (New York: Wiley and Putnam, 1844), 49.

94. Ibid., 58.

95. Ibid., 45.

96. Hodgson published *Memoir on the Megatherium and Other Extinct Gigantic Quadrupeds of the Coast of Georgia: With Observations on its Geologic Features* (New York: Bartlett & Welford, 1846) in which he credits Couper with "his observations on the geology of the sea-coast of Georgia, which are so full and completely scientific."

97. "Letter of James Hamilton Couper, Esq.," in Hodgson, *Notes on Northern Africa*, 68.

98. Couper, like Hodgson and Dwight, adds descriptions of his subject's milieu and physical characteristics. "The churches (mosques) are built of dried bricks . . . they contain a recess, towards the east or rising sun, towards which the *Al-Mami* turns his face, when he prays—towards Mecca . . . The hair of the natives is curled and woolly; and both men and women wear it in long plaits" (72–73).

99. See Michael Gomez's essay in this volume for an analysis of this sense of superiority.

100. Hodgson, *Notes on Northern Africa*, 11.

101. Alexis de Tocqueville, *Democracy in America*, ed. J. P. Mayer (New York: Harper & Row, 1969), 344.

102. Hodgson, *Notes on Northern Africa*, 59.

103. Ibid., 53.

104. *Christian Advocate* (Philadelphia), July 1825.

105. *Wilmington Chronicle*, January 27, 1847.

106. "Uncle Moreau," 307 [209].

107. "Secretary's Report," 201–6 [216–17].

108. Ibid., 205 [218].

109. "Uncle Moreau," 308 [211].

110. "It is also to be observed that those proprietors who were most anxious to emancipate their slaves were the very ones from whom the slaves received the most consideration." Early Lee Fox, *The American Colonization Society, 1817–1840* (Baltimore: The Johns Hopkins Press, 1919), 21. Fox offers the example of "an interesting native African sold to a South Carolina [*sic*] slaveholder [whose] name was Moro."

111. Hietala, *Manifest Design*, 11. See his chapter 2, "Texas, the Black Peril, and Alternatives to Abolitionism."

112. Henry Clay, *Speech of the Hon. Henry Clay before the American Colonization Society in the Hall of the House of Representatives*, quoted in Sanneh, *Abolitionists Abroad*, 193.

113. Sanneh, *Abolitionists Abroad*, 193.

114. Eric Burin, *Slavery and the Peculiar Solution: A History of the American Colonization Society* (Gainesville: University Press of Florida, 2005), 22. See also Douglas R. Egerton, "'Its Origin Is Not a Little Curious': A New Look at the American Colonization Society," *Journal of the Early Republic* 5, no. 4 (1985): 463–80.

115. Fox, *American Colonization Society*, 176.

116. Ibid., 142.

117. Ibid., 125.

118. Omar seems to have equivocated with Gurley, who found Omar "much interested in the plans and progress of the American Colonization Society," though unwilling to "return to his own country." "Secretary's Report," [218].

119. Theodore Dwight was educated at Yale and Isaac Bird at Yale and Andover, where "powerful clergymen . . . had registered their dissent from abolitionism before 1835." Larry E. Tise, *Proslavery: A History of the Defence of Slavery in America, 1701–1840*, 267.

120. "O Sheikh Hunter I cannot write my life (*Hayati*), I have forgotten much of my talk as well as the talk of the Maghreb" (*Life*, 59).

121. Reynolds, *Interpreting the Self*, 42–43.

122. James Olney, *Autobiography: Essays Theoretical and Critical* (Princeton, NJ: Princeton University Press, 1980), 159.

123. *Narrative of the Life of Frederick Douglass*, 31–32.

124. Sollors, "The Blind Spot of Multiculturalism," B4.

125. W. E. B. Du Bois, "The Negro in Literature and Art," *Annals of the American Academy of Political and Social Science* 49 (September 1913), 236.

126. Sylviane A. Diouf, *Servants of Allah: African Muslims Enslaved in the Americas* (New York: New York University Press, 1998), 18.

127. For a wide-ranging examination of the French slave trade, see also Christopher L. Miller, *The French Atlantic Triangle: Literature and Culture of the Slave Trade* (Durham, NC: Duke University Press, 2008).

128. As Timothy Marr notes, "Despite being politically relegated to the fringes of the hemisphere, the history of Islam's displaced yet looming absence has nevertheless frequently taken form as a spectral presence throughout the Americas since their first 'discovery.'" "'Out of This World': Islamic Irruptions in the Literary Americas," *American Literary History* 18, no. 3 (2006): 524.

129. M. I. Finley, *Ancient Slavery and Modern Ideology* (London: Chatto, 1980), 117.

130. Tocqueville brilliantly observes how the endgame of slavery witnessed a literalization of its metaphors. He tells the story of a white man in the South, who near death, could not overcome the laws' impediments to freeing his own slave children. "He imagined his sons dragged from market to market, exchanging a stranger's rod for a father's authority. . . . I saw a prey to the agony of despair, and then I understood how nature can revenge the wounds made by the laws." Tocqueville, *Democracy*, 362. For an analysis of the patriarchal metaphor in a European context, see Ala Alryyes, *Original Subjects: The Child, the Novel, and the Nation* (Cambridge: Harvard University Press), especially chapters 2 and 3.

The *Life*

The Life of Omar Ibn Said,
Written by Himself

Translated by ALA ALRYYES

1.

The

Life

of

Omar ben Saeed,

called

Morro,

a Fullah Slave, in Fayetteville, N.C.

Owned by Governor Owen.

Written by himself, in 1831, & sent to Old Paul,

or Lahmen Kebby, in New York, in 1836.

Presented to Theodore Dwight by Paul in 1836.

Translated by Hon. Cotheal Esq, 1848.—

(The beginning at the other end.)

The Life of Omar ben Saeed, called Morro, a Fullah Slave, in Fayatteville, N.C., Owned by Governor Owen, Written by himself in 1831 & sent to Old Paul, or Lahmen Kebby, in New York, in 1836, Presented to Theodore Dwight by Paul in 1836, Translated by Hon. Cotheal, Esq., 1848.[1]

---

1. A nearly identical version of this translation and a short introduction were published as *The Life of Omar Ibn Said, Written by Himself* in *The Multilingual Anthology of American Literature: A Reader of Original Texts with English Translations*, ed. Marc Shell and Werner Sollors (New York: New York University Press, 2000), 58–93.

بسم الله الرحمن الرحيم صلى الاه على سيدنا
محمد تبرك الذي بيده الملك وهو على كل
شيء قدير الذي خلق الموت والحياة ليبلوكم
ايكم احسن عملا وهو العزيز الغفور
الذي خلق سبع سموات طباقا ما ترى في خلق
الرحمن من تفاوت فارجع البصر هل ترى من
فطور ثم ارجع البصر كرتين ينقلب اليك
اليك البصر خاسئا وهو حسير ولقد زينا
السماء الدنيا بمصابيح وجعلناها رجوما
للشياطين واعتدنا لهم عذاب السعير
وللذين كفروا بربهم عذاب جهنم وبئس
المصير اذا القوا فيها سمعوا لها شهيقا وهي تفور

In the name of God, the merciful, the compassionate.[2] May God bless our Lord (*sayyidina*)[3] Mohammad:

Blessed be He in whose hand is the *mulk* and who has power over all things.

He created death and life that He might put you to the proof and find out which of you had the best work. He is the Mighty, the Forgiving One.

He created seven heavens arrayed one above the other. You will not see a flaw in the Merciful's creation. Turn up your eyes: can you detect a single crack?

Then look once more and yet again: your eyes in the end will grow dim and weary.

We have adorned the lowest heaven with lamps, missiles to pelt the devils with. We have prepared the scourge of Fire for these, and the scourge of Hell for those who deny their Lord: an evil fate!

When they are flung into its flames, they shall hear it roaring

2. Omar does not identify this Qur'anic fragment as *Surat al-Mulk*. This is noteworthy in the context of a slave narrative. The noun *al-mulk* comes from the tripartite Arabic root: "malaka," meaning both to own and to have dominion. The title of the *sura* is therefore the perfect allusion to slavery: absolute power through ownership. The verb and the noun conflate persons and things.

3. I misread *sayyidina* in the earlier translation.

وهي تعود نفسها تنيز س النعيم كلما الفي
بيها سالهم ثم نئدها الربا فقد نذ يرقالوا
بلى فد جاءنا نذير وكذبنا فلنا ساتزل الله
من شيء ان انتم الا في ضلك كبير فقالوا
لوكنا نسمع او نعقل ما كنا في عذ اب الشعير
واعترفوا بذ نبهم ولسحقا لاصحاب الشعير
ان الذين يخسون ربهم بالغيب لهم مغفرة
وعزر كبير واسروا قولكم واجهروا انه عليم
بذات الصدور الا يعلم س خلق وهو لليف
الخبير هو الذ ي جعل لكم ذ لولا جا مسوا في منا
كبها وكلوا من رزق اليه النسور ٤ انتم
س في السما ان يخسف بكم الارض فاذا هي

نمور

and seething, as though bursting with rage. And every time a multitude is thrown therein, its keepers will say to them: "Did no one come to warn you?"

"Yes," they will reply, "he did come, but we rejected him and said: 'Allah has revealed nothing: you are in grave error.'"

And they will say: "If only we listened and understood, we should not now be among the heirs of the Fire."

Thus shall they confess their sin. Far from God's mercy are the heirs of the Fire.

But those that fear their Lord although they cannot see Him shall be forgiven and richly rewarded.

Whether you speak in secret or aloud, He knows your innermost thoughts. Shall He who created all things not know them all? Gracious is He and all-knowing.

It is He who has made the earth subservient to you. Walk about its regions and eat of His provisions. To Him all shall return at the Resurrection.

Are you confident that He who is in heaven will not cause the earth to cave in beneath you, so that it will shake to pieces and overwhelm you?

واذا اهلي تصورا فما انتــم من العذاب عان يرسل

عليكم حاصبا وستعلمون.. كيف نذير

ولغم عذب الذين من قبلهم وكيف كان

تغيّر اولم يروا الى الطير وفهم صافانٍ

ويقبضن ما يمسكهن الا الرحمــن

انه بكل شيء بصير امن هذا هو يرزقكم

ان امسك رزقه بل لزوا في عتو ونجور ايمن

يمشي مكبا على وجهه اهدى ام من

يمشي سويا على صراط مستقيم قل هو

الذي انشاكم وجعل لكم السمع والابصر

والافيدة قليلا ما تشكرون قل هو الذي ذرعكم

فرالارض واليه تحشرون ويقولون متى هذا

[so that it will shake to pieces and overwhelm you?]

Are you confident that He who is in heaven will not let loose on you a sandy whirlwind? You shall before long know the truth of my warning.

Those who have gone before them likewise disbelieved: but how grievous was the way I rejected them!

Do they not see the birds above their heads, spreading their wings and closing them? None save the Merciful sustains them. He observes all things.

Who is it that will defend you like an army, if not the Merciful? Truly, the unbelievers are in error.

Who will provide for you if He withholds His sustenance? Yet they persist in arrogance and in rebellion.

Who is more rightly guided, he that goes groveling on his face, or he that walks upright upon a straight path?

Say: "It is He who has brought you into being, and given you ears and eyes and hearts. Yet you are seldom thankful."

Say: "It is He who placed you on the earth, and before him you shall all be assembled."

ويقولون متى هذا الوعد ان كنتم صادقين

قل انما العلم عند الله وان ما انا الا نذير مبين

فلما راوه زلفة سيئت وجوه الذين كفروا وقيل

هذا الذي كنتم به تدعون قل ارايتم ان اهلكني

الله ومن معي او رحمنا فمن يجير الكافرين من

عذاب اليم قل هو الرحمن آمنا به عليه الله قل ار

ايتم ان اصبح ماؤكم غورا فمن ياتيكم بماء

معين

They ask: "When will this promise be fulfilled, if what you say is true?"

Say: "God alone has knowledge of that. My mission is but to warn you plainly."

But when they see it drawing near, the unbelievers' faces will turn black with gloom, and a voice will say: "This is the doom which you have challenged."

[Say: "Consider: if all the water that you have were to sink down into the earth, who][4]

Say: "Consider: whether Allah destroys me and all my followers or has mercy upon us, who will protect the unbelievers from a woeful scourge?"

[Say: "God alone has knowledge of that.][5]

Say: "Consider: if all the water that you have were to sink down into the earth, who would give you running water in its place?"

---

4. Omar here inserts a fragment from the last verse of the *sura*.

5. Omar repeats a part of an earlier verse above, and omits the subsequent verse which reads: "Say: 'He is the Lord of Mercy: in Him we believe, and in Him we put our trust. You shall soon know who is in evident error.'"

يا الشيخ ظننته انه لا يستطيع

ان يتعتب الحياة انى ناس

كثيرا الكلام مع ...علم

العرب يا اخوة لا تلوموني

الحمد لله حمدا كثيرا

يوب من النعيم ما تزايد

من التحير ا ا

ي ا ي ا ي ا ي و

O Sheikh Hunter[6] (*Hanta*) I cannot write my life, I have forgotten much of my talk as well as the talk of the Maghreb.[7] O my brothers, do not blame me.

Praise be to Allah, much praise, He grants of bounty in abundance.

6. Words indicating English names of persons and places have been transliterated from Arabic by the translator.

7. Presumably Arabic.

بسم الله الرحمن الرحيم الحمد لله ٤٤ والاحسان

من فد مرو البود والس والا جلال والكرم الحمد لله

الذ ٤ خلق الخلق لمعرفا ته ٤ حتى زود ا جعل الدم وانولهم

ٯ عمرالي شيخ حننته سالتى ان اكتب الحيا ت

اذ لا يستطيع ان اكتب الحيا ت اخ ٯ انى مثير ا الكلا م

دع الكلا م العرب اذ لا يقوم نحو بالا قليلا لا اللغوى الا قليط ا

يا اشرت دسالتك بالله لا تلوموا اذ اان العين ضعيف الجسد كذا ار ٤

اسمى عمرابى سيد مكان مولدد وقوت تور بسى البى جى

طلب العلم بند وقوت شيخ يسمى محمد سيد

النوتى وشيخ سليمان كهبه وشيخ جبريل عمجال

ا ٯ يثبت طالب العلم خمس وعشر مى سنة جا ٤

ٯ مخا فدت سنة جا ٤ ٯ بطد نا جيش كبير

ٯتل الانسان كثير ا حثد ٤ يمشى حبسى البى با عوا ٤ زبد

النصر ٯ استر ٯ يمشى ال الشبعنة الكبير الي الكبير

In the name of Allah, the Gracious, the Merciful. Thanks be to Allah, for his goodness of old, his generosity and favor. To him is majesty due. Thanks be to Him who created the creation for His worship, so He may judge their deeds and words.

_⸎_

From Omar to Sheikh Hunter: You asked me to write my life. I cannot write my life for I have forgotten much of my talk [language] as well as the talk of the Arabs. Also I know little grammar and little vocabulary. O my brothers, I ask you in the name of Allah, not to blame me for my eye is weak and so is my body.

My name is Omar Ibn Said; my birthplace is Fut Tur, between the two rivers [or seas].[8] I sought knowledge in Bundu and Futa with a Sheikh called Mohammad Said, my brother, and Sheikh Suleiman Kimba and Sheikh Jebril [i.e., Gabriel] Abdal. I continued seeking knowledge for twenty five years, [then] I came to my place [and stayed] for six years. [Then there] came to our country a big army. It killed many people. It took me, and walked me to the big Sea, and sold me into the hand of a Christian man (*Nasrani*) who bought me and walked me to the big Ship in the big Sea.[9]

8. Fut Tur, or Futa Toro, lies between the Senegal and the Gambia rivers in western Africa. Michael A. Gomez notes that "In the middle Senegal valley a strong Muslim polity was established as early as the eleventh century. Subsequently, a dynasty of fluctuating loyalty to Islam was founded in the early sixteenth century, but it was overthrown in 1776 by a militant Islamic theocracy. Futa Toro, as the state came to be known, was ethnically Fulbe." Michael A. Gomez, "Muslims in Early America," *Journal of Southern History* 60, no. 4 (November 1994): 677. Gomez's essay is reproduced in this volume. The title-page of the manuscript refers to the author (in English) as "Omar ben Saeed, called Morro, a Fullah slave."

9. If consent and the freedom of movement are inextricably related, how poignantly ironic Omar's intense repetition of the verb "walk" is. The repetition of the word calls forth the processions of chained slaves—the physical repetition of nameless slaves—to which he probably submitted.

يمشي في البحر الكبير تشدو ونصف شجر جا عبر المكان

يسمى ه السنتش. في كلام نصراني با عوا اشتري

رجل من غير ضعيف سوء يسمى ؟ و تمشي كابر

جدالا خاف الله بيخ : اذ رجل صغير لا يستطيع

عن يعمل عملا شد بدا يفر س يد نه ونمس

الى شهر ٤ يمش الوسكان يسمى ويدل

رعى بيوت، وشهرا ٤ اذ خل في البيوت حتى يصلى

وعلى صبية يركب الخيل صبية جا في المكان ابو

يتكلم ابو ان راعى رجل سوء اثى والبو السمح

رجل يسمى همته رجل ٤ انم واحد منهم يركب

الخيل مع الكلب كثير انه. نيمشت معه

اثنا عشر اميال، في مكان يشمى، في يدل

والى بيوت كبير انه لا يستطيع ان يخرج انه. وبيوت

الكبير يسمى جميل. في كلام نصراني سن عشر

يوم وليله

We sailed in the big Sea for a month and a half until we came to a place called Charleston. And in a Christian language, they sold me. A weak, small, evil man called Johnson, an infidel (*Kafir*) who did not fear Allah at all, bought me.

I am a small man who cannot do hard work; I escape[d], from the hands of Johnson after a month, and walked to a place called Faydel.[10] I saw houses after a month; I entered the houses to pray. I saw a young man who was riding horses, then his father came to the place. He spoke to his father that he saw a Sudanese man in the house.[11] A man called Hindah together with another man riding a horse with many dogs took me walking with them for twelve miles to a place called Faydel.[12] They took me to a big house [building]. I could not come out of the big house—called *jeel* [i.e., jail] in the Christian language—for sixteen days and nights.

10. Fayetteville, North Carolina? Some of the Arabized names are difficult to interpret; for example, "Hindah," the leader of the chase party.

11. It was, and is, common to refer to black people in Arabic as "Sudanese" even if they did not hail from the Sudan. *Aswad* in Arabic means black.

12. The description of the group that "escorts" him, with mounted men and dogs, indicates perhaps a chase posse for escaped slaves.

فى اليوم الجمعة جاء الى الكبير واقتح الباب البيوت
رعنى رجال كتير وكلهم نصرانى ناد ثم عير اسمك
عمر عير دبيد واقرا بيسمع حكاه م النصى انى رعنى
رجل يسمى باب ممجد يا يتعظم اخرج البيوث
الكبير واذ زعغنا كتيرا يمشى معهم الى مكانهم
اتبت. و المكان ممده اربع ليال ونهار رجل يسمى
نويم عوي جوز بنتة ممجده بنسه ممجده
سالتنج زعغت يمشي. و المكان يسمى بليد
نعم زعغت يمشى معهم اتبت. و المكا
نويم عوي الى الان د

قبل ان جاء خ.من اليه دخل عوي اشترى رجل
يسمى مثل جاء خ مدادسلتخ ايسمش الى مكان د النش
ان خ كا لا كا لا لا لا لا ان جمشي من المكان
نا المسني اذ اتبت
نا البد نويم عوي

64

On Friday,[13] a man came and opened the door of the big house, and I saw many men whose language was Christian. They called to me: is not your name Omar, is it not Said? I did not understand [hear] the Christian language. I saw a man called Bob Mumford speaking [to the jailer?]. He took me out of the big house. I consented very much to walk with them to their place. I stayed in Mumford's place for four days and nights. A man called Jim Owen, the husband of Mumford's daughter, Betsy Mumford, asked me: "Do you consent to walk to a place called Bladen?"[14] I said, "Yes." I agreed to walk with them. I have stayed in Jim Owen's place until now.

Before I came into the hands of General Owen, a man called Mitchell came to buy me. Mitchell asked me: "Would you walk to a place called Charleston?" I said: "No, no, no, no, no, no, no—I will not walk to the place Charleston; I will stay in the hands of Jim Owen."

13. Or could it be Sunday, the Christian Sabbath?
14. Bladen County, North Carolina, is south of Fayetteville.

يا اهل نوف يا اليس يا اهل سوف يا البيت يا اهل مزه

يا اهم هل بيدكم رجل طبيب يتسمعى

ديم عويم مع ندوف عوم كنها رجل صالحيه

يا هم اكل اني اكلن كل من يلبس اعمى يلبس

ديم مع اخوف يفرعم في الا نجيل الله ريف انا لفظ

ومالكنا و مطلح حوالنا حد الا و ما الا وظلا

الا و جوجراء فدق هد ايفتح قلب الى سبيل

الهدى الى سبيل يسوع المسيح الى نزر عليهم

قبل ان جاء الى بلد النصرانى دين دين محمد

رسول الله صلى الله عليه وسلم يمشى الى

المسجد قبل طلوع الفجر يغسل وجه ورعس

واليدي ورجلين بصلاى و فى الظهر يصلى

و فى العصر يصلى و فى المغرب يصلى و فى العشاء

يصلى

O, people of North Carolina; O, people of South Carolina; O, people of America, all of you: are there among you men as good as Jim Owen and John Owen?[15] They are good men for whatever they eat, I eat; and whatever they wear they give me to wear. Jim with his brother read from the Bible (*Ingeel*) that Allah is our Lord, our Creator, and our Owner and the restorer of our condition, health and wealth by grace and not duty. [According?] to my ability, open my heart to the right path, to the path of Jesus Christ, to a great light.

Before I came to the Christian country, my religion was/is the religion of Mohammad, the prophet of Allah, may Allah bless him and grant him peace.[16] I used to walk to the mosque (*masjid*) before dawn, and to wash my face, head, hands, feet. I [also] used to hold the noon prayers, the afternoon prayers, the sunset prayers, the night prayers.

15. John Owen (1787–1841), brother of Jim Owen, governor of North Carolina from December 1828 to December 1830.

16. Omar's construction is ambiguous; he does not use the past construction (*kana*) to indicate his previous religion. A literal translation would read: "Before . . . my religion is the religion of Mohammad, etc."

اعطى زكات كل سنة ودهب وفضة وزرع

ويفرق ويضع وماعز الا ارزوفهم وص...

كلهم اعطى زكاة يمشي الى الجهاد كل سنة

الى الكبار يمشي الى المكة ومدينة ...

ابوك يجد ست ولد مع خمس بنت وام ثلاثة

ولد وبنت واحد اف يوم تركت في بطاط سنة

سبع وثلاثين سنة هقام في البلاد نصراني

اربع وعشرين سنة

وسنة واحد الى مع ثمانين مائة

واحد مع ثلاثين سنة

يسوع المسيح

يا اهل نوح ابنه يا اهل سوى نجيلين

يا اهل قرى كاهم الاول الولد ءيم عربي يسمى

خامس مع اخوة البنت يسمى ما الله نجيح

I used to give alms (*zakat*) every year in gold, silver, harvest, cattle, sheep, goats, rice, wheat and barley—all I used to give in alms. I used to join the *Jihad* every year against the infidels (*Kuffar*). I used to walk to Mecca and Medinah as did those who were able.[17] My father had six sons and five daughters, and my mother had three sons and one daughter. When I left my country, I was thirty-seven years old. I have been residing in the Christian country for twenty four years.

In the year eight hundred and thirty and one (1831) [after] Jesus Christ.

O, people of North Carolina; O, people of South Carolina; O, people of America, all of you: The first son of Jim Owen is called Thomas and his sister is called Maas Jen [Martha Jane?]

17. Omar seems here to enumerate some of the tenets and duties, or *arkan* and *furod*, of Islam, respectively, rather than assert what he has done. More precisely, I think he is mixing a description of his particular deeds, such as giving alms, with catechizing, such as "one should go to Mecca and Medinah if able."

هذا الجيل جيل جيد ٠ ثوم غويش نل غويش
تلد اثنان ولد وبنت واحد ولد الاول يدسمى نعيم
والا نخرون وبنة يدسمى ٠ مولسه ٠ سيد نعيم ونشبد
عومة تلد اثنان ولا وخمسن بنانة الاول نوثم
نوون وماسة ومريم وشبابة وما ئتا
وليسه هذا الجيل جيل جيد جدا ٠

ونذ ون عمر جس زوبذ نمه د س سى او شحة ما
زوجة صالحة تلد ثلاثة واثنان والبنات ثلا ث
وبقى اثنان

يا اهل نرقن يا اهل نوف نا ايش اهل ويك
هل ويتكم اهل يتكم اهل وي
الى الجيل الجيد خراف الله جدا

This is a good generation (*Geel*). Tom Owen and Nell Owen had two sons and one daughter. The first boy is called Jim and the other John; the girl is called Melissa. Master (*Sayyid*) Jim and his wife Betsy Owen have two sons and five daughters. They are Tom, John, Martha, Miriam, Sophia, Margaret and Lisa. This generation is a very good generation.

And John Owen's wife is called Lucy. A good wife, she had three children and then two. Three died and two remained.

O, people of America; O, people of North Carolina: do you have, do you have, do you have, do you have such a good generation that fears Allah so much?

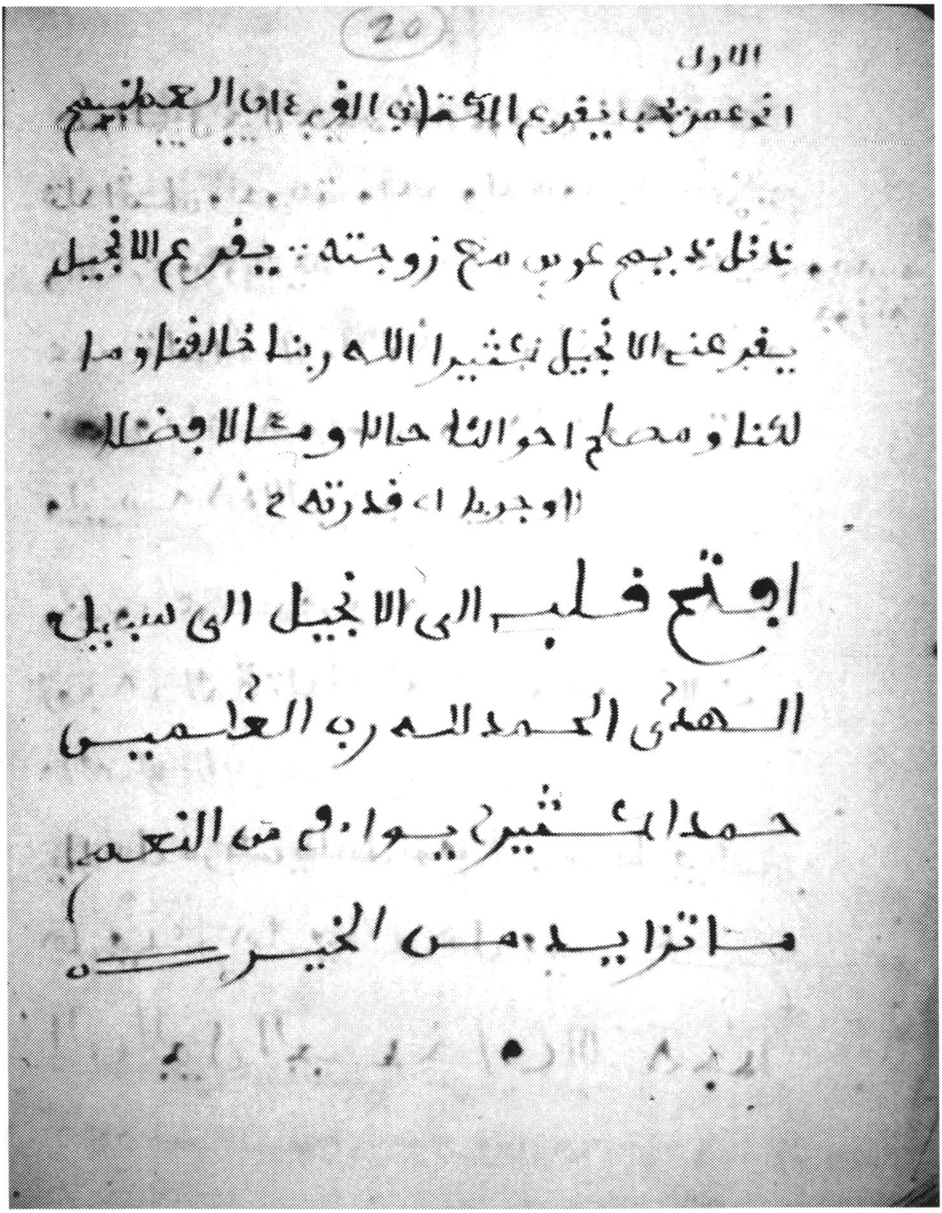
الاول
انو عمر نحب يقرء الكتاب الفرءان العظيم
نذكر يبم عرس مع زوجته :: يقرء الانجيل
يقرء عن الانجيل تبشيرا الله ربنا خالقنا وما
لكنا ومصالح احوالنا حالا ومئالا وفضلا
الوجود ا فدرته
افتح قلبي الى الانجيل الى سبيل
الهدى الحمد لله رب العلمين
حمدا كثيرا يوافي من النعم
ما تزايد من الخير

I am Omar, I love to read the book, the Great Qur'an.

General Jim Owen and his wife used to read the Bible, they used to read the Bible to me a lot. Allah is our Lord, our Creator, and our Owner and the restorer of our condition, health and wealth by grace and not duty. [According?] to my ability, open my heart to the Bible, to the path of righteousness. Praise be to Allah, the Lord of Worlds, many thanks for he grants bounty in abundance.

من اجل ان الشرع بموسى اعطى والنعمة

والحق كانا بيسوع المسيح ::

الاول عبد

ان يصلى فان الحمد لله رب العالمين الرحمن

الرحيم ملك يوم الدين اياك نعبد واياك

نستعين . اهدنا الصراط المستقيم صراط

الذين انعمت عليهم غير المغضوب

عليهم ولا الضالين ١٤ امين يا

والان قول ربنا يسوع المسيح

يا ابانا الذي في السموات يتقدس اسمك تاتي

ملكوتك تكون مشيتك كما في السما وعلى الارض

خبزنا الذي للغد اعطنا اليوم واغفر لنا ما علينا

كما نغفر نحن لمن لنا عليه ولا تدخلنا التجارب

لكن نجنا من الشرير وجان لك الملك والقوة والمجد الى الابد يا ..

Because the law (*Shar'a*) was to Moses given, but grace and truth were by Jesus the Messiah.

First, [following] Mohammed. To pray, I said: "Praise be to Allah, Lord of the Worlds; the Compassionate, the Merciful; Sovereign (*Malik*) of the Day of Judgment; It is you we worship, and to you we turn for help; Guide us to the straight path; The path of those whom you have favored with grace; Not of those who have incurred Your wrath; Nor of those who have strayed. Amen."

And [but?] now,[18] I pray in the words of our Lord Jesus the Messiah: "Our Father, who art in heaven, hallowed be thy name, thy Kingdom come, thy Will be done, on earth as it is in Heaven. Give us this day our daily bread and forgive us our trespasses as we forgive those who trespass against us, and lead us not into temptation but deliver us from the evil one for thine is the Kingdom, the power, and the glory for ever and ever. Amen."[19]

18. The Arabic construction *wa alān* is ambiguous in that it can be translated as the inclusive "and now" or the exclusive "but now."

19. I give here, of course, a translation of Omar's Arabic rendering of the Lord's Prayer. Noteworthy is the fact that Omar uses the Protestant version.

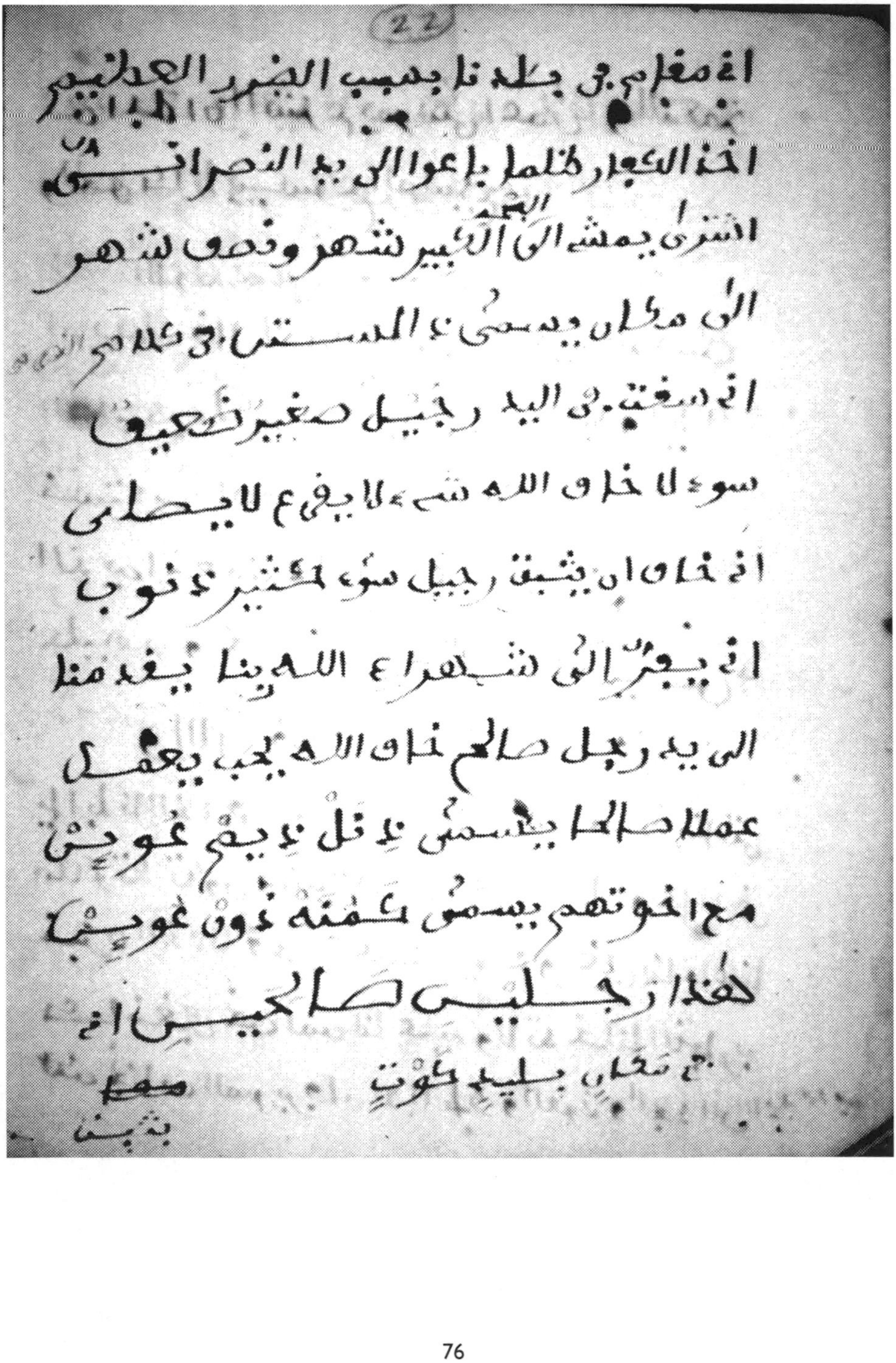

I reside in our country here because of the great harm. The infidels took me unjustly and sold me into the hands of the Christian man (*Nasrani*) who bought me. We sailed on the big sea for a month and a half to a place called Charleston in the Christian language. I fell into the hands of a small, weak, and wicked man who did not fear Allah at all, nor did he read nor pray. I was afraid to stay with such a wicked man who committed many evil deeds so I escaped. After a month, Allah our Lord presented us into the hands of a righteous man who fears Allah, and who loves to do good deeds and whose name is General Jim Owen and whose brother is called Colonel John Owen. These are two righteous men. I am in a place called Bladen County.

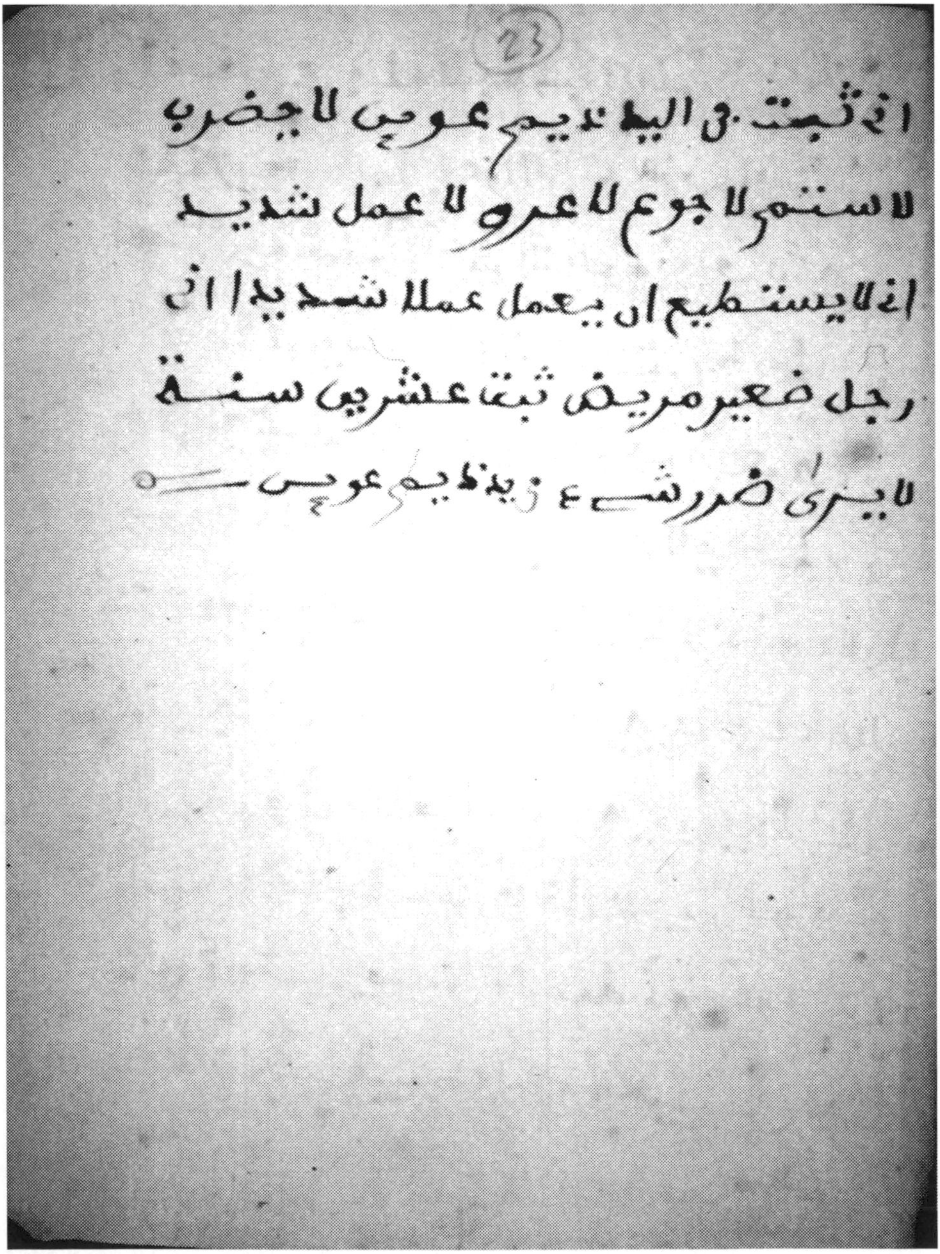

23

انه ثبتت في البلد ذيم عوجين لا يحضرب
لا ستتمر لا جوع لا عرو لا عمل شديد
انه لا يستطيع ان يعمل عملا شديدا انى
رجل ضعيف مريض ثبت عشرين سنة
لا يرى ضرر شيء في بلد ذيم عوجين

I continue in the hands of Jim Owen who does not beat me, nor calls me bad names, nor subjects me to hunger, nakedness, or hard work. I cannot do hard work for I am a small, ill man. During the last twenty years I have not seen any harm at the hands of Jim Owen.

The *Life*

Autobiography of Omar Ibn Said,
Slave in North Carolina, *1831*

Translated by ISAAC BIRD,

with an introduction and notes by J. FRANKLIN JAMESON

Most of the slaves who were imported into the American colonies, and into the United States before 1808, were brought from that part of the African coast which lies east of Cape Palmas, or still further south, but a considerable number came from the regions of the Gambia and Senegal rivers. These were mostly Mandingos, but partly Fulas. The Fulas are not precisely negroes, but seem to be a mixture of negro and Berber stock, and have long been devout Mohammedans. Among them, as among the Mandingos, education, to the point of reading the Koran and writing, was not infrequent.[1] Therefore it is not surprising that, among the American slaves, there were a certain number of literate Mohammedans; but there are only a few of whom accounts have appeared in print, and the only instance known to the present editor of an autobiographical sketch from the hand of one of them is that set forth below, from a manuscript in Arabic lent to him by its present possessor, his friend Mr. Howland Wood, curator of the American Numismatic Society, in New York.

The first story of an educated Mohammedan slave in America which has come to the writer's attention is that which is set forth in the rare pamphlet entitled *Some Memoirs of the Life of Job the Son of Solomon the High Priest of Boonda in Africa*.[2] This will be reprinted in one of those volumes of documents illustrating the history of the slave trade which are being prepared for the Carnegie Institution of Washington by Miss Elizabeth Donnan, associate professor in Wellesley College; it suffices here to say that Job, a slave in Maryland in 1731–1733, was, like the writer of the sketch below, a Fula from the kingdom of Futa, in what is now French Senegal, who wrote Arabic and was familiar with the Koran—indeed he could repeat the whole of it.

Another educated and originally Mohammedan Fula of whom there is an account in print is a slave called Old Paul, or Lahmen Kebby, of whom the Rev. R. R. Gurley, secretary of the American Colonization Society, reports in 1837, in the *African Repository*,[3] that "more than a year ago" he was preparing to embark at New York for Liberia. The fullest account of him, however, is given in the

---

1. Mungo Park, who in 1795 traveled in this region, having for some time a local schoolmaster as his companion, describes the status of education. *Travels in the Interior Districts of Africa* (London, 1816), I. 468–73. See also Comte Mollien's *Voyage dans l'Intérieur de l'Afrique en 1818* (Paris, 1820), II. 99.

2. By Thomas Bluett of Maryland (London, 1734). Later portions of his career are narrated by Francis Moore in his *Travels into the Inland Parts of Africa* (London, 1738).

3. XIII. 204.

Methodist Review for January, 1864,[4] in an article by Theodore Dwight (1796–1866), who for many years was recording secretary of the American Ethnological Society. Dwight was deeply interested in West Africa and made special efforts to obtain information from or respecting Mohammedan slaves in the United States. "But there are insuperable difficulties in the way in slave countries, . . . which quite discouraged a gentleman who made exertions in the South some years since, and compelled him to abandon the undertaking in despair, although he had resided in Africa, and had both the taste and the ability necessary to success."[5] Old Paul, he says, "was liberated in 1835, after being about forty years a slave in South Carolina, Alabama, and other southern states, and spent about a year in New York, under the care of the Colonization Society, while waiting for a vessel to take him back to his native country." Dwight had many talks with him, took copious notes of his information about Senegambia, and printed three or four pages from them in the proceedings of the American Lyceum in 1836.[6] Paul came from Futa, as Job and Omar did. "Paul was a schoolmaster in Footah, after pursuing a long course of preparatory studies, and said that he had an aunt who was much more learned than himself, and eminent for her superior acquirements and for her skill in teaching. Schools, he said, were generally established through the country, provision being made by law for educating children of all classes, the poor being taught gratuitously." He gave Dwight an account of their manuscript books, and a list of some thirty that were in his mother tongue (Sarakullé), though written in Arabic characters.

Finally, the early *Transactions* of the American Ethnological Society[7] show that there was read, in one of their meetings in 1843, "A letter from J. Hamilton Couper, Esq., of Georgia, to William B. Hodgson, giving an account of an aged Foulah slave now living in that State, together with his African reminiscences."

The manuscript translated below is written, in good Arabic script, on some fifteen pages of quarto paper, and is inscribed in English as having been "Written by himself in 1831 and sent to Old Paul, or Lahmen Kebby, in New York, in 1836, Presented to Theodore Dwight by Paul" in that same year, and translated into English in 1848 by Alexander I. Cotheal, who for many years was treasurer of the

---

4. "Condition and Character of Negroes in Africa," *Methodist Review*, XLVI. 77–90, especially pp. 80–84.

5. This means William B. Hodgson, of Georgia, who had been U.S. consul in Tunis for some years.

6. This periodical, for this year, the editor has not found.

7. I. xi.

Ethnological Society and was a fancier of Arabic manuscripts.[8] In February, 1863, the *Bulletin* of the society states: "Another Arabic MS. was again exhibited by the Recording Secretary, written in 1836 [*sic*], by the remarkable old slave Morro [Omar], in Fayetteville, N. C., which contains a connected narrative of the writer's life, according to a translation made by Mr. Cotheal, and formerly read to the society." In 1864 Dwight published in his article in the *Methodist Review* some extracts from that quite imperfect translation.[9] Some time after this he obtained a better version from Rev. Isaac Bird (1793–1876) of Hartford, who had been for a dozen years (1823–1835) a missionary in Syria,[10] and had a good knowledge of Arabic. It is this translation, slightly revised through the kindness of Dr. F. M. Moussa, secretary of the Egyptian Legation in Washington, which is here presented. The manuscript and both translations were given to Mr. Wood by a friend, who bought them at an auction.

Besides what Omar tells of his life, some additional facts may be found in an article in the New York *Observer* of January 8, 1863, entitled "Meroh, a Native African," and signed "A Wayfaring Man." The writer, who was the Rev. William S. Plumer (1802–1880),[11] Presbyterian pastor in Allegheny and professor in the Western Theological Seminary 1854–1862, says that he first met the man in Wilmington, North Carolina, in 1826, and had seen him once or twice since, and that he was born about 1770 on the banks of the Senegal.

> I write his name Meroh. It was originally Umeroh. Some write it Mora; and some put it in the French form Moreau. It is commonly pronounced as if spelled Moro.[12] Meroh's father in Africa was a man of considerable wealth. He brought up his children delicately. Meroh's fingers are rather effeminate. They are very well tapered. His whole person and gait bear marks of considerable refinement. At about five years of age he lost his father, in one of those bloody wars that are almost constantly raging in Africa. Very soon thereafter he was taken by an uncle to the capital of the tribe. Here he learned and afterward taught Arabic, especially some

---

8. See the account of his library in James Wynne, *Private Libraries of New York*, pp. 161–172.

9. XLVI. 88.

10. H. H. Jessup, *Fifty-three Years in Syria*, pp. 42–46.

11. Letter of Mr. Bird, among the manuscripts.

12. Mr. Bird says, in the letter just mentioned, "The name Moro is doubtless the same as Amrou or Omar, the final *o* or *u* being only a vowel point."

prayers used by Mahomedans. He also learned some rules of arithmetic, and many of the forms of business. When a young man he became a dealer in the merchandise of the country, chiefly consisting in cotton cloths.

Mr. Plumer adds that when "Meroh" first landed in Charleston (which, it will be observed, was apparently in 1807, the last year in which importations of slaves were legal) he was sold to a citizen of that city who treated him with great kindness, but soon died. He mentions that when confined in the Cumberland County jail, the poor man, finding some coals in the ashes, wrote in Arabic on the walls what were understood to be appeals for succor; that when he came to General Owen's family he was at first a staunch Mohammedan and kept Ramadan; that through the kindness of his friends an English version of the Koran was procured for him, and was read to him, along with the Bible, but that gradually he became a Christian; that he was baptized and received into the Presbyterian Church at Fayetteville by the Rev. Dr. Snodgrass (which fixes the date of such reception to 1819–1822), but later was transferred to a Wilmington church.

In a letter from Augusta, Georgia, May 21, 1837, Rev. R. R. Gurley reports,[13] "In the respected family of General Owen of Wilmington I became acquainted with Moro or Omora, a Foulah by birth, educated a Mahometan and who, long after he came in slavery to this country, retained a devoted attachment to the faith of his fathers, and deemed a copy of the Koran in Arabic . . . his richest treasure." He adds that, when Paul was about to embark from New York for Liberia, Moro or Omar "corresponded with him and presented him with one of his two copies of the Bible in that language." Omar speaks of them, in a letter from which Gurley quotes, as "two Arabic Bibles, procured for me by my good Christian friends," meaning doubtless the Owens. The copy which he retained, an Arabic Bible of the edition of Newcastle-upon-Tyne, 1811, is now in the Library of Davidson College, in Charlotte County, North Carolina, well worn, and bearing the inscription, "Old Uncle Moreau's Arabick Bible, Presented to the Williams Missionary Association, Davidson College, by Mrs. Ellen Guion, Charlotte, N. C., April, 1871."[14] Mrs. Guion was a daughter of Governor John Owen.

Miss Anna Guion Stith, of Wilmington, a connection of the Owen family, recalls from tradition that when Omar, arrested at Fayetteville as a vagrant, and

---

13. *African Repository*, XIII. 203–204.
14. Letter of the librarian, Miss Cornelia Shaw.

put in jail and advertised for sale as a slave, had "astonished the natives" by writing in Arabic on the walls, General James Owen, brother of Governor John Owen, out of curiosity, when visiting Fayetteville, went to the jail to see this remarkable man, became interested, and purchased him, carrying him to his country home, "Milton," in Bladen County, where he enjoyed life, without being treated as a slave, had a seat by himself in the country church, etc.; he spent his later years mostly at "Owen Hill," Governor Owen's estate, where he occupied his own home in the yard, and had his meals· prepared by the Owens' cook and brought in by a little negro, and where he was buried. He lived till after the Civil War. A daguerreotype of him is in the possession of Miss Mary Owen Graham, of Charlotte, North Carolina, who also has (inaccessible at present) some of his Arabic manuscripts, and who has kindly written the editor at length concerning him.

The earlier pages of the manuscript are occupied with quotations from the Koran which Omar remembered, and these might be omitted as not autobiographical, and are indeed separated from what follows by blank pages; but it has been thought best to print the whole. These remembrances from the past were a part of the man, and help to give the narrative greater completeness as a "human document" of unusual and indeed somewhat pathetic interest.

> In the name of God, the merciful the gracious.—God grant his blessing upon our Prophet Mohammed. Blessed be He in whose hands is the kingdom and who is Almighty; who created death and life that he might test you; for he is exalted; he is the forgiver (of sins), who created seven heavens one above the other. Do you discern anything trifling in creation? Bring back your thoughts. Do you see anything worthless? Recall your vision in earnest. Turn your eye inward for it is diseased. God has adorned the heavens and the world with lamps, and has made us missiles for the devils, and given us for them a grievous punishment, and to those who have disbelieved their Lord, the punishment of hell and pains of body. Whoever associates with them shall hear a boiling caldron, and what is cast therein may fitly represent those who suffer under the anger of God.—Ask them if a prophet has not been sent unto them. They say, "Yes; a prophet has come to us, but we have lied to him." We said, "God has not sent us down anything, and you are in grievous error." They say, "If we had listened and been wise we should not now have been suffering the punishment of the Omniscient." So they confess they have sinned in destroying the followers of the Omniscient. Those who fear their Lord and profess his name, they receive pardon and great honor. Guard your words (ye wicked), make it known that God is all-wise in all his

manifestations. Do you not know from the creation that God is full of skill? that He has made for you the way of error, and you have walked therein, and have chosen to live upon what your god Nasur has furnished you? Believe on Him who dwells in heaven, who has fitted the earth to be your support and it shall give you food. Believe on Him who dwells in Heaven, who has sent you a prophet, and you shall understand what a teacher (He has sent you). Those that were before them deceived them (in regard to their prophet). And how came they to reject him? Did they not see in the heavens above them, how the fowls of the air receive with pleasure that which is sent them? God looks after all. Believe ye: it is He who supplies your wants, that you may take his gifts and enjoy them, and take great pleasure in them. And now will you go on in error, or walk in the path of righteousness. Say to them, "He who regards you with care, and who has made for you the heavens and the earth and gives you prosperity, Him you think little of. This is He that planted you in the earth, and to whom you are soon to be gathered." But they say, "If you are men of truth, tell us when shall this promise be fulfilled?" Say to them, "Does not God know? and am not I an evident Prophet?" When those who disbelieve shall see the things draw near before their faces, it shall then be told them, "These are the things about which you made inquiry." Have you seen that God has destroyed me or those with me? or rather that He has shewn us mercy? And who will defend the unbeliever from a miserable punishment? Say, "Knowledge is from God." Say; "Have you not seen that your water has become impure? Who will bring you fresh water from the fountain?"

O Sheikh Hunter,[15] I cannot write my life because I have forgotten much of my own language, as well as of the Arabic. Do not be hard upon me, my brother.—To God let many thanks be paid for his great mercy and goodness.

In the name of God, the Gracious, the Merciful.—Thanks be to God, supreme in goodness and kindness and grace, and who is worthy of all honor, who created all things for his service, even man's power of action and of speech.

15. The address to some one named Hunter remains obscure. The document, for whomever written in 1831, was sent to Paul in 1836. Omar's own language was probably Fula.

From Omar to Sheikh Hunter.

You asked me to write my life. I am not able to do this because I have much forgotten my own, as well as the Arabic language. Neither can I write very grammatically or according to the true idiom. And so, my brother, I beg you, in God's name, not to blame me, for I am a man of weak eyes, and of a weak body.

My name is Omar ibn Seid. My birthplace was Fut Tûr,[16] between the two rivers. I sought knowledge under the instruction of a Sheikh called Mohammed Seid, my own brother, and Sheikh Soleiman Kembeh, and Sheikh Gabriel Abdal. I continued my studies twenty-five years, and then returned to my home where I remained six years. Then there came to our place a large army, who killed many men, and took me, and brought me to the great sea, and sold me into the hands of the Christians, who bound me and sent me on board a great ship and we sailed upon the great sea a month and a half, when we came to a place called Charleston in the Christian language. There they sold me to a small, weak, and wicked man, called Johnson, a complete infidel, who had no fear of God at all. Now I am a small man, and unable to do hard work so I fled from the hand of Johnson and after a month came to a place called Fayd-il.[17] There I saw some great houses (churches). On the new moon I went into a church to pray. A lad saw me and rode off to the place of his father and informed him that he had seen a black man in the church. A man named Handah (Hunter?) and another man with him on horseback, came attended by a troop of dogs. They took me and made me go with them twelve miles to a place called Fayd-il, where they put me into a great house from which I could not go out. I continued in the great house (which, in the Christian language, they called *jail*) sixteen days and nights. One Friday the jailor came and opened the door of the house and I saw a great many men, all Christians, some of whom called out to me, "What is your name? Is it Omar or Seid?" I did not understand their Christian language. A man called Bob Mumford[18] took me and led me

---

16. Futa Toro, one of the Fula states of that time, now a part of French Senegal. A description of it as it was at a time not much later than that at which Omar left it can be found in Comte Mollien's *Voyage dans l'Intérieur de l'Afrique*, I. 269–297.

17. Fayetteville.

18. Sheriff of Cumberland County, of which Fayetteville is the county seat.

out of the jail, and I was very well pleased to go with them to their place. I stayed at Mumford's four days and nights, and then a man named Jim Owen,[19] son-in-law of Mumford, having married his daughter Betsey, asked me if I was willing to go to a place called Bladen.[20] I said, Yes, I was willing. I went with them and have remained in the place of Jim Owen until now.

Before [after?] I came into the hand of Gen. Owen a man by the name of Mitchell came to buy me. He asked me if I were willing to go to Charleston City. I said "*No, no, no, no, no, no, no,* I not willing to go to Charleston. I stay in the hand of Jim Owen."

O ye people of North Carolina, O ye people of S. Carolina, O ye people of America all of you; have you among you any two such men as Jim Owen and John Owen?[21] These men are good men. What food they eat they give to me to eat. As they clothe themselves they clothe me. They permit me to read the gospel of God, our Lord, and Saviour, and King; who regulates all our circumstances, our health and wealth, and who bestows his mercies willingly, not by constraint. According to power I open my heart, as to a great light, to receive the true way, the way of the Lord Jesus the Messiah.

Before I came to the Christian country, my religion was the religion of "Mohammed, the Apostle of God—may God have mercy upon him and give him peace." I walked to the mosque before day-break, washed my face and head and hands and feet. I prayed at noon, prayed in the afternoon, prayed at sunset, prayed in the evening. I gave alms every year, gold, silver, seeds, cattle, sheep, goats, rice, wheat, and barley. I gave tithes of all the above-named things. I went every year to the holy war against the infidels. I went on pilgrimage to Mecca, as all did who were able. — My father had six sons and five daughters, and my mother had three sons and one daughter. When I left my country I was thirty-seven years old; I have been in the country of the Christians twenty-four years. — Written A. D. 1831.

---

19. James Owen (1784–1865), M. C. from North Carolina 1817–1819, and afterward president of the Wilmington and Raleigh Railroad and major-general of militia.

20. Bladen County, N.C.

21. John Owen (1787–1841), brother of the preceding, governor of North Carolina from December, 1828, to December, 1830.

O ye people of North Carolina, O ye people of South Carolina, O all ye people of America—

The first son of Jim Owen is called Thomas,[22] and his sister is called Masa-jein (Martha Jane?). This is an excellent family.

Tom Owen and Nell Owen have two sons and a daughter. The first son is called Jim and the second John. The daughter is named Melissa.

Seid Jim Owen and his wife Betsey have two sons and five daughters. Their names are Tom, and John, and Mercy, Miriam, Sophia, Margaret and Eliza. This family is a very nice family. The wife of John Owen is called Lucy and an excellent wife she is. She had five children. Three of them died and two are still living.

O ye Americans, ye people of North Carolina—have you, have you, have you, have you, have you among you a family like this family, having so much love to God as they?

Formerly I, Omar, loved to read the book of the Koran the famous. General Jim Owen and his wife used to read the gospel, and they read it to me very much,—the gospel of God, our Lord, our Creator, our King, He that orders all our circumstances, health and wealth, willingly, not constrainedly, according to his power.—Open thou my heart to the gospel, to the way of uprightness.—Thanks to the Lord of all worlds, thanks in abundance. He is plenteous in mercy and abundant in goodness.

For the law was given by Moses but grace and truth were by Jesus the Messiah.

When I was a Mohammedan I prayed thus: "Thanks be to God, Lord of all worlds, the merciful the gracious, Lord of the day of Judgment, thee we serve, on thee we call for help. Direct us in the right way, the way of those on whom thou hast had mercy, with whom thou hast not been angry and who walk not in error. Amen."—But now I pray "Our Father," etc., in the words of our Lord Jesus the Messiah.

I reside in this our country by reason of great necessity. Wicked men took me by violence and sold me to the Christians. We sailed a month

22. According to Miss Graham's recollection, the genealogical details which Omar here inserts are nearly though not quite correct, assuming that the "Tom Owen and Nell Owen" of whom he speaks in the next paragraph were Colonel Thomas Owen of Revolutionary days and his wife Eleanor Porterfield Owen, father and mother of the two brothers with whom his later years were so pleasantly spent.

and a half on the great sea to the place called Charleston in the Christian land. I fell into the hands of a small, weak and wicked man, who feared not God at all, nor did he read (the gospel) at all nor pray. I was afraid to remain with a man so depraved and who committed so many crimes and I ran away. After a month our Lord God brought me forward to the hand of a good man, who fears God, and loves to do good, and whose name is Jim Owen and whose brother is called Col. John Owen. These are two excellent men.—I am residing in Bladen County.

I continue in the hand of Jim Owen who never beats me, nor scolds me. I neither go hungry nor naked, and I have no hard work to do. I am not able to do hard work for I am a small man and feeble. During the last twenty years I have known no want in the hand of Jim Owen.

Contextual Essays

Muslims in Early America

Michael A. Gomez

During the post-1492 contact between the Old World and the New, Christianity and Judaism were introduced into the latter and indeed facilitated the western hemisphere's political subjugation and cultural transformation. These religions were carried by European colonizers, whose success in subjugating and transforming the Americas has resulted in careful study of the cultural institutions that accompanied them—at the expense of non-European systems of belief that were also imported into the New World. Specifically, Africans, transported via the transatlantic slave trade, brought with them their own religions, which were transferred into the New World with varying results, depending upon the unique blend of acculturative forces operating in the various areas of destination.[1]

One of the belief systems introduced into the Americas by Africans was Islam. However, the dawn of Islam in the Americas and its association with Africans have yet to receive the scholarly attention that is merited. This is particularly true of North American historical studies, in which one rarely reads of the early existence of Islam in what would become the United States.[2] Such neglect is most regrettable, given the possibility that one of America's most illustrious sons, Frederick Douglass, may have himself been a descendant of Muslims.[3]

This essay is a preliminary study of Islam in early African American history. Because of the limited data available at this stage of research, the arguments presented are necessarily more tentative than conclusive; nonetheless, available evidence does permit several statements on Muslims in early America. First of all, their numbers were significant, probably reaching into the thousands. Second, Muslims made genuine and persistent efforts to observe their religion; and even though they perpetuated their faith primarily within their own families, in some cases they may have converted slaves who were not relatives. Third, Islam and ethnicity were important in the process of social stratification within the larger

African American society. And finally, cultural phenomena found in segments of the African American community, such as ostensibly Christian worship practices and certain artistic expressions, probably reflect the influence of these early Muslims.

The study of Muslims in the American colonial and antebellum periods has yet to be undertaken seriously because materials on the subject are scarce. This scarcity of primary data is a function of two factors. First, colonial and antebellum observers, who were largely ignorant of the Islamic faith, did not accurately record the variegated cultural expressions of African slaves. The cumulative evidence suggests that such observers could distinguish the Muslims from other slaves but had neither the skills nor the interest to record detailed information about them. The other factor contributing to the scarcity of data is the reluctance of the descendants of these early Muslims to be forthright in answering questions about their ancestors.

Another reason for the lack of scholarly inquiry into Islam in early America is the absence of a satisfactory dialogue between historians of Africa and of North America. Efforts to address this problem have begun and can be seen in the work of such historians as Peter H. Wood and Daniel C. Littlefield. However, a great deal remains to be done, and the current exercise is an attempt to foster a process by which Americanists and Africanists come to view the colonial /antebellum world as it really was. As such, the present approach is not unlike the "Atlantic community" perspective advocated by scholars such as Philip D. Curtin, except that it is informed by a greater emphasis on the African component. Further, the present study is an effort to establish a more reliable context for the investigation of Muslims in early America and thus assist in the much needed exchange and collaboration between Africanists and Americanists.[4]

The primary documentation for this inquiry includes autobiographical and biographical sketches, newspaper articles and advertisements for runaway slaves, slaveholders' records, and the testimony of slaves and their descendants. Complementing the primary sources are secondary materials, of which Allan D. Austin's *African Muslims in Antebellum America* (1984), a mixture of primary sources and analysis, is the most comprehensive treatment of the subject to date. As it relates to North America, the work focuses on seven individuals who achieved a level of notoriety sufficient to warrant commentary by observers.[5] Although the book is very useful, readers should keep in mind that the author is neither an Africanist nor an Islamicist.

In addition to Austin's book there are biographies of two relatively prominent Muslims. In 1968 Douglas Grant published *The Fortunate Slave*, an account of the life of Ayuba ibn Sulayman, more commonly known as "Job Ben Solomon." The book's most important contribution concerns the activities of Ayuba following his repatriation to West Africa, but it is riddled with language suggesting paternalistic condescension. In contrast is the very fine effort of Terry Alford, entitled *Prince Among Slaves* (1977), a biography of Abd al-Rahman, or Abdul Rahahman. Alford's study is valuable in that it provides considerable insight into an African Muslim's reaction to enslavement. Beyond Grant and Alford, the more scholarly writings of Ivor Wilks, published in Philip D. Curtin's *Africa Remembered* (1967), address the experiences of Abu Bakr al-Siddiq and Salih Bilali.[6]

In addition to information in print, an interview with Cornelia Bailey, a direct descendant of Bilali (a prominent Muslim slave), was conducted for the purposes of this research. Her comments are critically treated and provide important insights into Bilali, the Muslim community in early coastal Georgia, and the question of the Muslim legacy.[7] All of these secondary materials focus on individuals, or a set of individuals, and, with the exception of Austin's book, make little attempt to treat the more complex issue of the general experience of Muslims in North America. In order to address this more complex issue, it is necessary first to establish the African context.

The evidence for the presence of Muslims in colonial and antebellum America comes from both sides of the Atlantic. On the African side, the historical research provides a reasonably clear picture of the political and cultural milieu out of which American-bound captives emerged. Several different types of sources yield information on the presence and activities of Muslims upon landing in the New World: the ethnic and cultural makeup of the African supply zones; the appearance of Muslim names in the ledgers of slave owners and in the runaway slave advertisements in newspapers; references to Muslim ancestry in interviews with ex-slaves and the descendants of Muslims; stated preferences for certain "types" of Africans by the slaveholding community; recorded observations of Islamic activity; and profiles of certain Muslim figures. Within the last genre are documents written in Arabic by Muslims themselves, a rare phenomenon. While very general statements can be ventured as estimates of the Muslim population in America, the data on this subject are almost entirely qualitative, so that attempts at quantification are only speculative at this point.

Islam had penetrated the savanna south of the Sahara Desert by the beginning of the ninth century as a consequence of Berber and Arab commercial activity. Some sub-Saharan African (or "Sudanese") merchants living in the *sahel* ("shore" or transition zone between the desert and the savanna) and the savanna began to convert, so that Islam became associated with trade, especially long-distance networks of exchange. In some societies, political rulers also converted to the new religion with varying degrees of fidelity, so that Islam became a vehicle by which alliances between commercial and political elites were forged. Islam continued to grow slowly throughout West Africa into the sixteenth century and dramatically increased its adherents during the nineteenth and early twentieth centuries, as Islam took on the form of anticolonial cultural resistance. This span of four centuries (beginning with the sixteenth) roughly corresponds to the period of the transatlantic slave trade. A consideration of the historical development of Islam in West Africa is therefore essential in trying to formulate an idea of the size and character of the Muslim presence in early America. More specifically, the political and cultural development of the zones in which Muslims and other Africans were procured provides the essential background for understanding their subsequent sojourn in America. With regard to those supply zones, the schema employed by Curtin will be adopted here. For, notwithstanding the discussion he stimulated in 1969 concerning the approximate number of Africans involved in the transatlantic trade, there is no reason to jettison his division of the conventional supply zones from which these captives came.[8]

The first of the zones, Senegambia, extends from the Senegal River to the Casamance River, and from the Atlantic coast to the upper and middle Niger valleys. This is an immense area; if operating in the interior, traffickers in human cargo had several outlets for their trade. They could, for example, sell their captives along the Gambia or Senegal Rivers; they could direct their caravans to other points along the West African coast; or, they could deal their cargoes into the transsaharan slave trade. That captives could originate from as far inland as the upper and middle Niger valleys indicates that there were at least three staging areas from which Africans in this zone were procured for the Atlantic trade: the coastal area, from the lower Senegal to the lower Casamance valleys; a mid-range area, encompassing the middle and upper Senegal and Gambia valleys; and the middle and upper Niger. The presence of Islam within this vast stretch of territory was relative to specific lands and periods of time.

With regard to the coastal areas, the Wolof had for the most part remained unconverted to Islam before the end of the eighteenth century, although Islam had penetrated the Senegal River from the north as early as the tenth century.[9] From the sixteenth to the nineteenth century, Islam was confined to the royal courts of such Wolof states as Jolof, Cayor, and Waalo; Muslim advisors serviced rulers who in turn practiced traditional religions and/or Islam. While the majority of the population did not practice Islam, the Muslim presence was nevertheless influential and resulted in a Muslim grab for political power in the last quarter of the seventeenth century.

In the mid-range of the Senegambian supply zone a substantial proportion of the population was Muslim. In the middle Senegal valley a strong Muslim polity

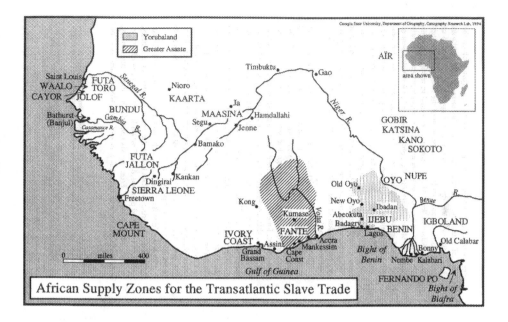

Georgia State University, Department of Geography, Cartography Research Lab, 1994

Yorubaland
Greater Asante

AÏR
area shown

Saint Louis
WAALO
CAYOR
FUTA
TORO
JOLOF
Senegal R.
Nioro
Timbuktu
Gao
Niger R.

KAARTA

Bathurst
(Banjul)
BUNDU
Gambia R.
Casamance R.
Ja
MAASINA
Segu
Jenne
Hamdallahi
GOBIR
KATSINA
KANO
SOKOTO

Bamako

FUTA
JALLON
Dingirai
Kankan
SIERRA LEONE
Freetown
Kong
New Oyo
Old Oyo
OYO
NUPE
Ibadan
Benue R.

Kumase
Abeokuta
Badagry
IJEBU
BENIN
IGBOLAND

CAPE
MOUNT
IVORY
COAST
Assini
FANTE
Grand
Bassam
Cape
Coast
Mankessim
Accra
Lagos
Bight of
Benin
Nembe
Bonny
Kalabari
Old Calabar

0   miles   400

Gulf of Guinea

FERNANDO PO
Bight of
Biafra

African Supply Zones for the Transatlantic Slave Trade

was established as early as the eleventh century. Subsequently, a dynasty of fluctuating loyalty to Islam was founded in the early sixteenth century, but it was overthrown in 1776 by a militant Islamic theocracy. Futa Toro, as the state came to be known, was ethnically Fulbe, or "Tukulor." (The latter term is used to distinguish the Muslim, sedentary, and—in some instances—ethnically mixed portion of the Fulbe from the pastoral, non-Muslim segment.) The upper Senegal and Gambia valleys contained proportionately fewer Muslims (and lower population densities), but again, by the eighteenth century, the Islamic factor had been present for several hundred years. This was largely due to the far-reaching tentacles of the old Malian empire (north and east of the Senegal River), of which the upper and middle Gambia composed the westernmost provinces before the empire's dissolution in the seventeenth century. In the upper Senegal around 1698, the Islamic factor eventually led to the creation of a Muslim polity known as Bundu, in which the population gradually became predominantly Muslim by the nineteenth century. Along the Gambia and further south to the Casamance, the various Mande-speaking populations, along with the Sereer, turned from traditional religions to Islam with the passing of time, facilitated by the presence of Muslim merchants among them.[10] Thus, the mid-range area represents a focus of Muslim power that increased throughout the duration of the transatlantic trade.

Far into the interior lay the western reaches of the Niger River, fabled for such cities as Ja, Jenne, and Timbuktu. The area was a mixture of Muslim and non-Muslim populations from the time of imperial Songhay (1464–1591) to the early nineteenth century, at which point the area known as Maasina fell to the armies of militant Fulbe Muslims. Between the fall of Songhay and the dawn of an Islamized Maasina in the early nineteenth century, the middle and upper Niger valleys witnessed an intense period of warfare with the rise of Segu in the early seventeenth. The non-Muslim Bambara of this well-known citadel, under the leadership of the Kulubali elite, went on to establish control throughout the upper Niger in the eighteenth century. The numerous war captives during this period were Muslim and non-Muslim alike, and many of them were eventually traded and transported to the western hemisphere.[11]

Thus, from the fifteenth through the mid-nineteenth centuries the Senegambian supply zone gradually became Islamized, more dramatically in the nineteenth than in earlier centuries, and during the nineteenth century the majority of the population became Muslim. But in order to assess the significance of this trend, several factors must be taken into consideration. First, Senegambia, by virtue of its location vis-à-vis Europe, was a principal supplier of slaves during the early phase of the Atlantic trade.[12] Second, the evidence from the clerically led revolt along the coast in the 1670s known as the *tubenan* movement suggests that the Wolof states of the Atlantic coast were deeply affected by the slave trade before the last quarter of the seventeenth century.[13] The Moor Nasir al-Din gained the support of the Wolof peasantry by condemning the participation of the Wolof elite in the slave trade, stating that "God does not allow kings to plunder, kill or make their people captive."[14] When the lieutenants of Nasir al-Din in turn betrayed the trust of the peasantry and began selling them into slavery, these officials were quickly overthrown. Their overthrow suggests the presence of effective opposition to the trade along the coastal area and leads to the conclusion that, beginning in the eighteenth century, the supply of slaves increasingly originated from farther inland, in the middle and upper Senegal and Gambia valleys. This shift in the slave supply is indirectly confirmed by the Islamic revolution of Futa Toro, which began in the 1760s and was, in part, the response of the Muslim community to its victimization in the trade.[15] Muslims seeking protection against enslavement created the Islamic polity of Bundu in part as an asylum from the slave trade.[16] In fact, there is growing evidence that the middle and upper Senegal valleys were more severely impacted by the transatlantic trade than previously understood.[17]

Finally, the non-Muslim Bambara of Segu were renowned warriors, so that a number of Muslims must have been fed into the trade as captives of war. Although the contribution of Senegambia to the trade declined dramatically after 1750, the *tubenan* movement along the coastal area meant that the bulk of the captives came from the mid-range and upper/middle Niger areas, in which Islam was relatively more widespread. After 1750 traders operating in the upper/middle Niger valleys simply redirected the considerable number of war captives to other points along the coast of West Africa.

The next supply zone was Sierra Leone, or what is now Guinea-Bissau, Guinea, Sierra Leone, and a small portion of Liberia, spanning the coast from the Casamance in the north to Cape Mount in the south. From the middle of the sixteenth century through the seventeenth, the region's principal sources for the slave trade were the non-Muslim Tenda and the "Paleo-Negritics," as Walter Rodney refers to them.[18] These people of the littoral were in fact the victims of raiding by Mande-speakers of the interior, who sold their captives to traders servicing, for the most part, the Spanish colonies. The French dominated the trade of the region for the first half of the eighteenth century and were succeeded by the English during its second half. For this period (1690–1800), Rodney estimates that 75 percent of the Africans sold into the trade came from the interior.[19] This observation suggests that a proportionate number of North American slaves who came from this supply zone during this time also originated in the hinterland.

The interior of present-day Guinea is dominated by the Futa Jallon massif. Originally inhabited by the Jallonke, these Guinea highlands received substantial numbers of Fulbe pastoralists from Maasina in the fifteenth and seventeenth/eighteenth centuries.[20] By the early eighteenth century, tensions between the Fulbe, who were largely Muslim, and the indigenous, largely non-Muslim Jallonke reached intolerable levels for reasons contested in the scholarly literature.[21] An alliance of Fulbe and Jallonke Muslims launched a holy war, or *jihad*, in the 1720s. After consolidating its power in 1747, the *jihad* expanded into adjacent lands and became a decidedly Fulbe-controlled operation. As a consequence of this movement, large numbers of captives were sold along the coast into the transatlantic trade.

A glance at the *jihad* suggests that the preponderance of captives sold into the trade were non-Muslims. However, the *jihad* was not one long, uninterrupted Muslim march to victory. Non-Muslim populations fought back; in particular, the incursions into Muslim-ruled territory by Kundi Burama of Wassulu lasted from the 1760s into the 1780s and wreaked havoc among the community of the Muslim faithful.[22] Paul E. Lovejoy records that the 1760s through the 1780s was the "most violent" phase of the conflict in Futa Jallon and resulted in a greater than 100-percent per annum increase in slave exports from the region.[23] It appears, therefore, that the Futa Jallon *jihad* was responsible for nearly all of the captives coming from the interior, which in turn accounts for Rodney's estimate that seventy-five percent of the eighteenth-century trade came from the interior.

The next supply zone was the Windward Coast, which at that time stretched from Cape Mount to the city of Assini (near the present-day Ivory Coast–Ghana border), and encompassed what is now Liberia and Ivory Coast. To date there is no evidence to suggest that Islam was significant here. However, the continuing expansion of the Futa Jallon theocracy, combined with the considerable commercial activity of Muslims from Kankan (in Guinea) to Kong (in Ivory Coast), indicates that some captives reaching the Windward Coast for sale must have been Muslim.

The Gold Coast, roughly occupying what is now Ghana, was visited along the Atlantic by European traders as early as the fifteenth century. Originally an exporter of gold and a net importer of slaves, the Gold Coast became a net exporter of slaves by the early seventeenth century.[24] In the first decade of the eighteenth century, Africans were exported from the region at a rate of 2,500 per annum; by the 1740s, the trade peaked at 9,100 per annum. The escalation of the trade resulted from the rising demand for slaves and the expansionist behavior by Asante, which pursued an imperialist policy from the time of its creation about 1680 until 1750.[25] One of the polities that succumbed to the power of Asante was the province of Gonja, a Muslim territory vitally connected to the middle Niger valley via Muslim commercial networks that led through Kong, Dagomba, Wa, and Mamprussi. In addition, Muslim traders from as far east as Hausaland conducted business on a regular basis in the capital of Kumase.[26] The Islamic presence in the interior was such that Lovejoy comments: "The Muslim factor was strong, providing commercial connections with the far interior, so that the Akan states were involved in continental trade on a scale that was at least equal to Oyo, Dahomey, and Benin and was perhaps even greater."[27] All of this suggests that Muslim captives constituted some percentage of the supply from the Gold Coast.

The Bight of Benin, from the Volta River to the Benin River, corresponds approximately to contemporary Togo, Benin, and southwestern Nigeria. The eighteenth-century struggles between the Yoruba (led by the state of Oyo) and Dahomey produced a great many captives, whose numbers were further augmented by Yoruba resistance to the ultimately successful expansion of Muslims from Ilorin. The latter were inspired by the 1804 *jihad* and subsequent caliphate of Usuman dan Fodio at Sokoto (in northern Nigeria). Again, as was true of the *jihad* in Futa Jallon, Muslims as well as non-Muslims lost their liberty and found their way into the transatlantic trade. The existence of large numbers of Muslim "Hausa" slaves (from northern Nigeria) in Bahia (Brazil) is confirmation of this observation.[28] In light of this information, it is reasonable to propose that a significant number of the captives exported from the Bight of Benin were Muslim.

The supply zones of Angola and Mozambique will not be reviewed here, as the Muslim factor was either nonexistent (as was true of Angola), or the total contribution to the North American slave population was negligible (the case with Mozambique). This leaves the Bight of Biafra, comprising what is now southeastern Nigeria, Cameroon, and Gabon. Here, large numbers of captives were procured via numerous, small-scale raids upon a densely populated region. Although there were some trade relations with Muslims to the north, it appears that the number of Muslims arriving on the coast for export was minimal.[29] As is true of Curtin's division of the supply zones, there are no compelling reasons to discard his computation of the relative contributions of these zones to the consequent African American population. According to his estimates, the distribution was as follows:

Senegambia	13.3%
Sierra Leone	5.5%
Windward Coast	11.4%
Gold Coast	15.9%
Bight of Benin	4.3%
Bight of Biafra	23.3%

Altogether, these six zones account for seventy-three and seven-tenths percent of the slaves exported to North America.[30] If the Bight of Biafra is eliminated from further consideration, it would mean that slightly over 50 percent of Africans imported to North America came from areas in which Islam was at least a religion of the minority. Given that between 400,000 and 523,000 Africans came to British North America during the slave trade, at least 200,000 came from areas influenced by Islam to varying degrees.[31] Muslims may have come to America by the thousands, if not tens of thousands. Beyond this general statement, a more precise assessment of their numbers is difficult to sustain at this time.[32]

However, it would be a mistake to focus simply on the Muslim population, for Islam's impact in West Africa was not confined to the converted, practicing community. On the contrary, many non-Muslims were acquainted with some portion of its tenets through the activities of Muslim traders and clerics. The Muslim trading networks, through which the Juula, Yarse, and Hausa merchants all supplied disparate West African communities with goods from as far away as the Mediterranean, also linked the savanna with the forest area, from Senegambia to Lake Chad.[33] The apolitical, nonproselytizing code of behavior of the merchants explains the receptivity of many non-Muslim as well as Muslim communities to their commercial activities.

In addition to, and often in conjunction with, the activities of Muslim traders, Muslim clerics performed religious offices throughout West Africa. Far removed from the lofty positions of the erudite in such cities as Kano and Jenne, numerous clerics of a more utilitarian calling were spread across the region's expanse. Literate in Arabic, these men performed religious and diplomatic services for royal courts and commoners alike. In particular, they provided amulets for both Muslims and non-Muslims; in fact, Muslim amulets, often containing Qur'anic inscriptions encased in sealed pouches, were very popular among non-Muslim populations, many of whom believed that letters possessed particular efficacy.[34] Mosques and *madrasas*, or Qur'anic schools, were invariably established in the Muslim part of town, or in the nearby Muslim village. As a result, many West Africans practiced indigenous religions but were nevertheless familiar with and influenced by Islam, having been exposed to Muslim dress, dietary laws, and overall conduct.

By the same token, it was not unusual for those who had converted to Islam to retain certain aspects of their previous belief systems, and Islam in West Africa underwent a number of reforms in an effort to achieve complete orthodoxy.[35] However, to the degree that these non-Islamic tendencies are not in conflict with the fundamental tenets of the faith (e.g., one God, Muhammad as God's messenger, daily prayer, fasting during Ramadan, etc.), the integrity of these practitioners and the veracity of their confession is not open to challenge.

To be sure, the Muslim presence in North America antedates the arrival of the English colonists. The Spanish first controlled Florida from 1565 to 1763, during which time St. Augustine and nearby Fort Mose featured a significant black population.[36] By the middle of the eighteenth century, the third largest African ethnicity in this metropolitan area was "Mandingo," a group that certainly contained Muslims.[37] As was true of the Spanish in Florida, the French in Louisiana also imported Muslims, as they received slaves from Whydah and Angola, but especially from Senegambia. Gwendolyn Midlo Hall argues that two-thirds of all Africans imported into Louisiana from 1719 to 1743 via the French came from Senegambia, while Rawley estimates that by 1803 some 28,300 slaves had entered Louisiana, many from Senegambia.[38] The Muslim population, while unquantifiable, must have been significant. The runaway notices support this probability, as in 1802 a Louisiana newspaper called for the return of "Pierre-Marc," who was "Sénégalais, âgé de 30 ans, parlant Mobilier, Espagnol, Français et Anglais"; and "Thomas, Sénégalais, âgé de 30 à 32 ans, . . . couleur rouge. . . ."; and again in 1806, when owners sought to find "Deux Negres bruts, nation Sénégal. . . ."[39] Hall writes: "The slaves of French Louisiana often kept their African names, many of which were Islamic. Some slaves with French names had Baraca, an Islamic religious title, as a second name."[40]

The existence of Islam in Spanish- and French-speaking North America is important and merits further investigation. The preponderance of the evidence, however, concerns English-speaking North America. The slave-owning society in Anglophone North America regularly distinguished among the various ethnicities within the African community. While these distinctions were generalized—they categorized African-born slaves according to region of origin and were therefore often inaccurate and misleading—at least whites understood that Africans were not a monolithic people. Some Africans, such as the Igbo and Ibibio of southeastern Nigeria, were reputed to be rebellious, unruly, and suicidal and were not highly prized in some North American areas. In contrast, Akan-speakers from the Gold Coast were regarded as more industrious and manageable.[41] In other words, the fundamental issue was the degree to which African labor could be successfully exploited. Within this context, slaves from Senegambia and Sierra Leone, often simply called "Mandingoes" by whites, were generally viewed by slave owners as preferable to others.[42] Within the categories of Senegambia and Sierra Leone were the bulk of the Muslim imports; both Hall and Austin maintain that the terms "Mandingo" or "Mandinga" were synonymous with Muslim by the nineteenth century.[43] While it cannot be demonstrated that all of these "Mandingoes" were Muslim, the aforementioned close association suggests that a substantial number must have been. The preference for "Mandingoes" by North American slave owners is reflected in the activity of eighteenth-century North American shippers who, although not responsible for the majority of slave importations into North America, nonetheless confined their activities to those areas of West Africa that were of greatest interest to planters and for that reason obtained the vast majority of their slaves from Senegambia and Sierra Leone.[44]

Advertisements for runaway slaves contain unique and substantial information on ethnic and cultural traits of individual slaves and are an underutilized source of data on American slavery. With regard to Muslims in early America, these advertisements occasionally provide names that are clearly Muslim but rarely identified as such.[45] Names such as "Bullaly" (Bilali), "Mustapha," "Sambo," "Bocarrey" (Bubacar, from Abu Bakr), and "Mamado" (Mamadu) are regularly observed in the advertisements for runaway slaves. Unless slave owners clearly understood the origin of these names, they would not necessarily associate them with Islam.[46] A good example is "Sambo," a corruption of the name Samba (meaning "second son" in the language of the Fulbe, an ethnicity spread throughout the West African savanna). The May 24, 1775, edition of Savannah's *Georgia Gazette* ran a notice for three missing men, including twenty-two-year-old "Sambo," reportedly "of the Moorish country."[47] This association with the "Moorish country" is more a reference to Sambo's Muslim identity than to his actually having hailed from North Africa. Similarly, the January 9–12, 1782, publication of the Charleston *Royal Gazette* sought the return of "Sambo" or "Sam," described as having a

"yellowish complexion . . . and his hair is pretty long, being of the Fulla country. . . ."[48] The connections among "Sambo," Islam, and the Fulbe become more
apparent when the preceding advertisement is juxtaposed with another notice in
which a decidedly Muslim name is identified with the same ethnicity. Thus, the July
29, 1766, edition of the Charleston *South-Carolina Gazette and Country Journal*
features an ad in which George Austin seeks the return of "Moosa, a yellow Fellow . . .
of the Fullah Country."[49] While the association between the name "Sambo" and
Islam is strong in the preceding examples, it does not at all follow that the name was
the exclusive property of Muslims. Rather, it is more reasonable to conclude that a
significant number of African-born males with this name may have been Muslim.

The appearance of incontestably Muslim names in the runaway notices is
relatively infrequent. More commonly, owners seeking the return of their slaves
associated them with particular supply zones (e.g., Gambia or Senegal), or they
provided an ethnic identity (Mandingo or Fula, for example). In the case of either
supposed area of origin or ethnic derivation, one cannot conclusively argue that
the individual in question is Muslim, but—given both the African background
and the tendency of American planters to conflate Muslims, ethnicity, and area of
origin—the probability that many of these people were Muslims is high.

Interestingly, examples of Muslim runaways come overwhelmingly from
South Carolina and Georgia, especially along the coast, and also from colonial
Louisiana.[50] This is probably because Charleston (and Savannah to a lesser extent)
was a preeminent slave port and was surrounded by major slaveholding areas
devoted to rice and indigo cultivation. Similarly, rice (and secondarily indigo) was
extremely important to early Louisianians for their own use, and when the first
two slavers arrived in Louisiana in 1719, they carried "several barrels of rice seed
and African slaves who knew how to produce the crop."[51] That is, slave ships
arrived with people from Senegambia, Gold Coast, and Sierra Leone who were
noted for their skills in this type of agriculture and therefore greatly in demand.[52]
In turn, these captives tended to come from Islamized areas. Given their preference for slaves from these areas and their distaste for Africans from the Bight of
Biafra, South Carolina and Georgia planters paid close attention to ethnicity. In
contrast, Virginians were not as discriminating.[53] Their relative lack of interest in
ethnicity—rather than an absence of slaves from those locations—may help to
explain the scarcity of references by Virginians to Muslims from Senegambia and
Sierra Leone.

Further examples of advertisements that clearly refer to Muslims include
the notice for "two Gambia Negroes, about 5 Feet 6 Inches high, the one his
Name is Walley [Wali], the other's Bocarrey. . . ."[54] In this notice, a connection is
established between the Gambia area and Muslims. At times a geographic or

ethnic affiliation is not given, only a name, as was the case in 1757, when a "negro man named Mamado" escaped from Rachel Fairchild; or again in 1772, when William Wood of Santee advertised for "A NEGRO FELLOW named HOMADY [Amadi, from Ahmad], Has a sulky Look and speaks bad English."[55] Enough time had passed for John Graham of Augustin's Creek and John Strobhar of Purrysburgh to learn the names of their absconded slaves and to seek the return of "Mahomet" and "Mousa" respectively, whereas John Inglis of Charleston could only state that three "new" men and one woman had escaped and that "two of the fellows are of a yellow complection and Moorish breed."[56]

In North Carolina in 1808, a one-hundred-dollar reward was offered for the apprehension of Arthur Howe, a white man who had taken away a slave named "Mustapha," commonly called "Muss," described as "polite and submissive" and a "handy fellow with most tools or about horses."[57] That same year, Charlestonian R. Heriot also suspected that "an African wench named FATIMA," who was about twenty years old and spoke "very little English," may have been "enticed away and is harboured by some worthless person or persons."[58] However, most Muslim slaves, as was true of slaves in general, were quite capable of stealing away on their own, as reflected in Godin Guerard's report from Georgia in 1792: "A MOOR SLAVE MAN, about 25 years of age, named MAHOMET who is badged by that name, but passes by the name HOMADY in common."[59]

The matter of absconding obviously involves the question of destination. Muslims were no different from other slaves in that they often sought refuge among American Indians. In 1781 "Hommady" had been absent from his owner in Savannah for three weeks and was "suspected to be harboured among the Indians."[60] Similarly, someone matching the description of the previously mentioned "Mahomet" belonging to John Graham of Augustin's Creek had "been seen at a settlement near the Indian Line on Ogechee very lately," three years after his initial flight.[61] While American Indian communities may have occasionally provided safe havens for slaves, some Muslims wanted to escape from America altogether, as was true of "A New Negro Fellow, called JEFFRAY, sometimes, BRAM, or IBRAHIM; . . . From some hints given by himself and others it is suspected he will endeavor to get on board some vessel."[62]

The preceding discussion concerns obscure individuals. But there are also accounts of Muslims who enjoyed some notoriety.[63] Austin has compiled data on some sixty-five Muslims, of whom only seven who came to North America are discussed in any detail. The question arises: of all the Muslims who came to America's shores before 1865, what was unique about these seven? An analysis of each case reveals that these people attracted attention for a variety of reasons. Umar ibn Said, or "Omar ibn Said," received the greatest amount of interest, apparently because of both his literacy in Arabic and his possible conversion to Christianity. This "Prince Moro," or "Moreau" as he was sometimes called, possessed an Arabic Bible.[64] In fact, he engaged in a campaign of sending such Bibles to West Africa in cooperation with another African Muslim of some renown, Lamine Kaba, or "Lamen Kebe."[65] This, coupled with his repatriation to Liberia in 1835 after nearly thirty years of slavery, probably explains the latter's fame. An article on the Soninke (or Sereculeh) language was also published based upon an interview with Lamine Kaba.[66]

In contrast to Omar ibn Said and Lamine Kaba, Salih Bilali, or "Tom," remained a devout Muslim; the source of his acclaim was his exceptional managerial skills. Born ca. 1765, he arrived in North America in 1800; by 1816, he was the head driver on a plantation at Cannon's Point, on the Georgia island of St. Simons. Such was his reliability that the owner left Salih Bilali in charge of the entire plantation for months at a time, without any supervision.[67] Likewise, Bilali (or "Ben Ali"), a contemporary of Salih Bilali, was also a dependable driver and managed a four-hundred-to-five-hundred-slave plantation on the Georgia island of Sapelo.[68] He is noted as well for an extant collection of excerpts from an Islamic (Maliki) legal text known as the *Risala* of Ibn Abu Zayd.[69] Furthermore, he served as the model for Joel Chandler Harris's caricature "Ben Ali."[70]

Abd al-Rahman, otherwise known as "Prince," was born in 1762 and arrived in New Orleans in 1788. Several remarkable stories surround him, but the one that probably catapulted him into national fame involves his encounter in Mississippi with a white man whom he had befriended in West Africa. Upon the latter's identification of Abd al-Rahman as royalty, a series of events were set into motion that ultimately led Abd al-Rahman back to Africa in 1829, where he died within months of arrival.[71] The motif of an unexpected, outside influence intervening in the life of an individual whose "true" status was previously unknown is repeated in the life of Ayuba ibn Sulayman, or "Job Ben Solomon," who was born ca. 1701, captured by traders in 1730, and brought to Maryland in 1732. Before two years had passed he was a free man, and in 1733 he was en route to West Africa via England as a result of the benevolence of a Royal African Company officer very much taken with the plea for liberty Ayuba had penned in Arabic.[72] Finally, the seventh Muslim of note is Yarrow Mahmud, or "Yarrow Mamout," who in 1819 was living in Georgetown when Charles Willson Peale painted his portrait—apparently because Mahmud had atypical features.[73]

The extraordinary or unusual circumstances in these seven individuals' lives—not their adherence to Islam—explain their relative prominence in the literature. Indeed, many of the accounts concerning them regularly refer to other enslaved Muslims, who, because they did not share in the special circumstance, did not receive significant recognition. Therefore, the attention that these seven are accorded in the literature is misleading because it conveys the idea that Muslims were very rare in number. A closer examination of the literature reveals the presence of more Muslims than previously known.

An investigation into the background of these seven Muslims supports the earlier discussion of the zones and conditions out of which most of the Muslim captives emerged. Ayuba ibn Sulayman, for example, originated from the upper Senegal valley, in the interior of the Senegambia supply zone, from where he traveled to the upper Gambia (ironically) to sell slaves. Unfortunately for him, he fell victim to slave raiders, who ultimately sold him into the transatlantic trade. Also captured and sold with him was Lamine N'jai, or "Lahamin Jay"; both would eventually return to West Africa.[74] Similarly, Omar ibn Said was born in Futa Toro, along the middle Senegal valley, and was captured and sold in the beginning of the nineteenth century. He himself writes that at the age of thirty-one, "there came to our place a large army, who killed many men, and took me, and brought me to the great sea, and sold me into the hands of the Christians."[75] Austin estimates that Omar arrived in Charleston in 1807, which means that the "large army" is probably a reference to the combined armies of Bundu, Kaarta, and Khasso, who invaded Futa Toro in 1806–1807.[76] This particular encounter is only one example of many such conflicts in the middle and upper Senegal valleys and demonstrates the susceptibility of the Muslim population to the slave trade.

Abd al-Rahman represents the Sierra Leone region in that he was born in Futa Jallon and in fact claimed to be the son of Almaami Ibrahima Sori, one of the most important leaders in Guinean history. In the course of a military campaign under his command, he and his army were defeated and captured. What immediately followed is unclear, but at least some of the captives, including Abd al-Rahman, were sold to the Malinke along the Gambia River. Eventually, he and fifty of his former soldiers were traded to an English slaver and transported to the western hemisphere. For Abd al-Rahman, then, his path led to the Gambia, whereas it is possible that other captives from the same company were taken to the Sierra Leone coast. In any event, Abd al-Rahman's personal account underscores the volatility of the region during the eighteenth century and supports the contention that many Muslims from Futa Jallon became captives of war and involuntary participants in the transatlantic trade. Nothing more is said of the other Muslims captured with Abd al-Rahman except for Samba, or "Sambo," as his name was corrupted, who was a part of the former's command in Futa Jallon and wound up on the same Natchez farm, thus explaining his mention.[77]

Like Abd al-Rahman, Bilali and Lamine Kaba were also originally from Futa Jallon. Like Ayuba ibn Sulayman, Omar ibn Said, and Abd al-Rahman, Bilali was

Fulbe.[78] Lamine Kaba, on the other hand, was from the clerically oriented community of the Jakhanke, along the southern reaches of Futa Jallon. His place of capture and point of departure are not clearly indicated, and similar information regarding Bilali is altogether missing. Lamine Kaba maintained that he was searching for writing paper along the coast when he was captured and subsequently enslaved.[79] The need for paper is consistent with the clerical nature of the Jakhanke, and his capture once again illustrates the insecurity of the Sierra Leone region.

Origins in the middle and upper Niger valleys are also represented in the list of Muslim notables. The case of Abu Bakr al-Siddiq, who eventually landed in Jamaica and is therefore not a focus of this study, nevertheless demonstrates that the tentacles of the transatlantic trade reached as far inland as the Niger buckle (the stretch of the Niger from Timbuktu in the west to the town of Gao in the east), as he was born ca. 1790 in Timbuktu and grew up in Jenne, in the upper Niger valley (in the floodplain).[80] Salih Bilali was also from the area, specifically Maasina, between the floodplain and the buckle. He was captured ca. 1790, during the period in which the Bambara were consolidating their control of the upper Niger. After his capture, Salih Bilali was taken south and sold at Anomabu, along the Gold Coast.[81] Sources have heretofore been interpreted to mean that captives coming out of the upper Niger valley were usually traded along the Senegambian coast.[82] The example of Salih Bilali, however, suggests that those trading in slaves from this area had a variety of options available to them for the disposition of their captives.

Finally, Yarrow Mahmud's origins are unspecified. His appearance, preserved for posterity by Peale, reveals features that are consistent with those of the Fulbe.[83] That he arrived in North America in the 1730s, as did Ayuba ibn Sulayman, suggests a middle or upper Senegal valley origin.

It is difficult to know the extent to which Muslims in early America had opportunities to engage in corporate expressions of their faith. At first glance, it seems highly improbable that the host society would allow Muslims to assemble for prayer. But evidence suggests that such assemblies may have taken place. First of all, there are recorded instances of Muslims performing *salat*, or prayer, as individuals. In some cases, such prayer was conducted in a threatening environment. Ayuba ibn Sulayman, for example, was chased by a white boy who threw dirt in his face and mocked him when he prayed. In other cases, Muslims were allowed to pray in the prescribed manner by their owners. Thus, Ayuba, after his unpleasant encounter with the white youth and subsequent flight, was returned to his owner, who provided him with a private place to pray.[84] There is also evidence that Abd al-Rahman continued to practice Islam and that after either a flirtation with Christianity or a conscious strategy of dissimulation to gain support for his repatriation, he immediately reaffirmed his Muslim beliefs upon returning to Africa.[85] Salih Bilali was a devout Muslim who fasted Ramadan; Bilali wore a fez and kaftan, prayed daily (facing the East), and also observed the Muslim feast days.[86] Charles Ball, a slave in Maryland, South Carolina, and Georgia for forty years, must have also witnessed certain Muslim practices among the slaves, for he wrote that "I knew several who must have been, from what I have since learned, Mohammedans; though at that time, I had never heard of the religion of Mohammed."[87] Ball, like many other observers, took cognizance of the unusual behavior but did not know enough about Islam to recognize what he saw.

Individual examples of adherence to Islam suggest that many more also practiced the religion, perhaps clandestinely or perhaps in full view of unsuspecting eyes such as Ball's. In any event, the possibility that Muslims congregated for prayer is enhanced by the tendency among slaves to steal away into secluded places for religious and social purposes.[88] It has generally been assumed that at such times slaves practiced their own brand of Christianity or even traditional African religions, but there is absolutely no reason to preclude Muslims from such activity. Indeed, the probability that Muslim worship took place in some sustained way is increased when the question of contact between Muslims is considered. Bilali and Salih Bilali, residing on plantations on neighboring sea islands, were considered to be best friends and were in contact with others who were apparently Fulbe. The sea island Muslim community on Sapelo and St. Simons islands was probably significant in size, as revealed by Bilali's statement when called upon by his owner to defend the island against the British in 1813: "I will answer for every Negro of the true faith, but not for the Christian dogs you own," he announced, going on to defend the plantation with a force of eighty armed slaves.[89] Religion and religious observances must have constituted an important, if not central, component of the Muslims' bond. Abd al-Rahman and Samba, his fellow Pullo (singular of Fulbe) and a slave on the same farm, were able to associate closely with each other, and the two communicated with at least one other "Mandinka" from Natchez.[90] As co-religionists, they surely sought opportunities to pray together. In addition to the well-known cases of Salih Bilali and Abd al-Rahman, other Muslim slaves may have resided together in significant numbers on the same plantations. For example, thirty-six slaves were taken from a plantation on Amelia Island, East Florida, in 1813 by white "patriots." Of the thirty-six, the following may have been Muslim: Jack and Samba and their two children Saluma and Pizarro; Adam and Fatima and their one-year-old Fernando; and thirteen-year-old Ottemar or Otteman. All of the adults were African-born, and the names "Samba," "Saluma," and "Fatima" make it entirely plausible that the two families were wholly Muslim. Furthermore, it is possible that even more were Muslim, as fifteen of the thirty-six were African-born. However, the names given to them by their owners, including "Hamlet," "Neptune," and "Plato," conceal their ethnic and religious affiliation.[91]

An even more intriguing case is the John Stapleton plantation at Frogmore on St. Helena Island, South Carolina. In May 1816, a list of the 135 slaves on the Frogmore estate was drawn up, and the following individuals were included: "Sambo," eighty-five years old and African-born; "Dido," a fifty-six-year-old "Moroccan"; "Mamoodie" and his wife, "Eleanor," both African-born and aged twenty-eight and twenty-nine, respectively; and the family of "Nelson," "Venus," and child "Harriett." Sambo and Dido were probably Muslim. Mamoodie and Eleanor had a child named Fatima who was born in 1814 (she died in infancy), so they were very likely to have been Muslim. The most interesting individuals are Nelson and Venus, who were twenty-nine and twenty-seven, respectively, and both African-born. In a subsequent slave list, drawn up in 1818, their other child "Hammett" appears. Hammett (Hamid or Ahmad) is a Muslim name, which strongly suggests that one or both of the parents were Muslim. Again, the remaining names on the 1816 list suggest no African derivations, but twenty-eight people are listed as African-born. Therefore, others may well have been Muslim as were Nelson and/or Venus, but the absence of corroborating evidence—such as a child with a Muslim name—prevents any such identification.[92] In any event, those who were Muslims would have sought out each other's company and would have searched for corporate ways to express their common faith.

Muslims sought not only to associate with one another but also to retain their common Islamic heritage. Dr. Collins, who wrote a manual on the medical treatment of slaves, stated that many slaves from Senegal "converse in the Arabic language . . . and some are sufficiently instructed even to write it."[93] Joseph Le Conte recalled "an old native African named Philip," a Muslim who, during the antebellum period, demonstrated the outward expressions of the religion "by going through all the prayers and prostrations of his native country."[94] Abd al-Rahman often wrote the *Fātiha* (opening *sura* or chapter of the Qur'an) for whites who believed that they were receiving the Lord's Prayer in an exotic hand. And Omar ibn Said penned his autobiography in Arabic.[95]

Many Muslims struggled not only to preserve their traditions but also to pass them on to their progeny. Thus, Bilali bestowed Muslim names upon his twelve sons and seven daughters; and, as they regularly communicated with one another in a "foreign tongue," he apparently had taught Pulaar (the language of the Fulbe) and possibly Arabic to all of his children except the youngest daughter.[96] Samba, the companion of Abd al-Rahman, had at least three sons and gave them all Muslim names.[97] The previously mentioned Nelson and Venus of St. Helena gave one of their children a Muslim name. In 1786 "Sambo" and "Fatima" escaped Edward Fenwicke of John's Island; Sambo was "of the Guinea country" and probably Muslim, but Fatima was described as "country born" (i.e., born in North America), so she either converted to Islam or had at least one Muslim parent.[98] The recurrence of Muslim names among American-born slaves corroborates the desire among many to keep their religion and culture alive.

The preponderance of runaway notices containing references to Muslims appear in South Carolina and Georgia newspapers. Consistent with this pattern, there is relatively more information on Muslims and their descendants living along the Georgia coast, both on the various sea islands and on the mainland near Savannah. The data provide an incomplete but substantive picture of African-born Muslims, their progeny, and associated communities of believers who pursued their religion with diligence and purpose in an atmosphere charged with the teachings of Christianity and the attraction of African traditional religions. There is also possible evidence of non-Muslim slaves converting to Islam. Finally, the grandchildren and subsequent progeny spoke of the African-born Muslims with pride, suggesting a strong and clear identification with an Islamic heritage, if not an actual embrace of the religion.

As noted earlier, Salih Bilali and Bilali served as drivers on very large plantations located on the Georgia sea islands of St. Simons and Sapelo. It appears that the number of Muslim slaves in this area was significant. For example, in May 1802, two Muslim men named "Alik" and "Abdalli" escaped from Sapelo Island; both were probably African-born, as one spoke "bad English," while the other's command of the language was only slightly better.[99] In March 1807, "Toney," "Jacob," and eighteen-year-old "Musa" also escaped from Sapelo Island, having belonged to Alexander Johnston.[100] Again, it is conceivable that all three men were Muslim.

John Couper (1759–1850) and his son James Hamilton Couper (1794–1866) owned a number of plantations on St. Simons Island and along the Altamaha River, including the well-known Hopeton plantation. In an 1827 document detailing the sale of Hopeton by John Couper to James Hamilton (a close friend) and his son James, 381 slave names are listed.[101] Of these names, "Fatima" is repeated six times, "Mahomet" twice, and there is one "Maryam." These were probably Muslims. However, the principal Muslim on the plantation was Salih Bilali, who is listed as "Tom" in the document. How many more Muslims there were at Hopeton cannot be discerned from the available data, but there were probably others whose Islamic identities are hidden behind such names as "Tom." Indeed, James Hamilton Couper himself wrote that "there are about a dozen negroes on this plantation, who speak and understand the Foulah language."[102]

Ben Sullivan was eighty-eight and living on St. Simons when interviewed by the Works Progress Administration (WPA) in the 1930s.[103] Sullivan was the grandson of Salih Bilali, and Sullivan's father's name was "Belali," a direct indication of Salih Bilali's desire to pass on his Islamic identity. Ben Sullivan remembered, in addition to his father and grandfather, two other Muslims in the community, "ole Israel" and "Daphne." Concerning the former, Sullivan reported, "Ole Israel he pray a lot wid a book he hab wut he hide, an he take a lill mat an he say he prayuhs on it. He pray wen duh sun go up an wen duh sun go down. . . . He alluz tie he head up in a wite clawt an seem he keep a lot uh clawt on hand." The book Sullivan refers to may have been the Qur'an. Similarly, Daphne prayed regularly, bowing "two aw tree times in duh middle uh duh prayuh," and was usually veiled.[104]

On nearby Sapelo Island was the large plantation of Thomas Spalding (1774–1851), the driver of which was Salih Bilali's coreligionist Bilali (pronounced "Blali" in the Sapelo community), also referred to as the "Old Man."[105] Bilali's large family of twelve sons and seven daughters all "worshipped Mahomet," as one observer stated in 1901, based on her memories of the late 1850s.[106] Some details of their religious practices are provided by Katie Brown, who at the time of the WPA interviews was "one of the oldest inhabitants" of Sapelo Island.[107] She was also the great-granddaughter of Bilali, or "Belali Mahomet." She enumerated Bilali's seven daughters as "Magret, Bentoo, Chaalut, Medina, Yaruba, Fatima, and Hestuh"; Katie Brown, whose grandmother was Margaret, went on to say: "Magret an uh daughter Cotto use tuh say dat Bilali an he wife Phoebe pray on duh bead. Dey wuz bery puhticluh bout duh time dey pray and dey bery regluh bout duh hour. Wen duh sun come up, wen it straight obuh head an wen it set, das duh time dey pray. Dey bow tuh duh sun an hab lill mat tuh kneel on. Duh beads is on a long string. Belali he pull bead an he say, 'Belambi, Hakabara, Mahamadu.' Phoebe she say, 'Ameen, Ameen.'"[108] In addition to religious observances, Bilali apparently adhered to Islamic prescriptions on marriage; Ms. Brown remarked that "Magret she say Phoebe he wife, but maybe he hab mone one wife. I spects das bery possible."[109] Information on Muslims' adherence to Islamic dietary proscriptions is meager; however, Cornelia Bailey provides a few glimpses with her observation that Bilali's children would not eat wild animals or fresh meat and that certain seafoods such as crab were avoided, as were certain kinds of fish.[110] Taken together, the testimonies of Ben Sullivan, Cornelia Bailey, and Katie Brown provide the contours of Muslim life in early Georgia—prayer mats, prayer beads, veiling, head coverings, Qur'ans, dietary laws, and ritualized, daily prayer characterized the lifestyle. The composite picture is consistent with a serious pursuit of Islam.

Bilali's daughters, who were also slaves and whose places of birth are not as clearly defined as their father's, were just as religious.[111] Shad Hall of Sapelo Island, another descendant of Bilali through his grandmother Hestuh, describes the daughters as follows: "'Hestuh an all ub urn sho pray on duh bead. Dey weah duh string uh beads on duh wais. Sometime duh string on duh neck. Dey pray at sun-up and face duh sun on duh knees an bow tuh it tree times, kneelin on a lill mat.'"[112]

A sense of a closely-knit family emerges from these WPA interviews. Katie Brown refers to Salih Bilali of St. Simons as "cousin Belali Sullivan." Shad Hall states that his grandmother Hestuh bore a son called "Belali Smith," who in turn was the grandfather of Phoebe Gilbert, also a Sapelo resident.[113] Phoebe Gilbert's other set of grandparents were Calina and Hannah, both of whom were Igbo. Sapelo inhabitant Nero Jones was also related to "Uncle Calina and An Hannah" and says that they were "mighty puhticuluh bout prayin. Dey pray on duh bead. Duh ole man he say 'Ameela' and An Hannah she say 'Hakabara.'"[114] The last quote is fascinating, for it strongly suggests that Calina and Hannah were Muslim converts, as the Igbo of southeastern Nigeria were not Muslim.[115] Likewise, the Igbo population in early America was substantial, but hardly ever associated with Islam.

Islam along coastal Georgia was by no means limited to the descendants of Bilali and Salih Bilali. The WPA interviews of Ed Thorpe of Harris Neck, Rosa Grant of Possum Point, and Lawrence Baker of Darien reveal that their ancestors were also Muslim. Like the "Bilali" families, these early Muslims also prayed three times daily in the prescribed fashion, ending their prayers with "Ameen, Ameen, Ameen." In fact, Rosa Grant says of her grandmother Ryna that "Friday wuz duh day she call huh prayuh day." This is not an allusion to daily prayer, as Ms. Grant had previously stated that her grandmother's prayers began "ebry mawnin."[116] Rather, this is a reference to the Muslim observance of Friday prayer, on which day Muslims congregate at noon. Whether Ms. Grant and others actually gathered for the prayer is not known, but at least she attempted to keep alive the significance of the day. Muslims contemporary with Bilali and with names similar to his might have lived in other areas along the Atlantic coast. Speculation on this point arises from the earlier mentioned possibility of Muslim ancestry in the lineage of Frederick Douglass. His great-great-grandfather was named "Baly," and his grand-parents were Betsy and Isaac Bailey of Talbot County along Maryland's Eastern Shore. Betsy Bailey's daughter Harriet gave birth to Frederick Augustus Bailey. William S. McFeely, the biographer of Douglass, writes:

> In the nineteenth century, on Sapelo Island (where Baileys still reside), there was a Fulfulde-speaking slave from Timbo, Futa Jallon, in the Guinea highlands, who could write Arabic and who was the father of twelve sons. His name was Belali Mohomet. . . ."Belali" slides easily into the English "Bailey," a common African American surname along the

Atlantic coast. The records of Talbot County list no white Baileys from which the slave Baileys might have taken their name, and an African origin, on the order of "Belali," is conceivable.[117]

Since Betsy Bailey was born ca. 1772, she was essentially Bilali's contemporary and therefore very unlikely to have been his descendant. However, McFeely's point concerning the structural similarities between Belali and Bailey, coupled with the absence of white Baileys in Talbot County, is intriguing, and the possibility of Muslim antecedents in this particular lineage cannot be ruled out.

In sum, the Muslim presence in coastal Georgia (and possibly elsewhere along the Atlantic) was active, healthy, and compelling. Clearly, the history of Africans along the South Carolina-Georgia continuum is more complicated than previously understood; its study can no longer be limited to the Gullah language and associated handicrafts and artifacts, notwithstanding their importance.

In relation to other Africans, Muslims were generally viewed by slave owners as a "more intelligent, more reasonable, more physically attractive, more dignified people."[118] The belief in the superiority of the "Mohammedans" was apparently a consistently held view throughout the colonial and antebellum periods. As an example, Salih Bilali is described as "a man of superior intelligence and higher cast of feature."[119] In part, this view of the Muslim was informed by the physical appearance of slaves funneled through the Senegambia and Sierra Leone supply zones, such as the Fulbe and such Mande-speakers as the Malinke, who were believed to be phenotypically closer to Europeans than were other Africans.[120] But the more precise reason for the preference for Muslims was that they tended to come from Senegambia, a region whose inhabitants, together with those from the non-Muslim areas of Sierra Leone, were valued for their expert knowledge of rice (and to a lesser extent indigo) cultivation.[121] Clearly, such experience influenced the desire of many Carolina and Georgia planters to purchase Africans from Senegambia and Sierra Leone.

As a result of their agricultural skill and the advantage it gave them, as well as for reasons to be explored shortly, many Muslims were given more responsibilities and privileges than other slaves. Alford writes that Muslim slaves were used as "drivers, overseers, and confidential servants with a frequency their numbers did not justify."[122] Examples of this general statement include the careers of Bilali and Salih Bilali, who were both placed in positions of high authority and who jointly used that authority to quell a slave insurrection. Zephaniah Kingsley, a slave owner who advocated the "benign" treatment of slaves, recorded that along the Georgia coast during the War of 1812, there were "two instances, to the southward, where gangs of negroes were prevented from deserting to the enemy by drivers, or influential negroes, whose integrity to their masters, and influence over the slaves prevented it; and what is still more remarkable, in both instances the influential negroes were Africans, and professors of the Mahomedan religion."[123] This is apparently a reference to Bilali and Salih Bilali. Not only did they crush the revolt, but, as previously noted, Bilali defended Sapelo Island in 1813 with eighty armed slaves and denied access to the English. The majority of these eighty slaves were probably Muslim, given the extensive nature of Islam in the area, combined with Bilali's statement that he could depend only upon fellow Muslims to aid in the armed defense of the island, as opposed to the general slave population.[124]

As the examples of Bilali and Salih Bilali suggest, there were certain tensions between Muslim and non-Muslim slaves, whether the latter were African-born or not. In the first place, there is evidence that some American-born slaves condescended to newly arrived Africans, Muslim or non-Muslim.[125] To the extent that African Muslims encountered such treatment, they would have experienced pressures to modify or discontinue their Muslim/African practices in order to conform to what was acceptable in the new setting or they would have found the resolve to remain faithful to their convictions.[126] The evidence shows that the majority of Muslims reaffirmed their faith. With this in mind, it is not surprising to read of Bilali's characterization of his fellow (or actually subordinate) slaves as "Christian dogs." Neither is it startling to read of Abd al-Rahman's comments to Cyrus Griffin, in which "he states explicitly, and with an air of pride, that not a drop of negro blood runs in his veins."[127] This attitude was confirmed by the children of Bilali, all of whom were Muslims, and who were described as "holding themselves aloof from the others as if they were conscious of their own superiority."[128] Bailey essentially confirms this, stating that not only did Bilali "keep his distance" from others because he "did not like mixing" with them but also that Muslims and non-Muslims as a whole tended to "keep to themselves," although they generally "got along" and could work with others for specific purposes or special occasions.[129]

The attitude of Muslim superiority, to the degree that it in fact existed, must first be explained within the context of the West African background. The probability that these people themselves had been slaveholders in the Old World influenced their view of slaves. Their African experience was shaped along the lines of highly stratified societies in which the servile population was seen as inferior. The ethnic factor is also relevant in that there is considerable data on the ethnocentricity of the Fulbe of West Africa, who were clearly present among the American Muslim population.[130] Bertram Wyatt-Brown, in discussing three related, yet distinct psychological responses by men to enslavement, cites Ibrahima as a prime example of a Fulbe man who, by virtue of his exclusionary early socialization vis-à-vis other ethnicities, embodied the first category of response, which was characterized by a "ritualized compliance in which self-regard is retained." That is, Ibrahima maintained his culturally inculcated dignity and pride as he reconciled himself to enslavement by remembering his *pulaaku*, the essence of the distinctive Fulbe character and prescriptive code of behavior. Hence, he never descended to the second category of response which "involves the incorporation of shame," or to the third category, described as "samboism" and "shamelessness."[131] Indeed, to Ibrahima's mind, the internalization of enslavement was characteristic only of other, lesser, non-Fulbe ethnicities.

A second factor in explaining Muslim attitudes of superiority concerns Islam itself. To live as a Muslim in eighteenth- and nineteenth-century West Africa was to live in an increasingly intolerant society. This was the period of the *jihad*, of the establishment of Muslim theocracies, of self-purification and separation from practices and beliefs that were seen as antithetical to Islam. Abu Bakr al-Siddiq summarized the perspective of the Muslim when he wrote:

> The faith of our families is the faith of Islam. They circumcise the foreskin; say the five prayers; fast every year in the month of Ramadan; give alms as ordained in the law; marry four free women—a fifth is forbidden to them except she be their slave; they fight for the faith of God; perform the pilgrimage to Mecca, i.e. such as are able to do so; eat the flesh of no beast but what they have slain for themselves; drink no wine, for whatever intoxicates is forbidden to them; they do not keep company with those whose faith is contrary to theirs, such as worshippers of idols.[132]

As the evidence grows that a substantial number of slaves practiced to varying degrees African traditional religions, we can assume that the Muslim would have felt besieged by the non-Muslim majority and would have been under considerable pressure to conform.[133] Notwithstanding such pressure, there are many accounts of the piety of these Muslims, who steadfastly pursued their religion under adverse conditions. In the same spirit as Abu Bakr al-Siddiq, Salih Bilali is described by his owner as "the most religious man that [I] had ever known."[134] Another observer depicted him as a "strict Mahometan," who refused alcohol and who held "in great contempt, the African belief in fetishes and evil spirits.'"[135] In like manner, Ayuba ibn Sulayman prayed daily in the Muslim fashion, despite sustained harassment by a white youth who was quite amazed and amused.[136] Fundamental differences between Islam and other systems of belief clearly could have further militated against a uniform experience of enslavement.

But a third factor in Muslim attitudes of superiority is as important as the first two; namely, a number of these Muslim slaves were from prominent backgrounds in West Africa. For example, Abd al-Rahman was a scion of Almaami Ibrahima

Sori. Ayuba ibn Sulayman's father was a leading cleric in the upper Senegal valley. Several Muslims, including Lamine Kaba, Bilali, and Omar ibn Said, boasted of extensive educations in West Africa. In fact, it was more common than not that West African Muslims had an Islamic education and were therefore literate, and the various documents that discuss notable Muslims invariably comment that they could write Arabic. Literacy within the West African Muslim community was widespread; most Muslim villages and towns maintained *madrasas* to which boys and girls from ages seven to fourteen went for instruction. At *madrasa*, the Qur'an was memorized and Arabic grammar was introduced. From *madrasa*, young men of sufficient means moved on to more advanced studies, often requiring travel from one town to another in order to study under the appropriate *shaykh*, or master teacher of a specific curriculum. The most advanced students would go on to towns such as Pir and Jenne, where there were concentrations of scholars. Thus, the educational process was well established, with a tradition reaching back to at least the fourteenth century.[137] Reducing an educated elite to the status of slaves—a status shared with those of humble birth—was especially demeaning.

Reflecting on the pastoral background of many Africans and referring to considerations of "class," it is important to note that some of the Muslim slaves, such as Ayuba ibn Sulayman, were completely unaccustomed to agricultural labor, as became evident very quickly.[138] Dr. Collins remarked that slaves from Senegal "are excellent for the care of cattle and horses, and for domestic service, though little qualified for the ruder labours of the field, to which they never ought to be applied."[139] The aristocratic and/or pastoral background of some West Africans, combined with the aforementioned agricultural expertise of others, meant that Muslims were, in the eyes of the host society, "better suited" for domestic and/or supervisory roles. This determination, it follows, widened the schism between Muslim and non-Muslim, because the former would more likely be assigned the less physically demanding jobs. Finally, some Muslims probably were deeply affected by the racist views of whites toward other Africans. That is, they would have been encouraged to distance themselves from the average African, even to the point of denying any similarity to them. Thus, there is Abd al-Rahman's claim that he had no "negro" blood. In fact, Abd al-Rahman claimed to be a "Moor," and he placed "the negro in a scale of being infinitely below the Moor."[140] The convention of claiming Moorish or Berber ancestry was not unique to Abd al-Rahman; apparently it was used occasionally by those who could neither deny nor fully accept their African ancestry. As a result, a few slaves maintained the following position, as expressed ca. 1937 by centenarian Silvia King of Marlin, Texas: "I know I was borned in Morocco, in Africa, and was married and had three chillen befo' I was stoled from my husband. I don't know who it was stole me, but dey took me to France, to a place called Bordeaux, drugs me with some coffee, and when I knows anything 'bout it, I's in de bottom of a boat with a whole lot of other niggers."[141]

While some evidence points to strained relations between Muslims and non-Muslims, there are also indications of cordiality between the two. For example, Abd al-Rahman himself married a Baptist woman in 1794, had several children with her, returned to Liberia with her in 1829, and expired in her arms a few months later. Charles Ball mentions his acquaintance and friendship with a number of Muslims.[142] These two examples illustrate that, despite evidence of Muslim attitudes of superiority, Muslims and non-Muslims interacted in fundamental ways.

Notwithstanding the vitality of the Islamic tradition and the strength of their bonds (especially in coastal Georgia), Muslims in early America faced certain distinct challenges to the preservation of their religion. Though they may have gathered in small numbers and clandestine places to pray, they could not openly maintain Qur'anic schools and did not have access to Islamic texts. Inevitably their collective memory eventually faltered. As an example of not having access to the necessary texts, Bilali, author of the "Ben-Ali Diary," put together passages from Ibn Abu Zayd's *Risala* in such a haphazard fashion that Nigerian clerics, upon reviewing the document, declared it to be the work of jinn (spirits).[143] Likewise, Salih Bilali, while claiming to possess a Qur'an, could not write Arabic coherently.[144] The gradual loss of Islamic knowledge, combined with the tendency to use Arabic exclusively for purposes of religion, undermined Islamic culture in early America.

Islam was in competition with other African religions practiced by the slaves, especially prior to the nineteenth century. In the North American setting, most Africans from various parts of the continent adhered to non-Islamic beliefs. In the process of intermingling, there were pressures to find points of agreement or similarity in religious expression, and the need to establish a community was intense. As the nineteenth century progressed, the host society, while at times amused by the varieties of religions practiced by the slaves, became increasingly concerned with controlling the religious expression of its captive population. Finally, the number of Christian converts among African Americans increased rapidly as a result of their own desire to embrace an Africanized version of Christianity and of a post-1830 campaign within the "militant South" to use religion as a means of social control. As Africanized Christianity became more of a force, Islam necessarily suffered.

The process by which Christianity began to compete with and eventually overtake Islam can be seen in the Sapelo community. The progeny of African-born Muslims (who tended to restrict their social interactions with non-Muslims) eventually began attending the Tuesday, Thursday, and Sunday night "prayer houses" that each community on the island had, while continuing their own Muslim gatherings. With the establishment of the First African Baptist Church in May 1866, however, the open and collective pursuit of Islam became increasingly rare, although it is difficult to say when, exactly, it ended on the island.[145]

The response of African-born Muslims, however, was another story. Despite pressure to convert to Christianity, the majority of African-born Muslims evidently resisted with success any and all coercion to abandon their faith. Examples inconsistent with this finding are few and include Abd al-Rahman, whose supposed conversion to Christianity is contradicted by his subsequent recommitment to Islam upon repatriation to Africa. And while it is true that Lamine Kaba and Omar ibn Said both professed Christianity, questions surround the conversion of the latter.[146]

Having stated that most African-born Muslims remained loyal to their religion, it should be noted that ethnocentricity, combined with other cultural differences, probably restricted Muslim efforts to proselytize among non-Muslims. Therefore, the continuity of the Islamic tradition was heavily dependent upon a cultural transfer within existing Muslim families and over generations. This was a formidable task, especially since the importation of non-Muslims into North America greatly exceeded that of Muslims in the late eighteenth and early nineteenth centuries, and thus many Muslims had little choice except to marry non-Muslims. Further, African-born Muslims may have been unable to communicate with their children and grandchildren because they could not all speak a common language well enough to convey detailed information and would therefore have been frustrated in their attempts to convey the tenets of Islam adequately.[147] Enslavement itself impeded such matters as formal Muslim education, circumcision, the formation of brotherhoods, the maintenance of moral proscriptions, and the observance of basic dietary laws. The children of African Muslims were probably socialized within the context of the larger, non-Muslim slave culture and were deeply influenced by this process. In short, Muslims would have had great difficulty in preserving Islam within their own families, assuming a stable slave family. Given the vicissitudes of slavery, such an assumption is most unwarranted.

Questions concerning the resilience of Islam take on significance with the children and grandchildren of African-born Muslims, and it has not been established whether these progeny were or were not Muslims. The Islamic heritage was certainly present, so that individuals bore Muslim names and retained a keen collective memory of the religious practices of their ancestors. However, whether they themselves practiced Islam is unclear. A reluctance to be unequivocal about religion as well as about other matters can be observed in the responses of Georgia coastal blacks to the queries posed by the WPA interviewers. Indeed, a careful reading of these interviews reveals considerable anxiety among the informants, which is understandable given the period's sociopolitical dynamics.[148] If they were practicing Muslims, they certainly would not have volunteered such information to whites in the rural South of the 1930s.

One account given by the interviewers underscores the ambiguity of religious affinities during this time and supports the contention that the informants did not tell all. The account concerns one Preacher Little, who was encountered on Sapelo Island and whose physical appearance, demeanor, and dress were initially described as "Mohammedan looking." Although the interviewers were subsequently assured that the minister was a Christian (and they went on to witness the minister preside over a religious service), their first impressions are instructive, especially since this encounter took place after the interviews with the descendants of Salih Bilali and Bilali.[149] Preacher Little could very well have been the embodiment of a certain Islamic-Christian synthesis. Indeed, this possibility is enhanced by the reflections of Charles Jones, who, in 1842, wrote that African-born Muslims related Yahweh to Allah and Jesus to Muhammad.[150] His observation contains a number of potential meanings, including the possibility that these Africans, while ostensibly practicing Christianity, were in reality reinterpreting Christian dogma in the light of Islamic precepts. If this were the case, then they were probably more Muslim than Christian in their worldview, given that Islam had already shaped their perspective. It is conceivable, therefore, that their descendants could have continued this kind of syncretism (or perhaps dissimulation).

A further example of this possible syncretism (or even dualism, in which a person keeps the two religions separate and pursues them as such) again comes from Sapelo and the descendants of Bilali. Cornelia Bailey's grandmother told her about the life of Harriet Hall Grovner, Bailey's great-grandmother and the granddaughter of Bentoo, Bilali's daughter. Harriet Grovner was a practicing Muslim until the First African Baptist Church was organized in 1866, at which time she joined. Although she became very active in the Sunday School, she may have continued to practice Islam.[151] This speculation is based upon evidence that she frequently stole into the woods to pray. It is not clear whether she continued such clandestine activity after 1866 or why she would have found it necessary to do so after that time, unless she was praying something other than Christian prayers. Harriet died in 1922 and until her death may have still been practicing Islam as the legacy of an African Muslim tradition. In view of the above discussion and examples, it is reasonable to conclude that Islam's long-term survival in America was highly unlikely. This conclusion, however, is based on the notion that Islam in early America was, at the very most, inconsequential. One would not, therefore, search for remnants of what supposedly never existed. This study does not purport to make conclusive statements concerning Islam's legacy in America. Rather, it argues that, given Islam's importance in African and African American history, there are several areas into which further investigation may prove very beneficial. First of all, the Muslim /non-Muslim distinction played a role in social divisions among slaves. Not all "lighter-skinned" house servants (and others with similar "privileges") were the result of black-white miscegenation; at least some were Fulbe and other Africans with "atypical" features. This point, in turn, leads to a much broader question on the role of ethnicity within the slave community and deserves further study.

Second, the very important research of Robert Farris Thompson on the relationship between African and African American art and philosophy has revealed that, at least in the area of quilt-making, African Americans exhibit clear Mande influences.[152] The Mande world contained a large number of Muslims, so that such evidence points to the possible continuity of an Islamically influenced cultural heritage, if not the religion itself. Such a possibility may be supported by intriguing archaeological evidence involving the "recovery of blue, faceted glass beads from slave cabins that were of European manufacture [that] may be related to the Moslem belief that a single blue bead will ward off evil spirits."[153]

Third, an investigation of the potential influence of Islam upon the practice of Christianity by African Americans in certain areas or communities would be instructive. On Sapelo Island, for example, the congregation of the First African Baptist Church always prays to the east, which is the direction in which the church is pointed.[154] Regarding personal prayer, individuals are instructed to pray to the east, given that the "devil is in the other corner." The deceased are also buried facing the east.[155] Such details reveal substantial influence indeed, which may even be reflected in the teachings and beliefs of the church. Islam may not have survived as a complete and coherent system of faith, but some of its constituent elements may yet continue to guide and sustain.

Finally, further investigation is required into the backgrounds of such men as Elijah Muhammad (born 1898) and Noble Drew Ali (born 1886), the latter having been the founder of the Moorish Science Temple in 1913 in Newark, New Jersey, and the possible forerunner to Elijah Muhammad's Nation of Islam. Both men were born during a time in which Islam may still have been practiced by African-born Muslims.[156] Both grew up during a period in which the children and grand-children of these earlier Muslims were, at the very least, highly cognizant of their Islamic heritage. Both were born in the South, Ali in North Carolina, Muhammad in Sandersville, Georgia. Elijah Muhammad is particularly intriguing, as he came from an area relatively close to the Georgia coast. He was born Elijah Poole; his father, Wali Poole, was a Baptist minister and sharecropper. The term *wali* means "holy man" or "saint" in Arabic and refers to individuals noted for pious living and miraculous feats. The runaway slave notices include references to a number of "Walleys," all of whom come from either Gambia or "Guinea," a possible indication of Muslim identity.[157] Did Elijah Muhammad's father take the name Wali (or was it given to him) as a reminder of an Islamic family heritage? Did Elijah Muhammad, when he converted to Islam in 1931, do so because the words enjoining him to Islam were in some way familiar, reminiscent of concepts and ideas he had been exposed to as a child? Further research may or may not reveal a clear linkage. If so, it would mean that Islam in America never really disappeared but rather underwent a brief hiatus and has reemerged under more appropriate conditions to resume its place as an important aspect of the history of the African experience in America.

NOTES

1. With regard to North America itself, compare the discussion of African cultural transfer in William D. Piersen's *Black Yankees: The Development of an Afro-American Subculture in Eighteenth-Century New England* (Amherst, Mass., 1988) with that found in Mechal Sobel's *The World They Made Together: Black and White Values in Eighteenth-Century Virginia* (Princeton, 1987), or her earlier work *Trabelin' On: The Slave Journey to an Afro-Baptist Faith* (Westport, Conn., and London, 1979). Margaret Washington Creel's *"A Peculiar People": Slave Religion and Community-Culture Among the Gullahs* (New York and London, 1988) is an equally important contribution within this framework. Finally, Michael Mullin's *Africa in America: Slave Acculturation and Resistance in the American South and the British Caribbean, 1736–1831* (Urbana and Chicago, 1992) provides an examination of the relationship between acculturative forces and slave revolts, among other things.

2. Henceforth, "America" will be used to designate that part of North America that became the United States.

3. Consider William S. McFeely's speculations in *Frederick Douglass* (New York and London, 1991), 3–5.

4. For example, see Peter H. Wood, *Black Majority: Negroes in Colonial South Carolina: From 1670 through the Stono Rebellion* (New York, 1974); Daniel C. Littlefield, *Rice and Slaves: Ethnicity and the Slave Trade in Colonial South Carolina* (Baton Rouge and London, 1981); Philip D. Curtin, *The Rise and Fall of the Plantation Complex: Essays in Atlantic History* (Cambridge, Eng., 1990); and Curtin, *Cross-Cultural Trade in World History* (Cambridge, Eng., 1984).

5. Allan D. Austin, *African Muslims in Antebellum America: A Sourcebook* (New York, 1984). The seven and their approximate lifespans are as follows: Omar ibn Said (ca. 1770–1864), Lamine Kaba (ca. 1780–?), Salih Bilali (ca. 1765–?), Bilali (contemporary of Salih Bilali), Abd al-Rahman (ca. 1762–1829), Ayuba ibn Sulayman (ca. 1702–1773), and Yarrow Mahmud (elderly when portrait made in 1819).

6. Douglas Grant, *The Fortunate Slave: An Illustration of African Slavery in the Early Eighteenth Century* (London, New York, and Toronto, 1968); Terry Alford, *Prince Among Slaves* (New York, 1977); and Ivor Wilks, "Abu Bakr al-Siddiq of Timbuktu" and "Salih Bilali of Massina," in Philip D. Curtin, ed., *Africa Remembered: Narratives by West Africans*

from the Era of the Slave Trade (Madison, Milwaukee, and London, 1967). Concerning Muslim names, there is no standard method of transliteration into English. For example, just as the word "muslim" is often anglicized as "moslem," so names such as "Sulayman" may appear as "Sulaiman" and "Muhammad" as "Mohammed." The approach used here is to employ a scheme of vowelization that most closely approximates standard Arabic. However, it must be kept in mind that Arabic names often underwent changes in West Africa, and in such cases, it is the African appellation that will be transliterated. That is, since it is common in West Africa to encounter "Mamadu" as opposed to "Mahmud" or "Ahmad," "Mamadu" will be used here. Finally, the names of some individuals are slightly different in English due to corruption and/or a lack of familiarity with the meaning and functions of the components of the name. For example, Ayuba ibn Sulayman belongs to the Jallo clan of the Fulbe, and sometimes Jallo will be attached to the end of his name. In many instances Jallo will be written as "Diallo," owing to the French influence. The anglicizing of African and Arab names is problematic, to be sure. For the purposes of this study, care will be taken to make a full identification of the individual in question.

7. I interviewed Cornelia Walker Bailey in July 1992 on Sapelo Island, Georgia. She was born in Bell Marsh on June 12, 1945. Bilali is her great-great-great-grandfather through his daughter Bentoo (Arabic "Binta"). Mrs. Bailey presently lives in Hog Hammock Community on Sapelo with her husband and family. The interview was taped, and notes were taken during the interview. Both the tapes and the notes are in the author's possession.

8. Philip D. Curtin, *The Atlantic Slave Trade: A Census* (Madison, 1969). In fact, the lines of demarcation between these zones conform reasonably well to the political and cultural transitions of precolonial Africa.

9. J. Suret-Canale and Boubacar Barry, "The Western Atlantic Coast to 1800," in J. F. A. Ajayi and Michael Crowder, eds., *History of West Africa* (2d ed.; 2 vols., New York, 1976), I, 466; and Paul E. Lovejoy, *Transformations in Slavery: A History of Slavery in America* (Cambridge, Eng., and other cities, 1983), 58.

10. Jean Boulegue and Jean Suret-Canale, "The Western Atlantic Coast," in J. F. A. Ajayi and Michael Crowder, eds., *History of West Africa* (3d ed.; 2 vols., New York, 1985), I, 519–30.

11. Lovejoy, *Transformations*, 72–73.

12. Curtin, *Atlantic Slave Trade*, chap. 4; and Lovejoy, *Transformations*, 35–37.

13. The term *tubenan* is from the Arabic *tawba*, "to repent"; the Wolof word *tub* essentially carries the same meaning. For more on the tubenan, or "guerre des Marabouts," see Philip D. Curtin, "Jihad in West Africa: Early Phases and Inter-Relations in Mauritania and Senegal," *Journal of African History* 12, no. 1 (1971), 11–24; and Boubacar Barry, "La guerre des Marabouts dans la région du fleuve Sénégal de 1673 a 1677," *Bulletin de l'Institut Fondaniental* (formerly *Français*) *d'Afrique Noire* 33 (July 1971), 564–89.

14. Suret-Canale and Barry, "Western Atlantic Coast," 470.

15. David Robinson, "The Islamic Revolution of Futa Toro," *International Journal of African Historical Studies* 8, no. 2 (1975), 185–221.

16. Michael A. Gomez, *Pragmatism in the Age of Jihad: The Precolonial State of Bundu* (Cambridge, Eng., and New York, 1992).

17. Abdoulaye Bathily, "La traite atlantique des esclaves et ses effets économiques et sociaux en Afrique: La cas du Galam, royaume de l'hinterland sénégambien au dix-huitième siècle," *Journal of African History* 27, no. 2 (1986), 269–93; see also Philip D. Curtin, *Economic Change in Precolonial Africa: Senegambia in the Era of the Slave Trade* (Madison, 1975).

18. Walter Rodney, *A History of the Upper Guinea Coast, 1545–1800* (Oxford, 1970), 95–113 (quoted phrase on 112).

19. Ibid., 244–55.

20. Ibid., 255; and Thierno Diallo, *Les institutions politiques du Fouta Djalon au XIXe siècle* (Dakar, 1972), 20–34.

21. See the following for a discussion of causal possibilities: Boubacar Barry, *Le royaume du Waalo: Le Sénégal avant la conquête* (rev. ed.; Paris, 1985); Suret-Canale and Barry, "Western Atlantic Coast"; William Derman with Louise Derman, *Serfs, Peasants, and Socialists: A Former Serf Village in the Republic of Guinea* (Berkeley, Los Angeles, and London, 1973); Joye Bowman Hawkins, "Conflict, Interaction, and Change in Guinea-Bissau: Fulbe Expansion and Its Impact, 1850–1900" (PhD dissertation, U.C.L.A., 1980); and Joseph Earl Harris, "The Kingdom of Fouta Diallon" (PhD dissertation, Northwestern University, 1965).

22. Suret-Canale and Barry, "Western Atlantic Coast," 493–95; and Alfa Ibrahim Sow, *Chroniques et récits du Fouta Djalon . . .* (Paris, 1968), 15.

23. Lovejoy, *Transformations*, 59.

24. Ibid., 56.

25. See Ivor Wilks, *Asante in the Nineteenth Century: The Structure and Evolution of a Political Order* (London, 1975); and Lovejoy, *Transformations*, 56.

26. Wilks, *Asante*; Peter B. Clarke, *West Africa and Islam: A Study of Religious Development from the 8th to the 20th Century* (London, 1982), 50–60; Melville J. Herskovits, *The Myth of the Negro Past* (New York and London, 1941); and Herskovits, *The New World Negro* (Bloomington and London, 1966), 90–93.

27. Lovejoy, *Transformations*, 56–57 (quotation on 57).

28. Joao Jose Reis, "Slave Rebellion in Brazil: The African Muslim Uprising in Bahia, 1835" (PhD dissertation, University of Minnesota, 1983).

29. Lovejoy, *Transformations*, 57–58; see also Paul E. Lovejoy, ed., *Africans in Bondage: Studies in Slavery and the Slave Trade* (Madison, 1986).

30. Curtin, *Atlantic Slave Trade*, 157.

31. See Paul E. Lovejoy, "The Impact of the Atlantic Slave Trade on Africa: A Review of the Literature," *Journal of African History* 30, no. 3 (1989), 365–94; James A. Rawley, *The Transatlantic Slave Trade: A History* (New York and London, 1991), 428; and Curtin, *Atlantic Slave Trade*, 83–91.

32. For example, see the unsubstantiated estimates of Austin that 10 to 15 percent of all imported Africans were Muslims. Austin, *African Muslims*, 32–36.

33. For information on the Muslim merchants of Juula, see Timothy F. Garrard, *Akan Weights and the Gold Trade* (London and New York, 1980); Ivor Wilks, "Wangara, Akan and Portuguese in the Fifteenth and Sixteenth Centuries," *Journal of African History* 23, no. 2 (1982), 333–49 (Part I) and no. 4, 463–72 (Part II).

34. Regarding the role of clerics and amulets, see Jack Goody, ed., *Literacy in Traditional Societies* (Cambridge, 1968); and Mervyn Hiskett, *The Development of Islam in West Africa* (New York, 1984).

35. For introductory discussions, see I. M. Lewis, ed., *Islam in Tropical Africa* (London, 1966); and Nehemia Levtzion, ed., *Conversion to Islam* (New York, 1979).

36. Jane Landers, "Gracia Real de Santa Teresa de Mose: A Free Black Town in Spanish Colonial Florida," *American Historical Review* 95 (February 1990), 9–30.

37. Jane L. Landers, "Black Society in Spanish St. Augustine, 1784–1821" (PhD dissertation, University of Florida, 1988), 27–28.

38. See Gwendolyn Midlo Hall's recent work, *Africans in Colonial Louisiana: The Development of Afro-Creole Culture in the Eighteenth Century* (Baton Rouge and London, 1992), 10–35; and Rawley, *Transatlantic Slave Trade*, 114–15.

39. *Moniteur de la Louisiane*, September 11, 1802, and July 30, 1806.

40. Hall, *Africans in Colonial Lousiana*, 166.

41. See Curtin, *Atlantic Slave Trade*, 156–57; Ulrich Bonnell Phillips, *American Negro Slavery: A Survey of the Supply, Employment and Control of Negro Labor* . . . (New York and London, 1918), 42–44; Darold D. Wax, "Preferences for Slaves in Colonial America," *Journal of Negro History* 58 (October 1973), 390–97; Herskovits, *Myth*, 50; Marguerite B. Hamer, "A Century Before Manumission: Sidelights on Slavery in Mid-Eighteenth Century South Carolina," *North Carolina Historical Review* 17 (July 1940), 232–36; Rawley, *Transatlantic Slave Trade*, 272–73; Elizabeth Donnan, "The Slave Trade into South Carolina Before the Revolution," *American Historical Review* 33 (April 1928), 816–17.

42. For example, see David Duncan Wallace, *The Life of Henry Laurens* (New York and London, 1915), 76–77; and Austin, *African Muslims*, 29.

43. Austin, *African Muslims*, 21. Hall argues that these terms were synonymous as early as the eighteenth century in Louisiana (*Africans in Colonial Louisiana*, 41–42).

44. David Richardson, "Slave Exports from West and West-Central Africa, 1700–1810: New Estimates of Volume and Distribution," *Journal of African History* 30, no. 1 (1989), 16; and Lovejoy, "Impact of the Atlantic Slave Trade on Africa," 374.

45. For examples of names that probably have African origins see Charles Lyell, *A Second Visit to the United States of North America* (2 vols., New York, 1849), I, 263. For discussions of names as ethnic markers, see John C. Inscoe, "Carolina Slave Names: An Index to Acculturation," *Journal of Southern History* 49 (November 1983), 527–54; and Cheryll Ann Cody, "There Was No 'Absalom' on the Ball Plantations: Slave-Naming Practices in the South," *American Historical Review* 92 (June 1987), 563–96.

46. See Lathan Windley, comp., *Runaway Slave Advertisements: A Documentary History from the 1730s to 1790* (4 vols., Westport, Conn., and London, 1983); and Inscoe, "Carolina Slave Names," 533–35.

47. Windley, *Runaway Slave Advertisements*, vol. 4: Georgia, 64.

48. Ibid., vol. 3: South Carolina, 593.

49. Ibid., 605.

50. The author has only partially examined early Mississippi and Louisiana newspapers. This assessment is therefore subject to revision upon completion of the larger project.

51. Hall, *Africans in Colonial Louisiana*, 10–11 and 122–26 (quotation on 10).

52. Charles Joyner, *Down by the Riverside: A South Carolina Slave Community* (Urbana and Chicago, 1984), 14–15; Wood, *Black Majority*, 58–62; and Littlefield, *Rice and Slaves*, 76–98.

53. See Curtin, *Atlantic Slave Trade*, 156–58; Rawley, *Transatlantic Slave Trade*, 334–35. Littlefield (*Rice and Slaves*, 31–32) disagrees with the view that Virginia planters were unconcerned about ethnic origins. To the contrary, Littlefield maintains (based upon Wax's article "Preferences for Slaves," previously cited) that Virginians were concerned about ethnicity and that they preferred the Igbo and others from the Niger delta. Rawley, in

turn, states that Virginians preferred those from Gold Coast and Windward Coast, accepted the Igbo in large numbers, and disliked those from Angola.

54. *South-Carolina Gazette*, October 19, 1738, in Windley, *Runaway Slave Advertisements*, vol. 3, 35.

55. *South-Carolina Gazette*, June 23, 1757, and March 1, 1773, in Windley, *Runaway Slave Advertisements*, vol. 3, 155, 320.

56. *Georgia Gazette*, September 7, 1774, March 15, 1781, and August 17, 1774, in Windley, *Runaway Slave Advertisements*, vol. 4, 56, 89, 54–55.

57. Edenton *Gazette and North Carolina Advertiser*, June 23, 1808.

58. Charleston *Courier*, June 19, 1808.

59. Savannah *Gazette of the State of Georgia*, June 7, 1792.

60. Savannah *Royal Georgia Gazette*, October 4, 1781.

61. Savannah *Georgia Gazette*, August 31, 1774.

62. Savannah *Gazette of the State of Georgia*, December 8, 1791.

63. Austin, *African Muslims*, vii.

64. "Autobiography of Omar Ibn Said, Slave in North Carolina, 1831," *American Historical Review* 30 (July 1925), 787–95 [reproduced here, 81–92]; and Austin, *African Muslims*, 445–54.

65. Austin, *African Muslims*, 409–11; and "Autobiography of Omar Ibn Said," 788 [84]; see also Theodore Dwight, "Condition and Character of Negroes in Africa," *Methodist Quarterly Review*, 4th Ser., 16 (January 1864), 77–90.

66. Theodore Dwight Jr., "On the Sereculeh Nation, in Nigritia: Remarks on the Sereculehs, an African Nation, accompanied by a Vocabulary of their Language," *American Annals of Education and Instruction* 5 (September 1835), 451–56.

67. See Wilks, "Salih Bilali of Massina," 145–51; Austin, *African Muslims*, 309–16.

68. Lydia Parrish, *Slave Songs of the Georgia Sea Islands* (Athens, Ga., 1992), 25–28; and Austin, *African Muslims*, 265–68.

69. The manuscript is entitled the "Ben-Ali Diary," in the holdings of the Georgia State Law Library. See also Joseph H. Greenberg, "The Decipherment of the 'Ben-Ali Diary,' a Preliminary Statement," *Journal of Negro History* 25 (July 1940), 372–75.

70. Joel Chandler Harris, *The Story of Aaron (so named), the Son of Ben Ali* (Boston and New York, 1896).

71. See Alford, *Prince Among Slaves*; [Cyrus Griffin], "The Unfortunate Moor," *African Repository* 3 (February 1828), 364–67; and Austin, *African Muslims*, 121–32.

72. See Thomas Bluett, *Some Memoirs on the Life of Job* (London, 1734); Francis Moore, *Travels into the Inland Parts of Africa* (London, 1738); Philip D. Curtin, "Ayuba Suleiman Diallo of Bondu," in Curtin, *Africa Remembered*; and Grant, *Fortunate Slave*.

73. Austin, *African Muslims*, 68–70. Austin includes Peale's comments on Yarrow Mahmud in this account.

74. J. M. Gray, *A History of the Gambia* (London, 1966), 212.

75. "Autobiography of Omar Ibn Said," 792–93 [89–92] (quotation on 793 [89]). See Alryyes, *Life*, 61 in this volume.

76. See David Robinson, *Chiefs and Clerics: Abdul Bokar Kan and Futa Toro, 1853–1891* (Oxford, 1975), 15–18; Robinson, "Islamic Revolution of Futa Toro"; and Austin, *African Muslims*, 450.

77. Alford, *Prince*, 3–28.

78. Austin, *African Muslims*, 268. Interestingly, Cornelia Bailey says that Bilali's ethnicity was never discussed in her family, so that the Fulbe connection was not an issue (interview, July 1992).

79. Dwight Jr., "On the Sereculeh Nation," 451–52. For more on the Jakhanke, see Lamin O. Sanneh, *The Jakhanke: The History of an Islamic Clerical People of the Senegambia* (London, 1979); and Thomas Hunter, "The Development of an Islamic Tradition of Learning among the Jahanka of West Africa" (PhD dissertation, University of Chicago, 1977).

80. Ivor Wilks, "Abu Bakr al-Siddiq of Timbuktu," 152–69.

81. Ivor Wilks, "Salih Bilali of Massina," 145; and Austin, *African Muslims*, 309–16.

82. Curtin, *Economic Change*, 159–68.

83. Austin, *African Muslims*, 68–70.

84. Grant, *Fortunate Slave*, 82–84.

85. Alford, *Prince*, 57; Austin, *African Muslims*, 6–7.

86. Austin, *African Muslims*, 265, 321.

87. [Charles Ball], *Slavery in the United States . . .* (New York, 1837; rpt., New York, 1969), 165.

88. John W. Blassingame, *The Slave Community: Plantation Life in the Antebellum South* (rev. ed.; New York and Oxford, 1979), 130–46; George P. Rawick, ed., *The American Slave: A Composite Autobiography*, vol. 1: *From Sundown to Sunup: The Making of a Black Community* (Westport, Conn., 1972), 32–45.

89. Austin, *African Muslims*, 268 (quotation), 313, and 324–25.

90. Alford, *Prince*, 43–44 and 77.

91. Augusta *Herald*, November 11, 1813.

92. John Stapleton Papers (South Caroliniana Library, University of South Carolina, Columbia), microfilmed on reels 6 and 7, of Series A, Part 2 of *Records of Ante-Bellum Southern Plantations from the Revolution through the Civil War*, Kenneth M. Stampp, general editor.

93. Dr. Collins, *Practical Rules for the Management and Medical Treatment of Negro Slaves* (1811), quoted in Grant, *Fortunate Slave*, 81.

94. William Dallam Armes, ed., *The Autobiography of Joseph LeConte* (New York, 1903), 29–30.

95. Austin, *African Muslims*, 129. See footnote 64.

96. Austin, *African Muslims*, 265 and 272–75 (quotation). Cornelia Bailey maintains that Arabic was not taught but that "some African" was spoken.

97. Alford, *Prince*, 77–78. Two of the sons were named "Sulimina" (but called "Solomon" and "Samba").

98. *State Gazette of South-Carolina*, July 31, 1786, in Windley, *Runaway Slave Advertisements*, vol. 3, 400.

99. *Columbian Museum and Savannah Advertiser*, May 11, 1802.

100. Ibid., March 27, 1807.

101. State of Georgia Archives, GRG2–009 and GRG2–029 (Georgia Department of Archives and History, Atlanta).

102. Austin, *African Muslims*, 321.

103. Georgia Writers' Project, *Drums and Shadows: Survival Studies Among the Georgia Coastal Negroes* (Athens, 1940), 178–83.

104. Ibid., 179–80.

105. Cornelia Bailey interview, July 1992. For more on Sapelo Island, see William S. McFeely, *Sapelo's People: A Memory of Slavery, an Appointment with Freedom* (New York and London, 1994).

106. Parrish, *Slave Songs*, 28n22.

107. *Drums and Shadows*, 159.

108. Ibid., 161.

109. Ibid.

110. Cornelia Bailey interview, July 1992.

111. Though Bilali was African-born, his wife and children may not have been. According to Cornelia Bailey, Bilali's wife, Phoebe, was "from the islands," meaning that she was either Caribbean-born or "seasoned" there. Since Bilali came with his entire family to Sapelo, this would mean that he also spent some time in "the islands." This, in turn, allows for the possibility that the family developed in the West Indies, rather than in Africa. (Cornelia Bailey interview, July 1992).

112. *Drums and Shadows*, 165–66.

113. Ibid., 164.

114. Ibid.

115. In response to a direct question about this, Bailey responded that Calina and Hannah were indeed Muslims and that they came to Sapelo via the West Indies. Thus, they could have converted to Islam while in the Caribbean. (Cornelia Bailey interview, July 1992).

116. *Drums and Shadows*, 120–21, 144–45, and 154–56.

117. William S. McFeely, *Frederick Douglass* (New York and London, 1991), 3–5 (quotation).

118. Austin, *African Muslims*, 29.

119. Newbell Niles Puckett, *Folk Beliefs of the Southern Negro* (Chapel Hill and London, 1926), 528; and Lyell, *Second Visit*, 1, 266.

120. Collins, *Practical Rules*, 37; and Austin, *African Muslims*, 81.

121. Joyner, *Down by the Riverside*, 14–15.

122. Alford, *Prince*, 56.

123. Zephaniah Kingsley, *A Treatise on the Patriarchal, or Co-operative System of Society as it Exists in Some Governments, and Colonies in America, and in the United States, Under the Name of Slavery, with Its Necessity and Advantages* (Freeport, N.Y., 1829; rpt., 1940), 13–14. See also Parrish, *Slave Songs*, 25; and Austin, *African Muslims*, 268.

124. Ella May Thornton, "Bilali—His Book," *Law, Library Journal* 48 (1955), 228–29 (quotation on 228); and Austin, *African Muslims*, 268. Cornelia Bailey disagrees that the Muslims of Sapelo enjoyed advantages over non-Muslim slaves and maintains that slave owners treated both groups the same (Cornelia Bailey interview, July 1992).

125. E.g., see Puckett, *Folk Beliefs*, 528–29.

126. See Blassingame, *Slave Community*, 73.

127. [Griffin], "Unfortunate Moor" 366.

128. Georgia Bryan Conrad, *Reminiscences of a Southern Woman* (Hampton, n.d.), 13.

129. Cornelia Bailey interview, July 1992.

130. For the Fulbe in West Africa, see Victor Azarya, *Aristocrats Facing Change: The Fulbe in Guinea, Nigeria, and Cameroon* (Chicago and London, 1978); Marguerite Dupire, *Organisation sociale des Peul* (Paris, 1970); Paul Marty, *L'Islam en Guinée: Fouta-Diallon* (Paris, 1921); and G. Vieillard, *Notes sur les coutumes des Peuls au Fouta Djallon* (Paris, 1939).

131. Bertram Wyatt-Brown, "The Mask of Obedience: Male Slave Psychology in the Old South," *American Historical Review* 93 (December 1988), 1228–52 (quotations on 1232).

132. Wilks, "Abu Bakr al-Siddiq," 162–63.

133. An important work on the role of African retentions in North America is Sterling Stuckey's *Slave Culture: Nationalist Theory and the Foundations of Black America* (New York and Oxford, 1987).

134. Austin, *African Muslims*, 316.

135. Ibid., 321.

136. Grant, *Fortunate Slave*, 82.

137. Paul Marty, *L'Islam en Guinée*, 108–47; Jean Suret-Canale, "Touba in Guinea: Holy Place of Islam," in Christopher Allen and R. W. Johnson, eds., *African Perspectives* (Cambridge, Eng., 1970); and Gomez, *Pragmatism*, 26–28. Curtin refers to literacy among Muslim slaves in Jamaica. See Philip D. Curtin, *Two Jamaicas: The Role of Ideas in a Tropical Colony, 1830–1865* (Cambridge, 1955), 24–25.

138. Grant, *Fortunate Slave*, 81.

139. Dr. Collins, *Practical Rules for the Management and Medical Treatment of Negro Slaves*, quoted in Grant, *Fortunate Slave*, 81.

140. [Griffin], "Unfortunate Moor," 366.

141. Rawick, ed., *American Slave*, vol. 4: *Texas Narratives*, Part 2 (Westport, Conn., 1972), 290.

142. Austin, *African Muslims*, 127–31; and [Ball], *Slavery in the United States*, 164–65 and 167; see also Ball, *Fifty Years in Chains, or the Life of an American Slave* (New York and Indianapolis, 1859).

143. Greenberg, "Ben-Ali Diary."

144. Austin, *African Muslims*, 321.

145. Cornelia Bailey interview, July 1992.

146. See Austin, *African Muslims*, 448. Omar ibn Said continued to implore the help of Allah and the prophet Muhammad with invocations found even within the margins of his Christian Bible.

147. Indeed, in the Georgia coastal area, none of the descendants of African-born Muslims claim to be Muslim themselves in the WPA interviews.

148. For example, Rosanna Williams of Tatemville, Georgia, became so alarmed at the questions of the interviewers that she asked: "Wut yuh doin? Is yuh gonuh sen me back tuh Liberia?" (*Drums and Shadows*, 71).

149. Ibid., 169–70 (quotation on 169).

150. Charles C. Jones, *The Religious Instruction of the Negroes* (Savannah, 1842), 125.

151. Cornelia Bailey interview, July 1922.

152. Robert Farris Thompson, *Flash of the Spirit: African and Afro-American Art and Philosophy* (New York, 1983), 218–23.

153. Theresa A. Singleton, "The Archaeology of the Plantation South: A Review of Approaches and Goals," *Historical Archaeology* 24, no. 4 (1990), 75.

154. Cornelia Bailey interview, July 1992.

155. See Margaret Washington Creel, *"A Peculiar People": Slave Religion and Community-Culture Among the Gullahs* (New York and London, 1988), 320. Creel maintains that the Gullah in general buried their dead so that the body faced the east; the practice may not, therefore, reflect a Muslim influence, but a west-central

African one. Very little has been written on the subject, however, and additional research is warranted.

156. Ben Sullivan, Rosa Grant, Katie Brown, Shad Hall, Nero Jones, and Lawrence Baker all remember seeing and hearing their grandparents pray, etc. Since many of these people were in their seventies and eighties when interviewed in the 1930s, it would mean that their grandparents were still alive in the 1870s and 1880s (in order for the grandchildren to be of sufficient age to remember the specifics of their religious practices). In fact, Rosa Grant was only sixty-five years old at the time of her interview.

157. E.g., Charleston *South-Carolina Gazette*, January 15–22, 1754, and February 3, 1757, and Savannah *Gazette of the State of Georgia*, January 13, 1785, all in Windley, *Runaway Slave Advertisements*, vol. 3, 125, 152, and vol. 4, 122. Sources for Elijah Muhammad and Noble Drew Ali include Theodore G. Vincent, *Black Power and the Garvey Movement* (Berkeley, 1971); E. U. Essien-Udom, *Black Nationalism: A Search for an Identity in America* (Chicago, 1962); C. Eric Lincoln, *The Black Muslims in America* (Boston, 1973); and Alex Haley, *The Autobiography of Malcolm X* (New York, 1965).

Contemporary Contexts for Omar's *Life* and Life

Allan D. Austin

Omar ibn Said's 1819 Taylor-Key letter enclosure and his 1831 *Life*, discussed in other essays in this volume, are the two longest of his extant American-African-Arabic manuscripts. There are sixteen others. Facsimiles of all but his *Life* and two lists of Owen family members may be found in my *African Muslims in Antebellum America: A Sourcebook* and *African Muslims in Antebellum America: Transatlantic Stories and Spiritual Struggles*.[1] The following is a mostly chronological consideration or recognition of twenty-four comparable manuscripts in Arabic and related material by other hands, and then of Omar's writings. All of the texts discussed below were written in the Americas (limited in this essay to writers from North America, Jamaica, and Panama—omitting, therefore, other manuscripts from Cuba, Haiti, Trinidad, Brazil, etc.) between 1734 and the 1860s.[2] All were written by West Africans educated in homelands at least two hundred miles from the Atlantic coast. Their firsthand descriptions are richly instructive as they tell about geographical sites, schools, and activities then unknown to the West and unknowable as fully today in their absence.[3] Only two of these writers report having met Western whites before their being taken to the coast.

The majority of these texts in Arabic were written by members of Omar's larger Fulbe (s. Fula—also Fulani, Fellatah, Pulo, or Peul) family. These include writers Job Ben Solomon, Ibrahima Abd al-Rahman, Bilali Muhammad, and Charno. Other Fulbe who were probably capable of writing but from whom no manuscripts have been found—Salih Bilali, Philip, and Yarrow Mamud—were students when captured.

Other writers, such as "Captain Anderson's Negro," a "Moor on the Mississippi," William Rainsford, Muhammad Kaba, King, and London, might have been Fulbe, but were called Mandingoes by eventual translators. Jonas Bath was a

Susu, Lamine Kebe said he had a "Manenca" mother and Serehule father, Anna Musa was a Kassonke. Abu Bakr al-Siddiq, called a Mandingo, was from a Jakhanke/ Juula family—he provided his interviewer with wonderfully informative trade routes across west Africa from Timbuktu to the Gambia and south to the Gulf of Guinea, suggesting sites of commerce and Islamic schools also followed by some Fulbe. The ethnicity or homelands of other reportedly literate slaves are less clear: Mohammed, who was returned to Africa from Antigua; an unnamed servant of early Caribbean historian Bryan Edwards; and Sambo, a runaway from South Carolina, for some examples.[4] Origins of yet other African-born Muslims who reportedly could write are unknown to date: Jupiter Dowda, slave manager in Mississippi and free in Pennsylvania; King, a plantation manager in South Carolina; and S'Quash, another plantation manager also in South Carolina.[5]

Most of these writings are essentially assertions of faith in Islam—as was true of four very recently translated letters by the almost unknown Sana Sy or See, laboring across the Caribbean in the 1850s.[6] None—with the possible exception of yet-unfound papers by a Georgia and Florida slave named London noted below— suggest conversion to Christianity. And none, it seems to me, expresses anti-African feelings. On the contrary, all appear to assert Muslim and African identities, perhaps accounting for their relative obscurity. Most importantly, for my purposes here, these attitudinal consistencies, whether in Fulbe, "Mandingo," or other West African Arabic writings where being Muslim was more important than ethnicity, imply that they are representative of the attitudes of thousands of enslaved African Muslims not otherwise noticed in their day. These writings are, therefore, significant contexts relevant to Omar's writings and life.

Most contemporary American notes on "literate" enslaved Muslims appeared only in local Southern newspapers, in private letters intended only for their recipients' eyes, or in the limited publications of the American Colonization Society and the tiny American Ethnological Society. There are two exceptions. Many newspaper articles followed Abd al-Rahman's last two years and travels from Natchez to Liberia between 1827 and 1829 and at least three of his manuscripts were preserved among several written for men who helped him return to Africa. White Northern, Christian, and abolitionist writers opposed to returning freed former slaves to Africa allowed only passing interest, as did Americans generally, except those involved in his travels. Little interest was shown in black Africa itself, as authorities declared the area had no history and maps had little to show beyond its shores. There was some interest, however, at least in Abd al-Rahman personally, among free African Americans in Boston, New York, and Philadelphia. These included the fiery pamphleteer David Walker in Boston and the eventual African emigrant John Russwurm in New York.

Like Abd al-Rahman, Omar ibn Said was famous. Omar's papers were saved by members of both the ACS and the AES mentioned above, by Christian missionary enthusiasts, and by his purchaser's family, the Owens. Bilali's manuscript was saved as an exotic Southern curiosity. The most persistent antebellum collector of Arabic-American manuscripts was William Brown Hodgson, who had served in consulates in Algiers (1826–29), Constantinople (1832–34), and Tunis (1841–42). A slaveholder who dressed at least one of his black servants in fancy Oriental garb, he was one of only a handful of Americans capable of translating Arabic in the antebellum era.[7] His translations of manuscripts by "Anderson's Negro," Abd al-Rahman, and London, and his notes on such writings, some of which were sent on to the American Ethnological Society, will be discussed below, as will William A. Caruthers's inclusion of a facsimile of Charno's writing in a traveler's tale.[8]

The majority of mentions of such writers or writings are short and hesitant — as though to suggest that Africans were capable of writing anything was to break some kind of ethnic (or economic) taboo. This fact offers a hint of how amazing it is that as much as is available has been recovered.

This lack of American (and European) curiosity about Africa and Muslim Africans may also be seen in the singular case of Irishman Richard Robert Madden in Jamaica, where he served as a British temporary magistrate attempting to solve issues relating to ending slavery in the Caribbean. As someone who had begun to learn Arabic, he became intensely interested in and published articles on the trials and writings of an important handful of African-born Muslims, otherwise almost completely unnoticed, to which we will turn below for their relevance to Omar's writings.

Finally, in this introductory catalog of antebellum Africans who learned to write to some extent in Africa, the unusual cases of Mahommah Gardo Baquaqua and Mohammed Ali ben Said, both of whom had some training in Arabic in Africa, but who wrote in English rather than Arabic in America, may be addressed and set aside here. Both were free when they wrote and had reasons to think their learning English would be useful. Mahommah Baquaqua was born in the Gulf of Guinea area now called Benin. He had been enslaved there and then in Brazil before being freed in New York from his slave-sailor condition. Baquaqua did not care much for school in Africa and had a hard time learning to write in New York but eventually produced several letters and assisted in the writing of his wide-ranging *Biography of Mahommah Gardo Baquaqua* (Detroit, 1854), all in English. This biography-autobiography is the only first-hand freedom narrative by a native of Benin once enslaved in Brazil, and the only known account of an African as a student in an antebellum American academy. Baquaqua's letters and book reiterate his desire—shared by nearly all of these writers—to see his mother and mother-land again, even if he had to go back to Africa as a Christian missionary or cook or servant. The last heard from him was a report from England saying he was attempting to return to his homeland.[9]

Mohammed Ali ben Said, born and later enslaved in Bornu (now Nigeria), was marched across the Sahara, sold in Istanbul, freed in Russia, renamed Nicholas, and taken as a servant around Europe before going to America. Said seems to have been something of a linguist. A lightly edited version of his autobiography, "A Native of Bornoo," printed in the *Atlantic Monthly* in 1867, and a longer, often differing version, published in Memphis in 1873, show how consistently curious he remained. These charming autobiographies tell about his country, the trials and pleasures he met on five continents before he became a soldier in the Union army (prudently left out of his late Southern publication), and how he later attempted to find teaching positions in black schools in the postwar South. There he expresses a desire to teach his fellow black people, but seems to have given up on the goal he had expressed earlier of returning to Bornu.[10]

Now back to those Arabic writers and writings. Job Ben Solomon, a Fula taken from the Gambia River to Maryland in 1731, but born not far from Omar's birthplace in what is now Senegal, was one of the lucky ones.[11] Like Omar, he ran away from an American purchaser, proved to be an interesting spiritual and literate soul to humane gentlemen, and was soon ransomed and freed in England. By 1735, he had been returned to Senegal after impressing English nobility and intelligentsia with his literacy and religious strength. Along his way he wrote often in Arabic, including a letter from Annapolis to his father in Africa and at least one rendition of the Qur'an from memory. Job encouraged the writing by an English friend of a biographical memoir in English—the first published narrative of an American-enslaved African (1734). Since, however, there is no known writing by Job produced in the New World, he is included here only as an early and significant representative of Omar's people, their literacy, and their desire to return to the land and religion of their parents.[12]

The next dated Arabic manuscript by a Muslim in America was that of a man described only as a Negro slave of Captain David Anderson. This was dated 1768 and was said to have been written in South Carolina, according to its translator, William Brown Hodgson. In an 1838 letter, Hodgson correctly noted that it included the *Fātiha*, *Suras* 114—the last, 113, 112, and part of 110 of the Qur'an. Apparently the original manuscript comprised more pages. These Qur'anic chapters are short, traditionally the first taught, and in many ways, as they assert the faith of the writer, very important chapters in the Holy Book. They might also be the ones resorted to by a Muslim near the end of his days. Anderson's slave was probably writing to console himself at a low point. One wonders whether he expected to have this writing translated. Nothing else has been found about it or its author.[13] As we shall see, Omar also wrote *Sura* 110 near the end of his days.

On the island of Jamaica, early in the nineteenth century, an unknown number of enslaved Muslims wrote in Arabic to one another urging adherence to the faith. One of their number was Muhammad Kaba from Futa Jallon, called by a late master a Mandingo, who shared what he knew about these writings around 1830.[14] More will be said about Kaba below.

In a diary note for 1822, a Quaker trader on the Mississippi River wrote of meeting an impressive man he called a Moor—which seemed to be the traveler's name for a Muslim. He got the man to write his "creed"—probably the *Fātiha*. Although the man said he had only been in America for ten years (thereby being one of thousands of illegally imported Africans), he did not conceal his disappointment with this country and, by implication, its religion. His is a critical assessment. According to his interviewer, "he will not allow that the Americans are as polite and hospitable a people as the Moors—nor that they enjoy a tenth part of the comfort [we] do—and that for learning and talents, [Americans] are far behind."[15] No unhappy immigrant could have made a prouder statement about his home-land. Visiting European and American reporters expressed similar conclusions about Mississippi River settlements of that time. Mark Twain similarly described what he left behind as he fled the Civil War.

In 1828, Ibrahima Abd al-Rahman from Futa Jallon, now Guinea, was un-doubtedly the most famous African in America and his passage across America was followed more closely than those of all but the most important white politicians in the country. His story offers important comparisons to Omar's. Abd al-Rahman, a father and cavalry captain in Africa was captured and sent to Natchez, Mississippi, in 1788. Around 1807, an Irishman who had met Abd al-Rahman in Africa tried publicly but unsuccessfully to free him. Twenty years later, an admiring (though soon treacherous) local newspaperman showed him some type in Arabic and encouraged his attempt to get in touch with his people in Africa. Possibly as a result of mistreatment of his offspring in 1826 and because, after nearly forty years of acknowledged honesty, responsibility, leadership, and hard work, he had had enough, Abd al-Rahman wrote to his father. The State Department in Washington sent his letter on to Morocco, the nearest Muslim nation with whom the United States had political relations. Both nations urged Abd al-Rahman's manumission, and his purchaser did so. But the "freeman's" beloved wife had to be ransomed from his hard-hearted master by gifts raised by sympathetic Natchezians. Following up on this local charitable campaign, Abd al-Rahman told and had his story told by American Colonization Society activists and missionaries hoping to use his return to Africa to both raise money to buy others of his enslaved family and to bring Christianity to Abd al-Rahman's homeland. Aged over sixty, his was an extraordinary journey from Cincinnati to Baltimore to Philadelphia to Boston to Hartford to New York to Virginia and many points in between. Everywhere he went, he impressed common onlookers and important listeners with his dress, dignity, and transatlantic story. He raised enough money to free eight of his off-spring and did get back to Africa and his co-religionists, but he died early in 1829.

As was the case with Omar, Abd al-Rahman's literacy impressed his audiences. A New York student of Arabic declared that the several writings Abd al-Rahman did for him in 1828 were written "with correctness and fluency."[16] He often wrote what he allowed several to believe was the "Lord's Prayer," in line with the argument that Abd al-Rahman would spread Christianity upon his return to Africa. Actually, four extant manuscripts, written for different recipients, include variations on the *Fātiha*.[17] Unknown to most of his backers in Natchez, Abd al-Rahman had given his opinion of Christianity to another newspaper editor: "I tell you the Testament very good law; you no follow it; you no pray often enough; you greedy after money. You good man; you join the religion. See, you want more land, more neegurs; you make neegur work hard, make more cotton. . . . Where you find dat in your law?"[18] In his country, he said, slaves did not work all day for the master, and, if they joined the religion of their masters they had a chance to be free. He could have added, or perhaps he did, that children of good, converted slaves would be free—as his should have been. But back in the North, though no longer a slave, Abd al-Rahman was beholden to Christians. He was writing at their request and knew what they wanted to hear or read.

Charno's literacy was known—at least among other slaves in South Carolina—but it did not bring him freedom.[19] In 1834, Charno's correctly written *Fātiha* was facsimiled and translated in a good-humored novel by a once fairly popular writer, William A. Caruthers. For his own amusement, as Caruthers says, he sought out a literate slave of whom he had heard and asked him to write. As a matter of fact, Caruthers's interest was not so casual. He wrote in other pieces about other Muslim Africans. No one else, however, seems to have become interested in this "Charno" and neither Caruthers nor anyone else seemed to have been aware that *chierno*, or *thierno*, was a Fula or Peul title for a learned man in West Africa. The writer's retention of this title represents a proud assertion of what he had been in Africa and must have provided some sustenance for his stay in America.[20]

Two Georgia Muslims, Bilali Mohammed and Salih Bilali, were not named but were mentioned in a pamphlet in 1828.[21] The former's supposed plantation diary in Arabic was noticed by a few people after the Civil War, but it is now known that this document was actually a unique Muslim-American pedagogical statement. Bilali Mohammed (named after Bilal, the Prophet's black first *muezzin* or caller to prayer) wanted not only to contact but to teach or re-teach Muslims about their obligations even in a non-Muslim world. As a result, his "diary" is one of the most significant available such texts composed on the North American mainland. Bilali Mohammed was the plantation manager on Sapelo Island where, according to his once well-known master Thomas Spalding, he was left, for months at a time, in charge of some five hundred rice- and cotton-raising slaves. By default, undoubtedly, when no other was available, Bilali acted as a kind of Imam or *qadi* (judge) to dozens of male and female Muslims. His manuscript is a roughly remembered manual on prayer rituals—written with help from others who were not above correcting in his margins. Thirteen pages have survived. Only recently, however, have scholars seriously attempted to translate it. Some scholars such as B. G. Martin, Ronald A. T. Judy, and Mohammed al-Ahari, an indefatigable tracer of lost Muslims, are still at work.[22] The following summary is based on the latter's preliminary translation.

There are, on average, fourteen lines to a page. Thus far, there seems to be agreement that page 1 begins with a customary *Bismillah* and an opening echoing that of the *Risala* of Muhammad bin Abdullah bin Yusuf bin Ubaid al-Qairawani— a famous essay on rules for followers, written before 1032 CE.[23] This is followed by an introduction to what is to come from one who has learned from others. Page 2 asserts adherence to the Faith, learned through the Prophet and his Companions, and the fundamental beliefs in Allah, punishment, the day of Judgment, and the possibility of Allah's forgiveness. Then the text has not been translated for several pages. Page 7 reminds the reader to be patient and to keep from disbelief and then launches into a description of ritual ablutions. This discussion continues on page 8. Page 9 repetitively asserts the obligation of worshiping Allah alone. Page 10 emphasizes prayer and Allah's titles; page 11 tells more about where and how to pray; page 12 reassures that prayers and faith will be repaid; page 13 that prayer is better than sleep for the true servant of Allah.

Bilali Mohammed's manuscript, written in the 1830s or 1840s in Georgia, on eighteenth-century paper from Venice, wrapped in leather and tied as it would have been in Africa, is a precious physical relic and a remarkable accomplishment. One wonders whether Mohammed somehow brought the paper from his native Futa Jallon to the Bahamas and then to Georgia. He evidently was a strong and serious person. Bilali Mohammed gave his children Muslim names, kept up his Muslim traditions, dress, praying, prayer rug, and prayer beads, and was buried with them. Such sentiments and practices, and these material manifestations of his faith, reflect the memories his grandchildren told to the Works Projects Administration (WPA) interviewers in the 1930s. The latter also recalled identifiably Muslim expressions and habits in the children and many neighbors.[24] His island of Sapelo was, to a great extent, an island of Islam. It remains partially so today as Sapelo's Baptist Church follows several Muslim traditions, beginning with prayers to the east and separation of men and women.[25] It seems clear that Bilali was attempting to leave his essay on faith in a strange land. His manuscript was, in any case, left (and one wonders with what stipulations) in strange hands, those of a nearby white author, Francis Goulding. Goulding seems to have done little with it beyond sharing what he speculated about it with folklorist and fiction writer Joel Chandler Harris (Uncle Remus's creater), who distorted Bilali's book and author into a plantation diary by an Arab slave trader who despised Africans.[26]

Salih Bilali (able to read but not write Arabic), born in Massina, near Jenne, now Mali, but kidnapped, barely in his teens, and taken to the Gulf of Guinea, was sent to the Bahamas and then to St. Simon's Island, Georgia, around 1800. Salih Bilali, a friend of Bilali Mohammed's, also seems to have been his island's Imam. Similar recollections to those regarding Bilali Mohammed from Salih Bilali's descendents about his Muslim practices—and those of other islanders— were also made in the 1930s by the WPA in *Drums and Shadows* and in Lydia Parrish's *Slave Songs of the Georgia Sea Islands*.[27] Unlike on Sapelo, which has not been bridged yet, descendents of Muslim slaves on St. Simon's have long since scattered as a result of modern developments on the island.

Salih Bilali's masters, first John Couper (1759–1850) and then his son James Hamilton Couper (1794–1866), were fairly famous Sea Island plantation masters and have been the subject of recent biographies that do not give credit for the owners' successes to this African. James Hamilton Couper—often cited as an ideal rice planter—wrote in a private letter about what he had been told about Salih Bilali's Africa, and what must have been true of thousands of unrecognized African and African American overseers and drivers, that his "Tom" (Salih Bilali) was a clear thinker, organizer, and taskmaster. Couper, too, left major plantation control to this slave.[28] In a private letter sent to W. B. Hodgson, mentioned above, Couper wrote that "Tom" was a devout Muslim. J. H. Couper's son later declared that Salih Bilali was the most religious man he had ever met.[29]

Lamine Kebe, a teacher and trader in Futa Jallon, Guinea, before being taken to the Carolinas around 1795, found that, for many years, his noted dignity, spirituality, and literacy did not help him escape from slavery and get back to Africa. Eventually, however, a "good" master did free him and sent him off to fend for himself.[30] In 1835 he met the American Colonization and American Ethnological Society member and secretary, Theodore Dwight, Jr., who became interested in his attempts to return, even as an old man, to his native land and religion. Dwight published an article on some of Kebe's pedagogical ideas and practices: about neither being too harsh nor too soft, on keeping students under one teacher, and on a kind of bilingual instruction he called "doubling"—using Arabic and local languages together. His assertions that there were many schools in his country and that many were taught by well-trained women were passed on by Dwight. The article closed with Kebe's list of textbooks—as far as Dwight could understand what he was being told—and a list of somewhat haphazardly chosen Serehule words. This is the only article on African teaching that I know of in antebellum American papers.[31] Dwight promised much more on his fascinating subject, as Kebe asked him to, but published only a wide-ranging essay on American ignorance about Africa and scattered sources, including part of an early translation of Omar's *Life*.[32]

Dwight's essay appeared in 1864, shortly before Dwight died and long after Kebe managed somehow to get to Liberia on his way back to his homeland in 1835. As Kebe told Dwight, Americans, even friendly ones, were ignorant about Africa. He might have added that they seemed to be deliberately or timidly so. Maps of the interior of the continent would remain blank when they might have been at least partially filled in by slaves in their midst. Even when they credited slaves, American intellectuals often mistook their intentions. Although Dwight appeared to sincerely believe that at least this African had the intellect to teach, he hoped that he or others like him would teach if not preach Christianity in their homelands and encouraged the sending of Bibles in Arabic to West Africa with that purpose in mind. This notion that Bibles in good Arabic might be used in spreading Christianity in West Africa was based upon missionary beliefs that those who received these precious gifts would soon convert to the "higher" religion of Christianity.[33] Missionary hopes in Kebe and Omar and their African educations did lead to a combined Syria Protestant College and missionary attempt to bring Christianity to West Africa.[34]

Kebe also said that some Africans wrote their own languages using Arabic characters, a practice called *ajami*. Examples of that fact have been discovered. In 1857, Hodgson had come upon (he does not say how or where) a manuscript in Arabic that he could not translate until he recognized, citing an old Spanish example, that the letters were being used phonetically; it turned out that the manuscript's author, London, an enslaved African-Georgian, was writing the Gospel of John and some hymns from the black English he was hearing. London was not copying, apparently, from any printed texts.[35] This manuscript, unfortunately, has been lost, as has its great value to linguists. Equally disappointing is the fact that no more has been passed on about this writer. Was London practicing his phonetic Arabic skills inspired by some music around him? Was he a lover of prayer and songs from whatever source? Was he simply a convert to Christianity? Or did he find it amenable to combine the religions of two people of the book as did many Georgians, according to the important church preacher-historian, Charles Colcock Jones, or as suggested by "Old Lizzie Grey" in the late 1850s, who "ever said that Christ built the first church in Mecca and he grave was da."[36]

On the island of Jamaica, Muhammad Kaba, once a trader in Futa Jallon, is especially remarkable. An old man in 1835, he had apparently been one of a group of enslaved Africans who strove, in the face of powerful planter and pastor repression of abolitionist political and religious activity, to support all the Muslims they could contact. At least one of their methods was the distribution of letters in Arabic urging strict adherence to Islam. How many other such letters were written and destroyed, confiscated, or lost on other Caribbean islands, or the mainland is to be wondered. In 1834, finally, letters between quasi-emancipated slaves were legal. Kaba, more than fifty years removed from Africa, wrote to another newly freed African, Abu Bakr al-Siddiq, some thirty years away from his homeland. He is cautious but pleased that the latter has been released. Abu Bakr's response is also cautious and unctuous in praise of the master who had freed him and of the friendly Richard Robert Madden, mentioned earlier, who would see the letter. In its last paragraph, however, Abu Bakr asked Kaba to write again in Arabic, as if something had been left out of the first. One wonders if there were later, more politically pointed letters from either hand.[37]

Also in Jamaica, in the 1830s, four supposedly converted Muslims were recognized and encouraged to express themselves openly to Madden, an Irish abolitionist and a Special Magistrate overseeing the Emancipation Act of 1833, who worked for the end of slavery and peonage on the island. Once Madden gained their trust, these men began to speak of their lives and thoughts. "William Rainsford," a forceful preacher from Kankan (present-day Guinea); "Benjamin Larten," a Qur'anic expert; Anna Mousa or "Benjamin Cochrane," a medical doctor from Mali; and the geographically knowledgeable Abu Bakr, all literate, all forced into unwanted baptisms in Jamaica (where half the imports may have been from the Senegambia to Gold Coasts and hinterlands from which Muslims would have been drawn), told significant and touching stories about their lives and their shared religion. "Rainsford" wrote a sermon, concluding with a declaration that the rich had a duty not to oppress the poor; Larten wrote out the Qur'an from memory; Mousa wrote one or two short autobiographies; and Abu Bakr composed a wonderful autobiography and list of trade routes in West Africa—all in Arabic. Madden did his best to translate them.[38]

Abu Bakr, who kept plantation records in English using Arabic letters, descended from a sophisticated, wealthy, and extensive Juula or Wangara trading family. Born in Timbuktu around 1794, he was undoubtedly a good student until some time in 1807 when he was captured because he was on the losing side in a war. His autobiography is very informative about his family, their trading ventures, and the conflict that led to his enslavement in what is now Ghana. A second translator of his autobiography, the Reverend George C. Renouard, who spent time with Abu Bakr in London in 1835, was very impressed with the man's intelligence and geographical knowledge. Abu Bakr reported that he had visited or heard about towns from Sin near the mouth of the Gambia to Katsina in Nigeria, more than 1,600 miles to the east, and from Timbuktu to the Guinea coast, about 900 miles to the south. He went further and informed Renouard about these locales' geographical interrelations with one another, laying out an area comparable to that of the United States east of the Mississippi and referring to a vast and apparently active network of communities reaching through and beyond many different peoples.

Renouard also admired Abu Bakr's faith, which Abu Bakr expressed concisely and proudly in the conclusion to his autobiography:

> The faith of our families is the faith of Islam. They circumcise the fore-
> skin; say the five prayers; fast every year in the month of Ramadan; give
> alms as ordained in the law; marry (only) four free women—[others are]
> forbidden to them except she be their slave; they fight for the faith of
> God; perform the pilgrimage (to Mecca)—i.e. such as are able to do so;
> eat the flesh of no beast but what they have slain for themselves; drink no
> wine—for whatever intoxicates is forbidden unto them; they do not keep
> company with those whose faith is contrary to theirs, such as worshippers
> of idols, men who swear falsely by the name of the Lord, who dishonour
> their parents, commit murder or robbery, bear false witness, are covetous,
> proud, insolent hypocrites, unclean in their discourse, or do any other
> thing that is forbidden; they teach their children to read, and (instruct
> them in) the different parts of knowledge; their minds are perfect and
> blameless according to the measure of their faith.

And then Abu Bakr added this poignant note:

> Verily, I have erred and done wickedly, but I entreat God to guide my
> heart in the right path, for He knoweth what is in my heart, and whatever
> (can be pleaded) in my behalf.[39]

A few months later, Abu Bakr was chosen by a self-proclaimed English explorer, John Davidson, to guide a private expedition from Morocco's Atlantic port of Wadi Nun to Timbuktu. It is known that Davidson and his men were killed before they got far, but two years later a report said that Abu Bakr had returned to the famous city of Jenne and to some part of his family.[40]

With the exception of these relief-filled introductory letters, it may be seen that all of these Jamaican and North American pieces are assertions of their writers' faith, often accompanied with wistful remembrances of their African homelands. Neither the blandishments of Christian allies nor the wonders the New World turned them away from their religion and land of their parents.

This brings us back to Omar. It is difficult to believe that his native attitudes were wholly dissimilar. This dignified, proudly mysterious, even controversial man wrote often and often at the request of his purchaser's admiring family, or of clearly impressed Christian ministers. Usually he wrote for people who could not read his language and who accepted his characterizations of the contents no matter what the latter were. Several of these writings have been referred to in more than forty articles from the 1820s to today.[41] These are mostly local North Carolina publications that may be seen in several ways: as one-sided episodes of encounters between Christians and Muslims, as mixtures of facts and fictions regarding American Christian slavery, and as effusions on the humanity and intelligence of Africans or the kindness of his purchaser.

It is to be expected that the earliest known Omar manuscript, two beautifully written pages from 1819, should be made up of a melding of Hadith and Qur'anic excerpts. It is a sophisticated prayer for assistance by a man in forced exile, as described by John Hunwick.[42] Shorter fragments survive as well. Omar wrote in Arabic in the Arabic Bible sent to him a little later by Francis Scott Key. Inside the front cover are four inscriptions in Arabic; the first and fourth read: "All Praises to Allah, [or God]," the second: "All good is from Allah," the third is illegible. These expressions are Qur'anic; perhaps they do not exclude the possibility of their referring to the God of all peoples who could read. The only page annotated by Omar begins similarly. It reads, "Praise God," then is illegible until halfway through Omar's third line, which appears to be a personal prayer he wrote often: "My name is Umaru, son of Sayyid; my mother is Umhan Yaznik. May God comfort her resting place."[43]

The first of Omar's three surviving renditions of the Lord's Prayer in Arabic was pasted in a scrapbook. It is mislabeled the Twenty-third Psalm by a handwritten note in English; a note on the reverse includes the year 1828. This prayer, often recommended for first converts to Christianity, is preceded here by the curious statement: "And this is how you pray, you."[44] Omar seems to be separating himself from Christians. On a facing page of the scrapbook appears another Arabic text labeled the Lord's Prayer; actually it is a list of nine James Owen family members written above a graphic design similar to that found in the 1819 manuscript.[45] A second Lord's Prayer manuscript was described and dated 1840 in an article, "A

Prince of Arabia," by Louis T. Moore, published in 1927. It begins exactly as does the Taylor manuscript: "Thanks be to God, whom creatures were created to worship. He is the Lord of actions and sayings. Whomever does good, does so for himself; and whomever does evil will have evil."[46] The third Lord's Prayer, undated, was preceded by the *Bismillah*: "In the name of God the Merciful, the compassionate, May God have mercy on the Prophet Mohammed." It is followed by Omar's usual benediction: "My name is Umaru, son of Sayyid; my mother is Umhan Yaznik. May God comfort her resting place."[47]

The first of Omar's Twenty-third Psalms was found in the same scrapbook as the 1840 text described above. This contains the *Bismillah*, the Twenty-third Psalm, followed by "All good is from Allah, and no other." Omar signed his name inside his drawing of a presumably magical pentacle or star.[48]

In 1855, John F. Foard, another Colonizationist, asked Omar for some of his writing. Omar sent him a manuscript that was translated by Princeton Professor R. D. Wilson in 1904, who observed: "Uncle Moro still retained a little weakness for Mohammed" because his Twenty-third Psalm was preceded by the *Bismillah*. The translator could make nothing of the writing in a box in the lower left, but it is Omar's benediction for his mother.[49]

Another manuscript given to a prominent minister's daughter by James Owen in 1857 was supposed to be the Lord's Prayer, but is not from the Bible at all. Omar reached far back to his Qur'an to recall *Sura* 110. Suggestively, this was one of the last recitations from Allah—as Mohammed declared—before the death of the Prophet. Omar must have felt as if he were near a similar crisis, as Alryyes suggests. He also signed this text: "My name is Omar."[50]

Two texts are undated. James Owen's daughter Eliza kept a scrapbook that included three manuscripts. One includes the *Bismillah*, Omar's arabesque, and the names of Eliza and five other children.[51] A second is a provocative statement. The *Bismillah* is extended to praise the Creator and "the Lord of actions and sayings." Line five has been translated: "You recognize as a servant and son [of God?] Jesus." Does Omar not do so? Another line has been trimmed too close to be legible.[52]

Thus far, it would surely be possible to discern in these documents Omar the Muslim under Omar the Christian. But translators—all Christian—of presently unavailable Omar manuscripts discovered a convert. Leaving aside Omar's "Autobiography" for the moment, let's glance at some translated items. Ralph R. Gurley, longtime Secretary of the American Colonization Society, ordered translations of two Omar letters to Kebe that supposedly urged the latter to "Lay aside Mahomet's prayer and use the one which our blessed savior taught his disciples— our Father, &c." And "God has been good to us in bringing us to this country and placing us in the hands of Christians. Let us now wake up and go to Christ, and he will give us light. God bless the American land! God bless the white people." This statement is so neatly developed that it appears these were someone else's words. Omar did go on, however, according to this translation, and declared reason enough to be happy with his situation:

> My lot is at last a delightful one. From one man to another I went until I
> fell into the hands of a pious man. He read the Bible for me until my eyes
> were opened, now I can see; thank God for it. I am dealt with as a child,
> not as a servant.[53]

Another missionary wrote that sometime around 1860, Omar's mistress gave the near centenarian a blank book for another autobiography. According to George E. Post, a missionary in Syria who saw it in 1868, Omar filled it with Arabic writing. Post found "the pith of the scheme of redemption, in a series of Scripture passages from the Old and New Testaments." Then he wrote that this was followed by an appeal to Omar's African relatives—who were not likely ever to see it:

> Salaams to all who believe on the Lord Jesus Christ. I have given my soul
> to Jesus the Son of God. O, my countrymen [of] Bundah [Bundu], and
> Phootoor [Futa Toro], and Phootdalik [Futa Jalon?], . . . Come, come,
> come, come to Jesus the Son of God, and ye shall find rest to your souls
> in the day of judgment.[54]

This account would seem to settle the question about Omar's ultimate religious stance. But this is, once again, an invisible writing so far as the original manuscript has yet to be seen. And it has to be dated; Post's dating may be inaccurate. It may or may not have been written before Omar wrote his *Sura* 110 around 1857. In fact, he died in late June or early July 1863.[55]

There are, finally, two interesting sidelights on Omar ibn Said's history. One account of him said that Omar had received a letter in Arabic from a man named Yang, a Muslim from Canton, China. Apparently a missionary had brought one of Omar's letters to Yang and the latter was moved to respond in kind.[56] Nothing more, however, seems to have come of this correspondence. But other letters by Omar were shown by Lamine Kebe's interviewer to Reverend Daniel Bliss, the president of the Syria Protestant College. The latter followed up on what had been learned from Kebe, as well as on what had been heard and read of Omar, by sending a case of Bibles in Arabic to Liberia to be distributed inland. This was to provide an opening into the Muslim hinterland for the young Arabic Studies program of the College of Liberia, and for its founder, the great black West Indian scholar Edward Wilmot Blyden, who began teaching Arabic in Liberia in 1867. It did not bring in converts but did provoke responses from Muslims from Kankan and elsewhere.[57]

It is true that a tradition was passed on that Omar's master and some noble ministers of the Gospel sensitively turned Omar away from his early stubborn faith in the "bloodstained Koran" and toward a marvelously pious later career worshipping "at the feet of the Prince of Peace."[58] What is evident, however, is that Omar was a spiritual soul who needed to pray regularly with others who prayed. He might have agreed to baptism in order to be allowed to pray and to enjoy a level of comfort and even prestige among Christian bookmen not available to other African-born servants. And he may have done so out of an appreciation for the genuine kindness of his purchaser and family and for some aspects of Christianity. His Arabic Bible was used so much that it had to be re-covered and, apparently, more than once. There is no evidence thus far, however, that Omar ever attempted to copy more than the same two pieces (the Lord's Prayer and the Twenty-third Psalm—neither of which imposes ideas that would be out of place in a Muslim's worship). Further, he did not change his name, as converts to Christianity regularly did, and he continued wearing Muslim-like coats and caps. A number of visitors to Fayetteville and to the Owens' other home in Wilmington asserted that Omar was a wonderful Christian. Several ministers mentioned holding uplifting moral and spiritual conversations with Omar, while at least one found his remarks on a tentative sermon useful. His last minister, Reverend Mathew Grier, in his article mentioned above, liked to think Omar was a mature Christian, but allowed a little doubt as he hedged and wrote that "by all outward signs" Omar seemed to be a "sincere believer in Jesus Christ." It seems, then, that those who knew him beyond translations of his writings recognized a subtle personality.

An 1825 article inadvertently may supply a shrewd clue to an understanding of the man: some enslaved Africans in North Carolina saw in Omar a "pray-god to the king," a *marabout* or kind of missionary, to non-Muslim rulers. Maybe he always felt or acted as a go-between. Omar's autobiography clearly establishes his African homeland, education, literacy, early adherence to Islam, and suggests a conversion to Christianity. As Omar grew older in America he also seems to have catered to an American need for dark impressions of Africa. Interviewers reported that he acted as if something too terrible to talk about had happened in his homeland in Bure (Futa Toro) and that he would not want to go home again.

Omar often wrote for others; he also undoubtedly wrote for himself, to maintain his faith through rewriting the words of Allah or God. As is indicated above, most of these manuscripts and stories from Omar and others are fragmentary.[59] All were passed on by non-Muslims, only a few of whom could translate and understand what they saw or heard. Nearly all were accompanied by commentaries, but this African was aware of that fact and—as Job and Lamine Kebe did—urged respect for his own thoughts and statements. Together, these writings offer a more complete picture of these writers, their peers, and their religions, cultures, attitudes, homelands, and adjustments in America than is otherwise available. But they also hint at some of America's adjustments to them. Without doubt, more such texts will be discovered as scholars and others delve more deeply into this nation's and continent's incompletely explored African, American, and Muslim past.

Notes

1. Allan D. Austin, *African Muslims in Antebellum America: A Sourcebook* (New York: Garland, 1984), and *African Muslims in Antebellum America: Transatlantic Stories and Spiritual Struggles* (New York: Routledge, 1997). These two texts, hereafter Austin (1984) and Austin (1997), include discussions of five more of his writings mentioned or translated but unhappily lost that help round out our understanding of Omar. The writings of other African Muslims caught up in the international trade in Africans, as well as contemporary notices of them by whites—also included in these two compilations—shed more light on the context in which Omar wrote his *Life*. Together, they print copies of eight other such manuscripts by five different hands and provide discussions of thirty-one other pieces by eleven hands. The 1984 text prints copies of two letters in Arabic by Job Ben Solomon not discussed here and one copy of an Abd al-Rahman manuscript not included in the 1997 text. On the other hand, the manuscript of "Captain Anderson's negro"—and references to manuscripts by Sana See or Sy appear only in the latter.

2. Important explorations of the Muslim presence and mentions of Arabic writers may be found in Michael A. Gomez, "Muslims in Early America," *Journal of Southern History* 60 (November 1994), 671–709 [reproduced here, 95–132]; and, reaching beyond North America, Sylviane A. Diouf, *Servants of Allah: African Muslims Enslaved in the Americas* (New York: New York University Press, 1998).

3. These are accompanied by a map of the known African birthplaces and travels of thirteen writers as students, teachers, traders, soldiers, or captives.

4. Austin (1984), 39–40.

5. Austin (1997), 33–37.

6. Moustafa Bayoumi, "Moving Beliefs: The Panama Manuscript of Sheikh Sana See and African Diasporic Islam," *Inventions* 5 (2003): 58–81.

7. See Alryyes, introduction to this volume, 9.

8. See also Austin (1997), 111–12.

9. Austin (1984), 585–654; the fullest, latest reprinting and annotation of Baquaqua's writings and life may be found in Robin Law and Paul E. Lovejoy, eds., *The Biography of Mahommah Gardo Baquaqua: His Passage from Slavery to Freedom in Africa and America* (Princeton: Markus Wiener, 2001).

10. Austin (1984), 655–89; Austin (1997), 172–86.

11. Editor's note: In her essay here, Sylviane Diouf notes that Solomon's given name in Africa was "Ayuba Suleyman Diallo." The BBC's arts editor recently reported that "the National Portrait Gallery launched a campaign to raise money" to buy a portrait of Diallo, which is the "first known portrait that honours a named African as an individual and an equal, and thereby gives a useful insight into Britain in the eighteenth century." See Will

Gompertz, BBC Gomp/arts blog, July 7, 2010, http://www.bbc.co.uk/blogs/thereporters/willgompertz/2010/07/all_about_the_subject.html

12. Austin (1984), 65–120; Douglas Grant, *The Fortunate Slave: An Illustration of African Slavery in the Early Eighteenth Century* (London, 1968). It must be noted that Job returned to Africa bearing many gifts from Englishmen, several of whom expected him to advance English commercial ventures—and, when, later in his life, Job ran into troubles, he did express a desire to revisit England.

13. Hodgson, "Letter to John Vaughan," Philadelphia, November 3, 1838, Savannah Historical Society, Misc. Oriental Mss. Manuscript reprinted in Austin (1997), 32.

14. Austin (1984), 543.

15. Thomas A. Teas, "A Trading Trip to Natchez and New Orleans, 1822 (Diary)," *Journal of Southern History* 7 (1941): 378–99.

16. Terry Alford, *Prince Among Slaves* (New York: Harcourt Brace Jovanovich, 1977), 161. These manuscripts have not been found.

17. Three reprinted in Austin (1984), 133, 158, 190; in Austin (1997), 74, 75. Hodgson noted that Abd al-Rahman added: "From the Surat revealed at Mecca. May Allah help Muhammad and his family, and give them health and abundant blessings. Thus saith the Scheikh to Mecca." Manuscript of writing for Condy Raquet, mayor of Philadelphia, and translation from American Philosophical Society Library, Philadelphia, Hodgson letter dated 21 September 1837.

18. Austin (1997), 76.

19. William A. Caruthers, *Kentuckian in New York*, vol. 1 (New York, 1834), 146–47.

20. See note on Charno from Caruthers, above.

21. Zephaniah Kingsley, *Treatise on the Patriarchal or Co-operative System of Society as it Exists in some governments, and Colonies of America and in the United States*, 2nd ed. (1829; repr., Freeport, N.Y.: Books for Libraries, 1970), 13–14.

22. Martin, "Sapelo Island's Arabic Document: The 'Bilali Diary' in Context," *Georgia Historical Quarterly* (Fall 1994): 589–601; Ronald A. T. Judy *(Dis)Forming the American Canon: African-Arabic Slave Narratives and the Vernacular* (Minneapolis: University of Minnesota Press, 1993); al-Ahari, personal communication, 1991.

23. The *Bismillah* is the customary opening verse of all but one of the Qur'anic chapters. It translates as "In the name of God, the most gracious, the most merciful."

24. Savannah Unit of the Georgia Writers Project of the Works Projects Administration, *Drums and Shadows: Survival Studies Among the Georgia Coastal Negroes* (1940; repr., Athens: University of Georgia Press, 1985).

25. Cornelia Walker Bailey, with Christena Bledsoe, *God, Dr. Buzzard, and the Bolito Man: A Saltwater Geechee Talks About Life on Sapelo Island* (New York: Anchor, 2000).

26. Austin (1984), 291.

27. *Drums and Shadows*, 178–82; Lydia Parrish, *Slave Songs of the Georgia Sea Islands* (New York: Creative Age Press, 1942), 24–25.

28. James Hamilton Couper, "Letter from James Hamilton Couper, Esq." William Brown Hodgson incorporated this letter in his pamphlet *Notes on Northern Africa, the Sahara, and the Soudan* (New York, 1844), 68–75. See Alryyes, introduction to this volume, 29. Couper's letter is reprinted in Austin (1984), 321–25.

29. James Maxwell Couper, undated personal letter to his grandchildren, copy sent to me by Mrs. Mary Thiesen, a descendent, 17 August 1981.

30. Austin (1984), 409–44; Austin (1997), 115–26.

31. Theodore Dwight Jr., "Remarks on the Sereculehs, an African Nation, Accompanied by a Vocabulary of their Language," *American Annals of Education and Instruction* 5 (1835): 451–56, and in Austin (1984), 414–20.

32. "Condition and Character of Negroes in Africa," *Methodist Quarterly Review* (Jan. 1864): 77–90. See Alryyes, introduction to this volume, 14, for more on Dwight's article.

33. Austin (1997), 125.

34. Austin (1984), 454.

35. Hodgson, "The Gospels, Written in the Negro Patois of English, with Arabic Characters, by a Mandingo Slave in Georgia" (New York: [American Ethnological Society?], 1857).

36. Austin (1984), 41.

37. Austin (1984), 541–44; Yacine Daddi Addoun and Paul E. Lovejoy, "Muhammad Kaba Saghanughu and the Muslim community of Jamaica," in *Slavery on the Frontiers of Islam*, ed. Paul E. Lovejoy, 201–20 (Princeton: Markus Wiener Publishers, 2004).

38. Richard Robert Madden, *A Twelve Months' Residence in the West Indies, during the Transition from Slavery to Apprenticeship* (Philadelphia, 1835). See Austin (1984), 544–50.

39. Renouard's translation is in Austin (1984), 550–65.

40. Austin (1984), 566–70.

41. Many of these are reprinted in Austin (1984), 468–505.

42. John Hunwick, "'I Wish to Be Seen in Our Land Called Africa': 'Umar b. Sayyid's Appeal to Be Released from Slavery (1819)," *Journal of Arabic and Islamic Studies* 5 (2003): 62–77. Appendix 1 includes Hunwick's translation of this text.

43. The Bible is held by Davidson College; facsimiles of these pages are reprinted in Austin (1984), and of the annotated page, Austin (1997).

44. John Owen Papers, North Carolina State Archives, Raleigh; in Austin (1997), 141. See also Alryyes, introduction to this volume, 26.

45. John Owen Papers; in Austin (1997), 142.

46. Davidson College; in Austin (1997), 143.

47. Davidson College; in Austin (1997), 146.

48. Eliza Owen scrapbook, photograph from Thomas Parramore, Raleigh, North Carolina; in Austin (1997), 150.

49. In Foard, *North America and Africa: Their Past, Present and Future and Key to the Negro Problem* (Statesville, N.C., 1904); in Austin (1997), 147.

50. University of North Carolina at Chapel Hill; in Austin (1997), 148.

51. Eliza Owen scrapbook owned by a Mrs. Trammell, Atlanta, photo from Thomas C. Parramore; in Austin (1997), 149.

52. Eliza Owen scrapbook owned by Mrs. Trammell, photo from Thomas C. Parramore; in Austin (1997), 151.

53. Ralph R. Gurley, "Secretary's Report," *African Repository and Colonial Journal* 13 (July 1837): 201–5; in Austin (1984), 468–70 [reproduced here, 213–20].

54. George E. Post, "Arabic-Speaking Negro Mohammedans in Africa," *African Repository* (May 1869): 129–33; in Austin (1984), 483–87.

55. Personal note citing burial plot assignment from Thomas C. Parramore.

56. Mathew B. Grier, "Uncle Moreau," *North Carolina Presbyterian* (23 July 1859); in Austin (1984), 480–83.

57. Henry M. Schieffelin, *People of Africa* (New York, 1871)—some of which were included with the Omar papers. See Austin (1984), 484.

58. From Gurley, "Secretary's Report"; in Austin (1984), 469. See also Appendix 4 in this volume.

59. Another pair of pages from Omar may be seen in a manuscript in the Spartanburg County (South Carolina) Historical Association. (It bears a date of 1853, written in a different hand, on its back.) The first page begins boldly with the *Bismillah*, and the remainder is in smaller handwriting. The second page begins with the *Bismillah* and a warning to believe in the Qur'an and its message on the power and mercy of God and the judgment (Night of Determination from *Surat al-Qadr*). This page is elaborately illustrated with three talismanic designs. This is a wholly Muslim statement. This manuscript was brought to my attention by Mohammed al-Ahari, who is working on a translation.

The United States and
Barbary Coast Slavery

ROBERT J. ALLISON

Omar ibn Said's questions to Americans, "Are you confident that He who is in heaven will not cause the earth to cave in beneath you, so that it will shake to pieces and overwhelm you? Are you confident that He who is in heaven will not let loose on you a sandy whirlwind?" would have been particularly troubling, coming from a Muslim slave in North Carolina.[1] Americans regarded their victorious wars against Algiers (1790s and 1815) and Tripoli (1801–1805) as a triumph against Islamic tyranny. Even the Pope had praised the American campaign against Tripoli for accomplishing in a short time what all the Christian nations of Europe had failed to do for centuries. And yet this same encounter with Islam forced Americans to confront their own moral flaws. Algiers and Tripoli, it is true, seized ships and made slaves of several hundred American sailors, but Americans had enslaved hundreds of thousands of Africans. The Americans could claim a victory over Algiers and Tripoli, but this victory forced Americans to see their own conduct in the mirror of Barbary Coast slavery.

The year before Omar ibn Said arrived in America, New York poet Joseph Hanson had celebrated the American victory over Tripoli in an epic poem, *The Musselmen Humbled, or, a Heroic Poem in Celebration of the Bravery Displayed by the American Tars, in the Contest with Tripoli* (1806). In Hanson's poem, the "audacious Tripolitans," a "cruel and unprincipled enemy," a "rude race of Barbarians" and a "despicable foe" "had expected to see American citizens submit to their insults and impositions. . . ." But the "valorous conduct of your brave Tars," inspired by "[j]ustice and freedom" had taught the "plundering vassals of the tyrannical Bashaw" of Tripoli "that on this side the Atlantic, dwells a race of beings of equal spirit to the first nations." He implored the "bright sun of peace and prosperity" to continue to shine upon America, and that "all, who feel the genial rays, be thankful of the blessings."[2] This confident expression of national purpose characterized much of American reactions to the Algerian and Tripolitan wars. The United States had gone to war against Tripoli when the Pasha, Yusuf Qaramanli, demanded a larger annual tribute, in return for which he would not attack American ships in the Mediterranean. He was prompted to do this after Algiers had captured a dozen American ships in 1785 and 1793, holding more than one hundred Americans hostage and forcing the United States to pay an annual tribute of $20,000, plus $800, 000 to release the prisoners. The U.S. also agreed to pay Tunis and Tripoli, but was slow to send its payments. The captivity of Americans in Algiers prompted the United States to begin building a navy in 1793 and also provoked paintings, literature, and political commentary drawing the distinctions between American and Algerian society. The contrast between American liberty and Algerian slavery, the dire fate of Christians held as slaves, presented a ready motif. Borrowing imagery as old as the Crusades, American writers and painters exploited this theme in works that affirmed their nation's purpose.

But some Americans looked more deeply into the subject. An American teenager in a Paris convent school reported a rumor to her father in 1787: "A Virginia ship comming [sic] to Spain met with a courser of the same strength. They fought and the battle lasted an hour and a quarter. The Americans gained and boarded the courser where they found chains that had been prepared for them. They took them and made use of them for the algerians [sic] themselves. They returned to Virginia from whence they are to go back to algers [sic] to change the prisoners to which if the prisoners will not consent the poor creatures will be sold as slaves. Good god [sic] have we not enough? I wish with all my soul that the poor negroes were all freed. It grieves my heart when I think that these our fellow creatures should be treated so terribly as they are by many of our country-men."[3] This letter from Martha Jefferson to her father, American Minister to France, Thomas Jefferson (who never responded in writing to this particular part of her letter), resembles the reaction of other writers to the dilemma of "American slavery" in Algiers. An anonymous 1801 novel, *Humanity in Algiers or the Story of Azem*, insisted that the Algerians "only retaliate on us for similar barbarities." The author warned, "Unconscious of our own crimes, or unwilling the world should know them, we frequently condemn in others the very practices we applaud in ourselves, and wishing to pass for patterns of uprightness, or blinded by interest, pass sentence upon the conduct of others less culpable than ourselves."[4]

Benjamin Franklin, as president of a Pennsylvania antislavery society, submitted a petition to Congress in 1790 calling for an end to the slave trade. Franklin may well have thought this petition would be his last public act (he would die in April of that year). Congressmen from Georgia and South Carolina attacked both petition and Franklin, insisting that Congress should not abolish the slave trade because their economies depended on slave labor, and, furthermore, slavery was a good thing. Without African slaves, how would Georgia and South Carolina produce rice? The Congressmen added that the slaves should be grateful to be brought out of the darkness of Africa to America, where they would become Christians. The nation's economy should not be sacrificed to the moral scruples of Quakers and other religious zealots.

Franklin saw the irony. Writing under the name "Historicus," he praised the congressmen's speeches. He was, he claimed, reminded of something he had read years before written by a consul to Algiers. Franklin then rewrote one of the pro-slavery speeches delivered in Congress, changing the word "Africans" to "Christians." The arguments justifying slavery in America, which these members of Congress wanted Americans to accept as both an economic necessity and a positive good, could just as easily justify the enslavement of Americans in Algiers, which Americans considered barbaric. This satire, Franklin's last published essay, showed how large a gap loomed between American professions of moral superiority and American practices. Had Americans really created a new world based on freedom, or was their society as debased and corrupt as the one they imagined in Algiers?[5]

The protagonist in Royall Tyler's novel, *The Algerine Captive*, is captured by an Algerian cruiser while on a slaving voyage to West Africa. Tyler, best known as the author of *The Contrast*, the first play written by an American and performed in the United States, a future chief justice of Vermont and a former suitor of John and Abigail Adams's daughter, sees his protagonist's slavery in Algiers as a punishment for his involvement in the slave trade and for American exploitation of slave labor. In *The Algerine Captive*, the Algerian "pirates" free the black slaves held by the whites, while making slaves of the white slavers.[6] Tyler's reversal of white and black roles became a staple of anti-slavery writing. A short play, Caleb Bingham's *Columbian Orator*, has two American captives in Tunis, the navel officer Kidnap and his negro slave Sharp, put to work by the Bashaw, who has Kidnap put under the "instruction" of his former slave. A 1797 poem, "The Patriot of Seventy-Six in Captivity," consists of two cantos, each telling the story of a veteran of Bunker Hill. In the first, a white veteran laments his imprisonment in Algiers, where he languishes in slavery while his countrymen enjoy the liberty his sacrifices helped to secure. In the second, a black veteran tells his story. His sacrifice had helped secure American freedom, and now he is a slave in America.[7]

Novelists and poets were not the only ones to see the irony of Americans lamenting their slavery in Africa. Diplomats and journalists also pointed to the reversal of roles for white Americans in North Africa. William Eaton, American consul to Tunis, wrote of slavery in North Africa: "Alas, remorse seizes my whole soul when I reflect that this is indeed but a copy of the very barbarity which my eyes have seen in my own country. And yet we boast of liberty and national justice. . . . Indeed, truth and justice demand from me the confession that Christian slaves among the barbarians of Africa are treated with more humanity than the African slaves among the professing Christians of civilized America."[8] Matthew Carey's 1794 *Short Account of Algiers* noted that "for this practice of buying and selling slaves, we are not entitled to charge the Algerines with any exclusive degree of barbarity. . . . Before we reprobate the ferocity of the Algerines, we should enquire whether it is not possible to find, in some other regions of the globe, a systematic brutality still more graceful?"[9] In Bostonian James Ellison's 1811 play, *The American Captive, or the Siege of Tripoli*, celebrating the American victory, Jack Binnacle, an American sailor held captive in Tripoli, waxed poetic about his country, telling the overseer El Hassan that America was "a charming place . . . ; no slavery there! All freeborn sons!" El Hassan asks, "No slavery, hey? Go where the Senegal winds its course, and ask the wretched mothers for their husbands and their sons! What will be their answer? *Doomed to slavery, and in thy boasted country, too!*"[10]

Humanity in Algiers, which circulated mainly in Vermont and upstate New York, made even more of the curious reversal, or the inverted world, Americans experienced in North Africa. The title tells us there was humanity in Algiers. Was there also humanity in America? The title character, Azem, was, like Omar ibn Said, a Senegalese. Unlike Omar, though, Azem had been enslaved in Algiers and had become free. Azem, accompanying his owner's family on their pilgrimage to Mecca, was freed for saving his master's daughter from a rapist. Returning to Algiers, Azem's owner sponsored his beginnings in the caravan trade between Algiers and Senegal. There he found his mother and learned that Alzina, a Senegalese slave he had been courting and trying to free in Algiers, was actually his sister. Back in Algiers, Valachus, Alzina's owner, rejects Azem's offer to purchase her. Valachus, with his own lustful designs, was "callous to the feelings of pity, and deaf to the voice of reason." Newly independent and flush with his own importance, as were the Americans, Valachus listens more to the call of passion than to that of compassion.

Morality and reason could not change Valachus, but the plague could. He finally freed Alzina as he lay dying. The reunion of Alzina, Azem, and their mother prompted a sermon from the mullah Omri: "And may every master, in whatever part of the inhabited globe he may reside, with cheerfulness practice that important percept of the Alcoran—'Masters, treat your servants with kindness.' So may the light of Islamism shine forth, in its full splendor, to the utmost ends of the universe! For thus saith the God of all men: Of one blood have I created all nations of men that dwell upon the face of the earth."[11] These precepts of "Islamism" showing that there was humanity in Algiers derive from the Christian Bible and were meant to shame Americans into recognizing their own moral failings.

The fictional world of *Humanity in Algiers* found a real-life elaboration in James Riley's *Loss of the American Brig* Commerce (1817), treating his own shipwreck on the Mauritanian coast in 1815. Riley's book, one of the most popular American books of the nineteenth century, was the most important and the most widely read book coming out of the encounter with the Muslim world. More than a million copies were sold before the Civil War. John Adams, Henry David Thoreau, and Abraham Lincoln read it. Lincoln listed Riley's book along with the Bible, *Pilgrim's Progress*, Parson Weem's *Life of Washington*, and Franklin's *Autobiography* as the books that had most influenced him. Riley's book was the only one on the list with a clear anti-slavery message.[12]

Riley and his crew barely survived the *Commerce*'s wreck. Captured by a desert tribe, they were put to work as slaves. With little food (though no less than anyone else in the nomadic band) and no protection from the sun (their clothes had all been taken by their captors), Riley and his men withered and burned. A black African slave, Boireck, entertained the other slaves and Berber women in nightly performances after the hard travel and labor of the day. He mocked Riley as "rais" or captain and imitated the now feeble Americans "who could not even bear the rays of the sun (the image of God, as they termed it)." One of Riley's crew complained that it was bad enough to be a slave, but being mocked by a Negro was more than an American should have to bear. Riley, however, had come to see the situation differently. "Let the negro laugh if he can take any pleasure in it . . . ; he is a poor slave himself, naked and destitute, and is only tying to gain the favors of his masters and mistresses, by making sport of us, whom he considers to be as much inferior to him as he is to them."[13] Riley understood that Boireck had found a survival mechanism and did not begrudge him. Riley, though, learned to survive in another way, putting his faith in God and maintaining his own dignity and composure so his men would not despair. He knew that he and his men must learn to endure their hardships and try to get a message to Mogadore, where a European ship or consul might ransom them.

Relief came from two desert traders, Sidi Hamet and his brother Said. Returning to Morocco from a trading venture into the Sahara, Sidi Hamet experienced the shock of recognition on seeing the emaciated and sun-burnt American—a merchant like himself—far from his family and home, now facing death in a strange and hostile land. He and Riley seemed to have lived parallel lives. Sidi Hamet had led a caravan of one thousand men and four thousand camels south from Morocco to Timbuktu. Disaster struck when they ventured down the Niger to buy slaves and gold. Every camel and nine-hundred-ninety-six men perished.

Sidi Hamet was ruined as a trader, but still alive and wondering why he had been spared. When he saw Riley, he understood: Allah had preserved his life so that he could save Riley's. He would redeem his own humanity by devoting his life to ransoming captives. Sidi Hamet bought Riley and the shipmates still in the Arab camp, leading them to the British consul at Mogadore. He then returned to the desert where he died trying to track down other shipwrecked Americans.

A North Carolina reader was so moved by the "benevolent Arab" that he named a son after him. Riley himself was inspired by his rescuer to pledge to devote his own life to ending the scourge of American slavery. In the year Riley returned to the United States, the Reverend Ralph Gurley formed the American Colonization Society (ACS), dedicated to the gradual abolition of slavery. Riley supported the efforts of the ACS, which began with the premise that slavery was morally wrong. But the ACS also believed that white Americans would not accept former slaves as their equals. The ACS proposed that the United States establish a colony for the freed slaves, either in the Louisiana territory, in the West Indies, or in Africa. In 1822, the ACS founded the colony of Liberia, naming its capital Monrovia for the American president, James Monroe. The greatest support for Colonization came from moderate slaveholders, such as Monroe, James Madison, Thomas Jefferson, and John Marshall. The first published notice of Omar ibn Said appeared in the ACS's newspaper, the *African Repository*, in 1828. As Alryyes's introduction here argues, however, Omar had no desire to emigrate.

Perhaps fearing the wrath of God, Jim Owen showed his benevolence to a Muslim slave in America, just as Sidi Hamet, chastened by the power of Allah in Africa, had shown his benevolence to James Riley. Owen stood in contrast to the "weak, small, evil man called Johnson," who had purchased Omar in Charleston. Johnson was, according to Omar, "an infidel who did not fear Allah at all." Omar, Jim Owen, Sidi Hamet, and James Riley all feared Allah, call Him by what name they would. All trembled, as Thomas Jefferson did, when they "reflect[ed] that God is just: that his justice cannot sleep forever."[14] In the year Omar arrived in America, in fact, President Jefferson urged Congress to make good on its power to end the African slave trade. A generation earlier, in 1776, Jefferson had denounced the "piratical warfare" of the Atlantic slave trade, charging George III with waging "cruel war against human nature itself, violating its most sacred rights of life and liberty" by allowing the slave trade to persist.[15] At the Constitutional Convention in 1787, Virginia slave owners George Mason and James Madison pushed to give Congress the power to end the slave trade. By doing so, they believed that American slavery could be put on the road to extinction.

But by the time Omar wrote his autobiography in 1831, the political dynamic had changed. In 1790, when Franklin ridiculed American pretensions to moral superiority, only South Carolina and Georgia defended slavery as a necessity. But the invention of the cotton gin, the opening of the rich cotton lands of Georgia, Alabama, and Mississippi after the defeat of the Creeks and removal of the Cherokees, Choctaws, and Chicasaws, made cotton the premier export crop and made the entire American economy dependent on slave labor. In 1790, Georgia and South Carolina congressmen were considered heretical for suggesting that slavery was a good thing. By 1830, it would have been heretical, and a political suicide, for a representative from the slave states to suggest that slavery was not a good thing. In 1828, the year the *African Repository* carried the first notice of Omar ibn Said, the Senate's committee on foreign relations considered support for the American Colonization Society. There was no Franklin now to respond when the senators from Georgia and South Carolina denounced the ACS for attacking slavery. It had been possible, just barely, for statesmen like Jefferson and Madison both to own slaves and to maintain that all men were created equal. By the 1820s, however, it became impossible for American political leaders to hold on to both the idea of natural equality and their own profits from slavery. Virtually all chose to do away with the pretence of equality and to hold on to slavery.[16]

Both slavery's defenders and its opponents attacked Colonization. In 1829 David Walker, an African American who had fled to Boston from South Carolina, wrote his *Appeal to the Colored Citizens of the World*. Walker blasted the American founders for their moral hypocrisy and justified rebellion against slaveholders. Walker also assailed Colonization. Premised on the belief that blacks and whites could not inhabit one society, Colonization reinforced the racist ideas it pretended to combat. In 1831 Nat Turner led a slave rebellion in Southampton County, Virginia. In response to this violent rebellion, and the threat of future ones, Virginia's legislature considered the gradual emancipation plan first proposed more than fifty years earlier by Thomas Jefferson. The plan failed. Virginia professor Thomas Roderick Dew argued in his *Review of the Debates in the Virginia Legislature* that Colonization would be hopelessly expensive. As the proponents of Jefferson's emancipation plan argued that it would not work without Colonization, Dew asserted that slaveholders should accept slavery as a good thing for themselves and their slaves.[17]

When Omar ibn Said sat down to write his autobiography, the country was increasingly in the hands of men like Johnson, the small, evil, weak man who had first purchased Omar in Charleston. The American slave states, insisting on their right to treat men, women, and children as property, had replaced Algiers as the locus of barbarism. Abolitionist Charles Sumner's 1846 speech, "White Slavery in Barbary States," looked back to the American encounter with Algiers to point out that the real barbarism was happening at that moment in the southern part of the

United States. In "The Heroic Slave," an unpublished short story Frederick Douglass wrote based on a revolt on the slave ship *Creole*, the white first-mate retells the story to a white audience in a Norfolk tavern. Defending himself against the charge of cowardice for having failed to suppress the rebellious blacks, he clarifies to his accuser the helplessness of the slave: "I've some doubts whether you, Mr. Williams, would find it very convenient were you a slave in Algiers, to raise your hand against the bayonets of a whole government." The white mate comes to admire the rebellion's leader, whose real name, Madison Washington, reminded Douglass's audience that Virginia statesmen were once committed to liberty.[18] But by the 1850s, abolitionist Wendell Phillips dubbed Virginia "only another Algiers." "The barbarous horde who gag each other," fulminated Phillips, "imprison women for teaching children to read, prohibit the Bible, sell men on the auction block, abolish marriage, condemn half the women to prostitution, and devote themselves to the breeding of human beings for sale, is only a larger and blacker Algiers."[19]

Perhaps, in the first years of the century, the benevolence of men like Jim Owen, combined with official government policy and private endeavors to eradicate slavery slowly by ending the slave trade and keeping slavery out of the territories, might have been enough. But these small steps against slavery, such as the Northeast Ordinance of 1787, the end of the slave trade in 1807, the abolishing of slavery in the northern states, and individual emancipations by men like George Washington and John Randolph, turned out to be the end of early American anti-slavery, not the first steps at the beginning of the long journey of ending slavery. By the 1830s official policy had changed and individual acts of benevolence were difficult to sustain.

Had Omar remained in Futa Toro, he would have continued to study Islamic texts, trying to live life according to the way Allah had pointed out. But a "big army" tore through his city and took him and many others away from their lives and homes. Ripped away from his homeland by the horror of war, he died in 1864 in the midst of another terrible war. Had he lived a few more months, he might have witnessed another great army tearing through his new home. The army which had raided Futa Toro had made him a slave. This army, led by William Tecumseh Sherman, came to liberate.

Was this the sandy whirlwind and the shaking of the earth Omar had warned Americans about? Omar in both instances perhaps would have fondly hoped and fervently prayed with Abraham Lincoln that "this mighty scourge of war may speedily pass away." But, as Lincoln said in March 1865, "if God wills that it continue, until all the wealth piled by the bondsman's two hundred fifty years of unrequited toil shall be sunk, and until every drop of blood drawn with the lash shall be paid with another drawn with the sword," believers in God, whatever name they have for him, must say that "the judgments of the Lord are true, and righteous altogether."[20]

NOTES

1. Alryyes, *Life*, 53–55.

2. Joseph Hanson, *The Musselmen Humbled, or, a Heroic Poem in Celebration of the Bravery Displayed by the American Tars, in the Contest with Tripoli* (New York: Southwick and Hardcastle, 1806), 4–5.

3. Martha Jefferson to Thomas Jefferson, Paris, 3 May 1787, *Papers of Thomas Jefferson* 11:334.

4. *Humanity in Algiers, or the Story of Azem* (Troy, New York: R. Moffit & Co., 1801), 3–4. On the captivity narrative as a genre, see especially Paul Baepler, *White Slaves, African Masters: An Anthology of American Barbary Captivity Narratives* (Chicago: University of Chicago Press, 1999), and Robert Allison, *Crescent Obscured: The United States and the Muslim World, 1776–1815* (Chicago: University of Chicago Press, 2000). For a more recent fictional perspective, see Orhan Pamuk, *The White Castle*, tr. Victoria Holbrook (New York: George Braziller, 1991).

5. Benjamin Franklin, "On the Slave Trade," *Writings of Benjamin Franklin*, ed. Jared Sparks (London, 1882), 2:517–21.

6. Royall Tyler, *The Algerine Captive* (New Haven, 1970, orig. pub. 1797).

7. "The American in Algiers; or the Patriot of Seventy-Six in Captivity" (New York, 1797).

8. William Eaton to Mrs. Eaton, Tunis, 6 April 1799, in [Charles Prentiss], *The Life of the Late General William Eaton* (Brookfield, Massachusetts, 1813), 154.

9. Matthew Carey, *A Short Account of Algiers* (Philadelphia, 1794), 16.

10. James Ellison, *The American Captive, or the Siege of Tripoli: A Drama in Five Acts* (Boston: Joshua Belcher, 1812), 37–38. Emphasis in original.

11. *Humanity in Algiers*, 98–99. The Biblical verses are from the Letter to the Ephesians 6:9.

12. R. Gerald McMurty, "The Influence of Riley's Narrative upon Abraham Lincoln," *Indiana Magazine of History* 30 (June 1934).

13. James Riley, *An Authentic Narrative of the Loss of the American Brig* Commerce (Hartford, Connecticut, 1817), 91–92. For more on Riley, see Allison, *Crescent Obscured*, 223–25.

14. Thomas Jefferson, *Notes on the State of Virginia* (1787), in Merrill D. Peterson, ed. *The Portable Thomas Jefferson* (New York: Penguin Books, 1975), 215.

15. Declaration of Independence, Jefferson's Draft. In Peterson, *Portable Thomas Jefferson*, 238. For an illuminating discussion of Madison and slavery, see Drew R. McCoy, *The Last of the Fathers: James Madison and the Republican Legacy* (Cambridge: Cambridge University Press, 1989), chapter 7.

16. Eugene Genovese, *The World the Slaveholders Made: Two Essays in Interpretation* (New York: Oxford University Press, 1969), 133. See also Robert Allison, "'From the Covenant of Peace, a Simile of Sorrow': James Madison's American Allegory," *Virginia Magazine of History and Biography* 99, no. 3 (July 1991), 327–29.

17. Kenneth S. Greenberg, *Confessions of Nat Turner and Related Documents* (Boston: Bedford Books of Sterne Martin's Press, 1996); Alison Goodyear Freehling, *Drift Toward Dissolution: The Virginia Slavery Debate of 1831–1832* (Baton Rouge: Louisiana State University Press, 1982); Thomas Roderick Dew, "Abolition of Negro Slavery," in Drew Gilpin Faust, ed. *The Ideology of Slavery: Proslavery Thought in the Antebellum South* (Baton Rouge: Louisiana State University Press, 1981).

18. David Herbert Donald, *Charles Sumner and the Coming of the Civil War* (Chicago: University of Chicago Press, 1960), 154; Frederick Douglass, "The Heroic Slave," in Philip S. Foner, ed., *The Life and Writings of Frederick Douglass*, vol. 5, 1844–60 (New York: International Publishers, 1975), 500.

19. Rayburn S. Moore, ed. "John Brown's Raid at Harper's Ferry: An Eyewitness account by Chas. White," in *Virginia Magazine of History and Biography* 67 (1959), 391n.

20. Abraham Lincoln, Second Inaugural Address, in James Richardson, *Messages and Papers of the Presidents* (Washington, D.C.: Bureau of National Literature and Art, 1908), 6: 277. Lincoln quoted Psalm 19:10.

"God Does Not Allow Kings to Enslave Their People"

Islamic Reformists and the Transatlantic Slave Trade

Sylviane A. Diouf

"Then there came to our country a big army. It killed many people. It took me and walked me to the big Sea, and sold me into the hand of a Christian man."[1] If quite succinctly, Omar ibn Said described vividly one of the main events that took place in 1807 in Futa Toro in northern Senegal. In April, the "big army" of the Bambara kingdom of Kaarta, made up of "infidels," as Omar mentioned at the end of his manuscript, marched over parts of the Islamic state of Futa Toro.[2] Abdel Kader Kane, its founder and *almamy* was killed, as were many men, while others were made prisoners.[3] Among them, it seems, was Omar, witness and probable participant—he mentioned he went to war repeatedly against the "infidels"—in one of the most emblematic in the succession of Islamic movements that swept Senegambia from the end of the seventeenth century to the end of the nineteenth century, and central Sudan in the nineteenth century. The old aristocracies, the European powers, the warrior elite, the clerical class, and the peasant masses saw their fates intertwined, and as a result, following each successful or failed movement, cohorts of Muslims whom the reformists had sought to protect were made prisoners and spent the rest of their lives enslaved in the Americas.

The figure of the reformist is part of a tradition in Islam: a Hadith establishes that a devout scholar will "set matters aright in evil times." Al-Maghili, the North African scholar, explained his role to Askia Muhammad ibn Abu Bakr Ture, the Songhay leader:

> Thus it is related that at the beginning of every century God sends men a
> scholar who regenerates their religion. Therefore, it is necessary that this
> scholar (who manifests himself) in every century acts in a way to enjoin
> what is right and forbid what is wrong, and reform people's affairs by
> establishing justice among them, in having right triumph over injustice,
> and the oppressed over the oppressor, in contrast to the conduct of the
> scholars of his age.[4]

Reformists were announced and expected, and they regularly appeared denouncing
tyranny, the degeneration of the religion, Christian enslavement of Muslims, and
later European penetration. As stated by al-Maghili, quoting a Hadith to Askia
Muhammad, the reformists could be perceived as personifying the idea that
"Islam started among the excluded and it will end among the excluded (as it
started)."

The first of the religious reform movements in Senegambia was launched by
Nasir al-Din, a *Zawaya* (marabout or cleric) Berber from Mauritania who, like
many reformists after him, belonged to the Qadiriyya Sufi order. His religious
movement started as a reaction against the Hassani or Bani-Hassan warriors
(Arabs originally from Yemen) whose exactions against the Berber maraboutic
clans made them appear as "infidels" to the Zawaya.[5] It was, fundamentally, a
nationalistic Berber movement against the Arabs who were dominating the entire
area. In Mauritania, Nasir al-Din's war, called *Sharr Bubba*, lasted thirty years
(1644–74).

The imam wanted to establish a rigorous Islamic theocracy, but his movement
was also a reaction against the commercial hegemony of Saint-Louis in present-
day Senegal. The port city had been established as a trade post by the French
under Louis XIV, in 1659, on a small island at the mouth of the Senegal River.
Saint-Louis was doing a brisk business in gum, millet, ivory, and captives, and this
new enterprise disrupted the traditional trade carried on through the Sahara by
the Berbers, whose commerce was also being upset by the Bani-Hassan's hegemony.
As shown by Boubacar Barry, the Berber had good reasons to want to replace the
Senegal River Valley rulers with ones who would be sympathetic to their cause and
help them revert to their old pattern of Saharan trade.[6] Nasir al-Din's movement
spread to the southern bank of the Senegal River at the beginning of 1673. It was
known, there, as the Marabouts' War or the Tuubnan movement, from the Wolof
tuub, to convert to Islam, itself a corruption of the Arabic to repent. This name
notwithstanding, it was a movement aimed more at reforming the practice of
Islam rather than at converting the so-called infidels.[7]

Nasir al-Din's first target in Senegal was the Denyanke regime of Futa Toro, established in the late fifteenth century by Koli Tenguela Ba, who had ushered in the collapse of the Jolof Empire, which in turn had resulted in the deportation of numerous people to the New World.[8] The Denyanke monarchy had been Muslim from the start, and some *satigi* (rulers) had gone to Mecca. Islam was also the religion of an important part of the Haalpulaar population—Tukulor and Fulbe—as mentioned in Arabic sources, oral tradition, and a 1606 account by Father Balthasar Barreira, a Portuguese Jesuit missionary: "[T]he banks of this river [Senegal] are inhabited by the *Fulos* [Fulbe], a warlike and policed people, which follows the sect of Mahomet."[9] However, with time, several satigi seemed to the most devout to be more nominal Muslims than true believers, and their regime engaged in activities that the religious groups condemned as anti-Islamic. Further, they had proved incapable or unwilling to protect their subjects from the slaving raids of the Moors and the Moroccans. With the help of the *ceddo*—a royal corps of enslaved warriors whose task it was to raid, pillage, and levy tribute on the peasant masses—the Denyanke sold their own Muslim subjects into slavery, which contradicted Islamic law.

Louis Moreau de Chambonneau, an employee of the French Compagnie du Sénégal and future director of the Concession du Sénégal—who witnessed the events and left the only first-hand account of the Marabouts' War—stressed the link that existed between the slave trade and the Islamic reform movement. He stated that the kings "often raid their subjects, under the pretext that they have talked badly of them, or that they have stolen or killed, or whatever other crime, so that no one feels safe for his possessions and his freedom since they take them captives. This has caused in large part the change of government into the Toubenan."[10] In conformity with Islamic prescriptions, Nasir al-Din first sent emissaries and marabouts to Satigi Sire Tabakali, asking him to pray more properly and more often, to content himself with three or four wives, to get rid of the *griots* (musicians), and to stop raiding, killing, and enslaving his subjects. If these demands were not met, the emissaries emphasized, the marabout had God's permission to depose the kings who did not change their ways, since they were enemies of God.[11] The satigi was certainly not impressed and let the marabout know that he had no intention of relinquishing power. Having failed in his first attempt to reform the regime by persuasion, Nasir al-Din went on to preach to the peasants. He condemned tyranny with firmness and eloquence, as relayed by Chambonneau: "God does not allow kings to pillage, kill or enslave their people, on the contrary, [God] has them to maintain and protect the people from their enemies, people are not made for the kings, but kings are made for the people."[12] Besides killings, reduction to slavery was certainly the most severe of the exactions committed by the rulers and aristocracy against the peasants; but there was also general tyranny and pillage that had been exacerbated by the transatlantic commerce. By providing firearms and goods, and encouraging greed and the exploitation of peasants, European traders had contributed to the development of a powerful militaristic class of wealthy aristocrats and elite enslaved warriors, whose interests clashed with those of the rural masses.[13]

The disruption brought by the transatlantic slave trade accentuated social differences even as it weakened local political authorities, reinforced royal power, and reduced the influence of the clerics. Muslim and non-Muslim rulers had traditionally relied on the advice and amulet protection of the marabouts, but as their power increased through trade with the Europeans, they tended to put some distance between themselves and the clerics, who demanded detachment from earthly riches. The transatlantic slave trade diminished some of the clerics' power and influence, but at the same time they gained new supporters and converts among the peasant masses. The marabouts' villages—which employed enslaved and free labor—were protected and appeared prosperous.[14] These safe havens were also perceived as being under the protection of God at a time when rulers did little to protect their subjects. By the 1670s—if the success of the tuubnan is any indication—people in certain areas started to see a correlation between personal safety (including from deportation overseas) and Islam.

Regardless of his discourse, Nasir al-Din should not be perceived as being against slavery per se. In the context of his time, such a position would have been indeed extraordinary. Domestic slavery was not questioned and nothing indicates that Nasir al-Din opposed the trade in non-Muslims. In point of fact, enslavement of so-called pagans is lawful in Islam, and it is, in theory, the only case in which a free person can be submitted to captivity. In seventeenth-century Senegal, Islam and the reformists who wanted to apply Qur'anic law to its fullest could only be appealing to the peasants, the main victims of the slave trade.

In short order, Nasir al-Din's troops of clerics, *talibs* (students, disciples), and commoners deposed the satigi of Futa Toro who fled to Gajaaga, the *damel* of Kayor, the *buurba* Jolof, and the *brak* of Walo.[15] Some battles were bloody; in other cases, the resistance was minimal. To ensure that Islamic law and the prohibition against selling free Muslims would be respected, the marabout replaced the monarchs with clerics, called in Wolof *buur jullit* or "leaders who pray." They put an effective stop to the slave trade, as Louis Moreau de Chambonneau lamented: "[T]he leading marabouts . . . despise us a lot because of the difference between our religion and their superstition. They tell the people that we trade in captives to eat them; since they became Masters of the country, up to now not one has entered our canoe; without the powerful, it is impossible for us to trade in anything."[16]

A year after he had established Islamic polities in northern Senegal, Nasir al-Din was killed in battle in Mauritania in 1674 and his revolution soon collapsed. With the help of the French and the Hassani warriors who were eager to resume the slave trade, the deposed aristocracies fought back and regained their lost power. Chambonneau, in his report to the directors of the Compagnie du Sénégal, draws a vivid portrait of the bloody events. Yerim Kode, the brak of Walo—who had been appointed by the tuubnan but turned against it—ravaged the country, burning, looting, killing, and taking "captives in great quantities."[17] He sold them to the French who promptly shipped them to the Antilles. The survivors were reduced to eating boiled grass, carrion, and pieces of leather. The famine was so devastating that entire families pawned themselves for food. As he traveled through Futa—which had been reconquered by Sire Tabakali with the help of the Hassan warriors—in July 1676, Chambonneau mentioned that if he had had enough goods, he could have bought six hundred more captives.

The political backlash inevitably hurt the Muslim clerics. The old aristocracies considered their egalitarian discourse dangerous, and their opposition to the trade in Muslims ran counter to Europe's slaving interests. Consequently, the repression that followed the Muslim revolution was particularly hard on them. It lasted for years, as pointed out by Jacques Joseph Le Maire, who emphasized in 1682 that the people of Walo had "no more marabouts in their country and those they can catch, they enslave."[18] This was true throughout the region. The slave dealer Jean Barbot mentioned that the people of Kayor had resolved "never more to entertain any Marabout, but to sell all such as they should find in their country for slaves."[19]

Although the Marabouts' War ended up in a resounding defeat and the deportation and enslavement of the peasants and Muslims it had sought to avoid, it had demonstrated that common people could fight the ceddo regimes with success; that the aristocracy, who—with the traders—was the beneficiary of the slave trade, could be overthrown. While some among the aristocracy and rulers became hostile to Islam, the religion started to be associated with the resistance of the peasantry against local oppression and foreign intrusion. The Marabouts' War became an inspiration for later movements.

As many marabouts and defeated Muslims were sent to the New World, some of the clerics settled in Bundu, between the Senegal and the Gambia rivers. Their leader was Malik Dawda Sy, a cleric from Futa who had studied at Kokki and Pir, the famous Qur'anic schools of Kayor. Bundu had started as a place of refuge for the Muslim reformists opposed to absolutism within a secular framework and to the effects of the transatlantic slave trade on Muslims, and it continued for years to welcome dissidents, persecuted peasants, and clerics. One of its most famous citizens in America was Ayuba Suleyman Diallo. Born in 1700, the year Malik Sy died, he was abducted in 1731 near the Gambia River where he had gone to buy paper and sell two captives. He was shipped to Maryland, enslaved on a tobacco plantation, and renamed Job ben Solomon. A letter in Arabic he sent to his father via a slave factor to be given to a slave captain eventually gained him his release. He went back to Bundu in 1734.[20]

In 1725 Futa Jallon, in present-day Guinea, also went through a reformist movement that installed an Islamic theocracy. One of its leaders was Almamy Mawdo Sory whose son, Ibrahima Abd-al Rahman, was made a prisoner of war in 1788 and deported to Mississippi. He spent thirty-nine years enslaved in Natchez before sailing to Liberia.[21] But by the end of the century, the stage of the Islamic revolutions had shifted back to the Senegal River. Since the first decade of the eighteenth century Futa Toro had undergone a prolonged crisis, due to a struggle for succession, and the ensuing civil strife sent numerous prisoners to the Americas. War also raged between European powers, and the slaving islands, Gorée and Saint-Louis, changed hands. The British seized Saint-Louis in 1758 during the Seven Years War and kept it until 1779.[22] Great Britain was eager to make the most of what it surely suspected, given prior experiences of conflict with France, was a temporary holding of Saint-Louis: her traders hastened to ship as many captives as possible to her Caribbean possessions. Its other objective was to weaken the Senegal River kingdoms—which had the power to cut off Saint-Louis from its slave supply upriver—by spreading terror and taking captives. Governor Charles O'Hara asked for and obtained the participation of the Moors of Brakna and Trarza, who invaded the southern bank of the Senegal River to round up captives with the weapons and ammunition provided by Saint-Louis.[23] On August 18, 1775, O'Hara wrote: "For the past two months, the Moors have totally submerged all nations of Blacks inhabiting the banks of this stream near the Senegal. They have killed and sold thousands of persons and forced others to flee the country."[24]

Omar ibn Said would have been five at the time and, according to contemporary sources, his father was killed "in one of those bloody wars that are almost constantly raging in Africa."[25] It is therefore possible that Omar's father was a victim of these particular events.[26] Records show that at least thirty-six ships left Saint-Louis, with more than 5,800 captives on board: 3,505 in 1775 and 2,305 the following year.[27] Except for 1774, it was the highest annual number of captives embarked from that port during the entire history of the transatlantic slave trade. Charles O'Hara's successor, Matthew McNamara, confirmed that the manhunt had been exceptional and emphasized that because of the huge number of Fulbe (and Tukulor) sent to the West Indies, the nation of Futa Toro was traumatized and that it would be difficult to engage in reconciliation.[28] During the British period, between 1758 and 1779, at least 181 ships sailed from Saint-Louis with over 27,300 captives (most coming from Khasso, Gajaga, and Bambuk) destined mostly to the Caribbean and to eight of the thirteen mainland colonies, with South Carolina receiving by far the highest number of all: 15 percent of the total deportees.[29]

To add to the suffering, a dreadful famine settled in the land, just as had happened after the Marabouts' War. The famine was the consequence of an invasion of locusts, recurrent droughts, wars, and the slave trade, which had wiped out entire villages of hard-working peasants.[30] The militaristic Denyanke aristocracy that had come back to power after the defeat of Nasir al-Din had been unwilling to protect the peasantry from the exactions of the Europeans and the Moors. But another group, despised by the nobility, who called its members "sons of hungry beggars," was gaining ascendancy: the so-called *torodbe* (sing. *torodo*, meaning "one who asks for alms"). The torodbe have become a hereditary clan situated in the upper echelon of Futa society, but originally, people belonging to the lower castes—including freed people—could join the group as long as they were willing to follow Islam and devote time to Qur'anic studies.[31] In the eighteenth century, as Tukulor and Fulbe societies were rigidly stratified into castes, the torodbe offered social promotion through learning, an avenue that was accessible to anyone, at least in theory. Not surprisingly, they brought dramatic change to the region, leading a movement that took its inspiration from the Marabouts' War and the successful Islamic theocracies in Bundu and Futa Jallon. The torodbe presented themselves as opposed to oppression wherever it came from, be it from non-Muslims or Muslims. Their religious philosophy meshed with the traditional African reluctance for despotism that had led, centuries before, to the establishment of various councils to counterbalance the power of the elected rulers.

At the head of the torodbe movement was the marabout Suleyman Bal.[32] A devout Muslim, he had studied in Kayor and traveled to Futa Jallon, where he became familiar with the institution of the *almamate*. He had also studied in Mauritania and had seen firsthand how his people were treated as captives. According to oral tradition, Bal first tried to persuade Satigi Sule Ndiaye to reform and to stop raiding and pillaging his own subjects.[33] But other methods were also employed. In Futa Jallon, Bal had "acquired some of the mystical and magical training associated with the area."[34] Traditionalist Shaykh Muusa Kamara mentions that Bal or his successor, Abdul Kader Kane, both well-versed in occult sciences, had written the verse "May you get out of our country or enter into our religion" in a pentagram, with the names of the Denyanke chiefs in the middle.[35]

Once he had established control over central Futa, one of Bal's major preoccupations was to put a stop to the Moors' slaving incursions, and he personally led several battles against them. His troops' success put a stop to the payment by Futa of the *mudo horma*, an annual tribute of gold to the Moors. Another concern was the protection of his subjects from British-occupied Saint-Louis. In 1775, in retaliation to Governor Charles O'Hara's deportation of *Futanke* (people from Futa) to the West Indies, Futa closed the traffic coming from Gajaga.[36]

After Bal's death in battle against the Moors in 1776, Abdul Kader Kane, now fifty years of age, was chosen to lead the movement as the first almamy. Kane, who came from a learned and devout family of pilgrims and teachers, had studied at Pir and Kokki, like Malik Sy and Suleyman Bal. He had then taught and been a judge in Bundu.[37] Once his power had been consolidated, Abdul Kader was strong enough to negotiate a favorable agreement with Louis XVI's France, which had in the meantime recovered Saint-Louis from the British. Signed in March 1785, it stipulated the conditions of trade between France and Futa, with tolls on each vessel and an annual due to be paid to Futa.[38] There was an absolute prohibition on the sale of Muslims. Non-Muslim prisoners of war were not included in the ban and could transit through Futa on their way to Saint-Louis.

Abdul Kader's second move was to neutralize the Moors of Trarza, who were a constant threat, meddling in Futa's affairs and kidnapping people for their own use or to sell to Saint-Louis.[39] He allied himself with the Moors of Brakna, and their joint troops routed the Trarza and killed their leader. René Claude Geoffroy de Villeneuve, a French doctor, who was during these events an Assistant to the Governor of Gorée Island, wrote: "These ferocious Moors attacked the subjects of the Almammy himself, of whom they took many, and continued to harass them until this virtuous prince having gathered his troops vanquished the Moors in a battle in which their king [Eli El-Kowri] lost his life."[40] His victory gained Abdul Kader many supporters and ensured peace on the northern front. Futa made the Moors pay tribute in horses and other goods.

The following year, due to renewed problems with Saint-Louis, Abdul Kader put a stop to all traffic, including the trade in mostly non-Muslims from the Bambara kingdoms in the east. According to French officials, the reason was purely commercial. Abdul Kader insisted on "some new and ridiculously exaggerated conditions for the liberty of the Galam [Gajaga] convoy" with which they did not want to comply.[41] Futa, in turn, accused the French of not paying the agreed-upon fees on millet, gum, and captives. Swedish naturalist Carl Bernhard Wadstrom, who witnessed the events, saw the move in more humanistic terms:

> In 1787, King Almammy had issued a law that honored him greatly, and by which it was forbidden that any slave pass through his states. There were many vessels anchored in the Senegal [River] that were awaiting slaves. This edict forced the traders to take another route and the slaves were brought to other places. The French, who could not complete their cargo,

sent remonstrances to the king who, however, did not listen to them since he sent back the gifts that the Compagnie du Sénégal had sent him.[42]

Futa's diligent opposition to the deportation of Muslims attracted settlers. A French trader, Pruneau de Pommegorge, stressed that Abdul Kader Kane had succeeded in peopling his kingdom by forbidding captivity and harassments, and, he added, his good administration had become a threat to his neighbors. He emphasized that this man, from an "almost savage" country, had given a lesson in humanity to more policed peoples.[43] Futa had become a safe haven for soldiers, farmers, herders, and people in search of safety from all over the area. Religious education spread and Qur'anic schools and mosques sprang up in villages and towns. Omar ibn Said, who lived almost his entire life in Senegal under the almamate, was one of the beneficiaries of this emphasis on Islamic instruction, and his long years of study with prominent teachers enabled him to maintain his Arabic literacy several decades after being abruptly removed from his intellectual and religious milieu.

The prohibition on the kidnapping and selling of Muslims was firmly maintained by Abdul Kader, who did not hesitate to intervene personally to retrieve them when necessary. After the French had bought three children from Futa, "Almammy, king of the Muslims," threatened the French in a letter to Commandant Blanchot, dated March 1789:

> We are warning you that all those who will come to our land to trade [in slaves] will be killed and massacred if you do not send our children back. Would not somebody who was very hungry abstain from eating if he had to eat something cooked with his blood? We absolutely do not want you to buy Muslims under any circumstances. I repeat that if your intention is to always buy Muslims you should stay home and not come to our country anymore. Because all those who will come can be assured that they will lose their life.[44]

This letter is a rare example of a written, overt threat against the transatlantic slave trade. The fact that it expresses concern exclusively for the Muslims accords with Islamic law, which Abdul Kader was known to apply to the letter. While he was protecting his own people, he had no problem making money on every French ship that transported millet, gum, and non-Muslim captives.

In addition to keeping the French and the Moors at bay, the almamate set out to subdue the rulers of the adjacent kingdoms deemed "pagans" or lax Muslims. Like Nasir al-Din, the torodbe specifically linked freedom from slavery and happiness with Islam, as reported in 1789 by Dominique Lamiral, an agent for the Compagnie de la Guyane, who worked in Senegal:

> The Fulbe . . . commanded by the priests, wanted to ravage everything
> not to take slaves, they said, but to force them [the people of Walo and
> Kayor] to submit to the cult of Mahomet: they cried liberty everywhere;
> they said that they had nothing against the people, that on the contrary
> they came to set them free. They said to them, so long as your king is not
> a marabout, you will not be free. Support us and you will be happy.[45]

The rulers of Walo, Jolof, Kayor, and later Khasso (in western Mali) and Bundu
swore allegiance and paid tributes to Futa. But when Amari Ngone Della came to
power in Kayor, contrary to his predecessor, he refused to submit to Abdul Kader
and to follow his purist brand of Islam. In addition, Amari Ngone had entered
into a feud with the clerics of the city of Louga who wanted to overthrow him;
their leader, Malamine Sar, was killed, while one of his sons was sold away into
slavery. Abdul Kader had sent one of his closest allies, Hamadi Ibrahima, to Kayor
with instructions to propagate Islam, and he too was killed with his family. Abdul
Kader was eager to avenge his coreligionists' deaths or sale into bondage and to
subdue Amari Ngone. According to Baron Roger, the French Governor of Senegal,
who wrote an historical novel based on pro-Abdul Kader eyewitness accounts of
the events, the marabouts' discourse against Damel Amari Ngone went thus:

> War to this king who is an enemy of God and humanity, who arbitrarily
> reduces in slavery the free people of his country! Who refuses freedom to
> the slaves who can read the Koran! Let's retaliate against the man who
> mistreats the marabouts! Death to him who sells Muslims as slaves to the
> Christians![46]

In conformity with Islamic customs, Abdul Kader and his council sent emissaries
to Amari Ngone. They asked him to better observe Islam and have the religion
respected in his land; to stop selling free men and Muslims to the Christians; and
to free the captives who had become Muslims. The king's response was that the
almamy should mind his own business, and, if he wanted war, the damel was
resigned to beat him.[47]

Abdul Kader Kane gathered a large troop—30,000 men, women, and children—
with a view to settle in Kayor.[48] At the time, Omar ibn Said was twenty-six, and
since he mentions that he went to war "every year" against the "infidels," it is
possible that he participated in this action, the most grandiose of Abdul Kader's
endeavors. The link between this campaign, which was also religious, and the
slave trade seems to have been clear in the minds of at least some participants. One
of them, Samba Makumba—captured at twenty-one—ended up enslaved in
Trinidad, where he was a founding member of the Free Mohammedan Society of

Port-of-Spain. He analyzed these events for a British traveler about forty years later:

> He [Samba Makumba] belonged to the tribe Fullah Tauro, which engaged in war with six other tribes in Africa to prevent them, as he said, from carrying on the slave trade. The Mahometans are forbidden to make slaves of those of their own faith, and when any of their people are concerned in this traffic, they believe their religion requires them to put a stop to it by force. It was for this purpose a war was commenced by the Fullahs against these other tribes and in this war Samba was taken prisoner and sold as a slave.[49]

According to Baron Roger, everyone in Futa was aware of the connection between freedom from deportation and enslavement and the torodbe revolution. In addition, he stated, those in Futa believed that "by forbidding the trade in slaves, Europeans have been inspired by their example. They are proud to have preceded us in the realm of reason, justice and humanity."[50]

The long walk to Kayor was a disaster. Amari Ngone's scorched-earth tactic decimated the Futa group, which was soundly defeated at Bunguye.[51] Abdul Kader was made a prisoner and pleaded for his men not to be sold to the Christians.[52] It was in vain. The French, who wanted to get rid of the almamy because of his opposition to the trade in Muslims and the high trade duties he demanded, had provided the damel with weapons and ammunition in exchange for the prisoners he was going to take. Scottish explorer Mungo Park met some survivors of the debacle as they boarded the slave ship *Charlestown* at Gorée in 1797. They were bound for South Carolina, but due to mechanical problems, landed in Antigua.[53] Many of the defeated Muslims took refuge in the Cap-Vert peninsula (now the region of Dakar), where they helped establish still another theocracy under the leadership of the marabout Dial Diop.

As some of his followers were swept into the transatlantic slave trade, Abdul Kader remained a prisoner for a few months before being released and sent back to Futa by a magnanimous Amari Ngone. Abdul Kader's defeat and consequent absence had weakened his power and allowed the crystallization of opposition. Nevertheless, he continued his leadership in the same uncompromising and inflexible manner as before. In 1802 he concluded yet another treaty with the French. Arrangements were made for the exchange of Muslim captives from Futa sold as prisoners of war by other states. But in retaliation against the almamy who had once again interrupted the trade on the river, Commandant Blanchot raided a few villages in 1804. In July 1805 Futa took its revenge and attacked Saint-Louis gum traders, killing thirty-six. On August 2, Blanchot sent six hundred men in twelve boats from Saint-Louis to Podor to burn a dozen villages. They killed two hundred people and took six hundred prisoners, who were sold as slaves along with sixteen Tukulor who were in Saint-Louis at the time.[54] Both parties finally agreed to a new treaty and Blanchot signed another accord with the almamy in 1806 that confirmed the terms of the 1785 treaty. Napoleonic France's river trade depended, once again, on the almamy's goodwill.

It was not an advantageous situation for the French, but it would not last for long. Within a year, Abdul Kader was gone. The last episode in the almamy's life was typical: it started with the defense of a Muslim community and ended with another contingent of captives shipped to the American plantations, Omar ibn Said possibly among them. The leader of Futa responded to the cry for help from a community in Bundu that felt oppressed by assembling an army to confront Almamy Sega Gay.[55] Gay was condemned by an Islamic tribunal and killed. The almamy appointed one of his protégés, Amadi Pate, at the head of Bundu, but he was eventually replaced by Amadi Aïssata, Sega Gay's brother.

While Abdul Kader was interfering in Bundu, he was deposed in Futa and replaced by Abdul Moktar Kudeje Talla. Futa traditionalist, Islamic historian, and genealogist Sire Abbas Soh states that Moktar Kudeje and his brothers based their decision to depose Abdul Kader on the fact that he was eighty years old and had been a captive in Kayor, which did not fit "a prince of the believers."[56] In addition, and maybe more importantly, Abdul Kader had alienated many with his insistence on the strict application of Islamic law. His rigid and rigorist approach had resulted in an authoritative regime that was largely resented. As reported by Shaykh Muusa Kamara: "To tell the truth, Almamy had made many enemies because he did not fear anyone when it came to executing Allah's law. He acted and judged only according to the law (al-haqq). He could not be corrupted and did not favor anyone when it was a matter of divine law. Nothing mattered to him but the law; this is why his enemies were opposed to him and plotted against him."[57]

Meanwhile, the leaders of Futa, Bundu, and Kamera, as well as Abdul Kader's old enemies, the Denyanke, asked the kingdom of Kaarta for help in getting rid of the almamy, once and for all. In April 1807, the Futa-Bundu-Kaarta-Kamera coalition faced Abdul Kader in Juude Guriki. The following description of his last moments was relayed by the leader of Kamera to the French Commandant of Bakel:

> When the Bambara charged the Almamy, several of the people who were around him fled, some whipped his horse so that he could escape from danger, but he managed to rein it in and persisted to wait for his enemies even though everybody had abandoned him. One of the Bambara, as he approached him, struck him with his rifle butt, which threw him on the

ground, but he did not recognize him and left him there as he took away his horse. Some time later, people from Bundu arrived and as they recognized Abdoul Kader, they alerted Almamy; he ran to his enemy and found him laying on the ground, his head in a pagne [a piece of fabric]. Salamalecum, he said. The other said nothing, he repeated his greeting, Abdoul still kept quiet. Ah! Ah! Amadi said, do you remember the incident with Almamy Sega, my brother? You did not think that this moment would arrive; I am going to send you to the same place where you sent my brother! He said so, and shot him and ordered all his people to shoot him. Abdoul Kader died without a murmur.[58]

According to tradition, the date of Abdul Kader's death, at eighty-one, was 7 Safar 1221, or Thursday, April 4; but a calendar that gives the concordance of Islamic and Christian dates, puts it at April 21, 1807.[59]

All the men with Abdul Kader were either killed or taken prisoner and sold. Omar ibn Said's account is too brief to provide any clue as to the exact circumstances of his own capture. He may have been among Abdul Kader Kane's close followers, or he may have been captured a little later. In any event, the fact that he "walked to the sea" suggests that he was taken prisoner during the dry season, when the Senegal River was not navigable.[60] At thirty-seven, Omar was already too old to be considered a good candidate for overseas sale; on the other hand, he was a good one for ransom. Since he belonged, according to his pastor, Rev. Mathew Grier, to a wealthy family, his relatives could probably have redeemed him, as was frequently the case with people whose family could either pay for their freedom or give some captives in exchange.[61] The fact that he was not redeemed may indicate that he was purposely taken out of the area before he could be freed. This often happened when people were deemed a threat, perhaps because of their political connections. The fact that Omar was captured during the particular events surrounding Abdul Kader's defeat may indicate that Omar was an active, well-known, or influential supporter of the almamy.

Once on the coast, Omar was detained in Saint-Louis, either in the fort that doubled as a slave *entrepôt* or in one of the private *captiveries* owned by the French, mulatto, and Wolof traders.[62] Only four American slave ships had arrived in the city in 1807. One left in March, before the events, and three sailed away between October and December, which means that Omar was confined for at least six months. It is possible that he would have been moved, by the end of his stay, to the northern part of the city. It was almost uninhabited and was routinely used as an open-air slave pen, called a *gallo*, from October onward, when the flow of captives brought from Gajaga exceeded the holding capacity of the city's cells.

The first American ship to leave Saint-Louis was the *Eliza* from Rhode Island, which sailed into Charleston on October 20 with seventy-nine people on board. Eleven had died during the voyage. Omar may instead have boarded the schooner *Hannah*, another Rhode Island ship that had embarked fifty-seven people and left on September 30.[63] The fifty-one survivors of a forty-one-day ordeal—Omar states he was "a month and a half" at sea—disembarked at Charleston on November 10. Finally, he could have been on the *Caroline*, which landed in Charleston on December 23, 1807, nine days before the official abolition of the U.S. international slave trade took effect.[64] In all, about 385 people who embarked in Saint-Louis reached Charleston that year. Whatever boat he arrived on, Omar was among the last captives to legally enter the United States.

That same year had seen the first of several Muslim uprisings in Brazil, a consequence of the launch, three years earlier, of the reformist movement led by Usman dan Fodio—whose family had emigrated from Futa Toro generations earlier—in Central Sudan (Nigeria). This jihad, too, that proclaimed its attachment to social justice, led to the deportation of numerous Muslim prisoners of war, especially to Bahia, where they continued to fight and organized the largest uprising in Brazilian history in 1835.[65]

As Omar was writing his autobiography in 1831, another war erupted between the Bambara and Futa and was followed a year later by a civil war; trade disputes, treaties, and bloody retaliations on both sides went on for decades between the almamate and Saint-Louis. And reformists, who stated that to live under a Muslim ruler was no guarantee of receiving social justice, continued to appear. As Abdul Kader's men had emphasized, without marabouts—and not just any Muslim—as rulers, the people could not be "happy." They stated that piety, honesty, benevolence, and fairness were the most decisive criteria for choosing a leader, as recommended by Suleyman Bal to his followers:

> Choose an imam, pious and ascetic, who is not interested in [the riches of] this world; and if you see that his possessions increase, depose him and confiscate all his belongings; and if he refuses to abdicate, fight him and exile him to make sure he does not establish a tyranny his sons would inherit. Replace him with another among the men of knowledge and action. . . . Bring to power one who deserves it, one who forbids his soldiers to kill defenseless children and old people, and to [rape] women, let alone kill them.[66]

The reformists saw the *sharia* as the ideal rule of law, the only one that could provide justice and fairness, contrary to what they denounced as the arbitrary and autocratic dictum of the secular Muslim and non-Muslim rulers. They made clear that Muslims were, by essence, free men and women and that they could not be sold under any circumstances to the Christians. Their enslavement, in other words, was illegal. In non-Muslim African societies, enslavement was not linked to religion. Prisoners of war, debtors, people accused of adultery or witchcraft, thieves, murderers, and political prisoners were all liable to bondage. With the advent of the transatlantic slave trade, however, several categories of crimes punishable by servitude were added as the powerful saw fit. Islamic law, on the contrary, insisted that only one category of people could be enslaved: the "unbelievers" and apostates. Not only did Islamic law reduce the motives for enslavement to religion only, but it also introduced the idea that all were equal in matters of law: as long as they were believers, the poor and the defenseless—and not only the powerful, the wealthy, and the nobility—were worthy of protection, too. To the reformists, ethnicity had no relevance; the only bond that mattered was Islam. By denouncing the corruption and injustice of the local rulers, which had increased with the transatlantic slave trade, and by attacking them, the Muslim reformists gained support among the poor, the lower castes, the peasants, and the uneducated— victims for centuries of various slave trades—to whom they offered, in theory, safety, literacy, and a possible upward mobility. The Muslim theocracies sought to bring unity, through violence as well as persuasion, to diverse populations, and they consolidated areas once divided into small polities; however, their rigorist application of Islam also alienated numerous would-be supporters.

Muslims made great efforts to protect their own, but based on religious tenets, "unbelievers" were fair game. Muslim traders and rulers were thus directly and actively involved in the slave trade. Moreover, those who professed reformism did not hesitate to sell their brethren who, according to them, did not follow Islam to the letter. They branded them as unbelievers or even worse, apostates, and therefore had no qualm selling them to the Christians.

By the middle of the nineteenth century, new reformist movements were launched by marabouts—warriors who had been inspired by the leaders of the past. They too preached the strict application of Qur'anic law, stressed the ideals of Islamic solidarity and justice, and worked for the overthrow of rulers they considered despotic and/or weak Muslims. Through war, conquest, and the enslavement of prisoners, these new reformers attempted to politically consolidate the region, which pitted them against the Europeans and somewhat facilitated colonial expansion by weakening the populations already exhausted by incessant wars. In 1864, the year Omar died enslaved in North Carolina, El Hajj Umar Tal, the reformist scholar and military strategist born in Futa Toro, was killed in an explosion of his own gunpowder. He had fought against the non-Muslim populations and the French and established a vast Islamic Tukulor Empire over parts of Senegal, Guinea, and Mali. Maba Diarrou Ba, Amadou Cheikhou, and Mamadou Lamine Drame took on his jihad and were the last reformist marabouts—warriors of stature in Senegambia. Drame was killed in 1887, and by 1891 Futa Toro and the rest of what were once Islamic polities were under French control.

NOTES

1. Alryyes, *Life*, 61. Another version of Omar's enslavement has been given by the Rev. Mathew B. Grier in the *North Carolina Presbyterian* (July 23, 1859): "While engaged in trade, some event occurred, which he is very reluctant to refer to, but which resulted in his being sold into slavery." This is evidently in total contradiction with Omar's direct account, as found in his autobiography written twenty years before. Grier's version is too vague to provide any clue as to the reason why Omar was sold away and it does not fit with what is known of Futa Toro at the time. It is very doubtful that Omar would have been sold to the Christians because of a commercial dispute. Omar's version of the events surrounding his captivity is the one used in this paper, as it has the advantage of being a personal, direct description as opposed to one of the many secondhand accounts of his life, some of them patently wrong. For different versions of Omar's life and origins (an Arab, a Freemason, a prince, the son of "the King of the Meli" of Central Africa), see Allan D. Austin, *African Muslims in Antebellum America: A Sourcebook* (New York: Garland Publishers, 1984), 445–523, and *The Life of Omar Ibn Said, Written by Himself*, with introduction and translation by Ala A. Alryyes, in *The Multilingual Anthology of American Literature: A Reader of Original Texts with English Translations*, ed. Marc Shell and Werner Sollors (New York: New York University Press, 2000). In 1889, Omar was said to have been a slave trader in the Congo (*News and Observer*, Raleigh, September 3, 1889). Later, he was presented as having been captured during a war between the "Foulas" and the "Hausas": George H. Callcott, "Omar Ibn Seid, a Slave Who Wrote an Autobiography in Arabic," *Journal of Negro History* (January 1954): 58–63.

2. Kaarta is located in the west of present-day Mali. Futa Toro is located on the southern bank of the Senegal River, in present-day Senegal.

3. *Almamy* is the title of a religious and political leader, from the Arabic *al-imam*.

4. Joseph M. Cuoq, *Recueil des sources arabes concernant l'Afrique occidentale du VIIIe au XVIe siècle (Bilad al-Sudan)* (Paris: CNRS, 1985), 405.

5. Nasir al-Din belonged to a Berber population, the Lemtuna, who had arrived in present-day Mauritania in the eighth century. The *Zawaya* are the religious leaders or marabouts, often of Berber origin. The Hassani or Bani-Hassan are the warrior group, of Arab (Yemeni) origin. The Berbers turned to clericalism in order to retain some power, as they were militarily defeated by the Yemeni Arabs in the seventeenth century. Both groups form the higher echelon of Mauritanian society. Arab and Berber groups, as well as the (non-indigenous) black populations they formerly enslaved—the *harratin* or "freedmen"—are called collectively Moors. The indigenous black populations, who were pushed south to the Senegal River Valley by the Arab invasions—the Soninke and Haalpulaarpeople who speak Pulaar, i.e., Tukulor and Fulbe—are not culturally or ethnically part of Moor society.

6. Boubacar Barry, *Senegambia and the Transatlantic Slave Trade* (Cambridge: Cambridge University Press, 1998), 50–54.

7. For a discussion of the "conversion versus reform" argument, see Lucie Gallistel Colvin, "Islam and the State of Kayoor: A Case of a Successful Resistance to Jihad," *Journal of African History* 15.4 (1974): 596.

8. For Koli Tenguela and early Futa Toro, see Al-Saʾdi, *Tarikh es-Soudan* (Paris: Maisonneuve, 1964), 127–28; Shaykh Muusa Kamara, *Florilège au jardin de l'histoire des Noirs. Zuhur al-Basatin. L'aristocratie peule et la révolution des clercs musulmans (Vallée du Sénégal)* (Paris: CNRS, 1998), 97–127; Djibril Tamsir Niane, "A propos de Koli Tenguéla," *Recherches africaines* 54 (October 1960): 33–36; Jean Boulègue, *Le Grand Jolof (XIIIe–XVIe siècle)* (Blois: Editions Façades, 1987), 156–60.

9. Nize Isabel de Moraes, *A la découverte de la Petite Côte au XVIIe siècle (Sénégal et Gambie) Tome I: 1600–1621* (Dakar: IFAN Cheikh Anta Diop, 1993), 111.

10. Louis Moreau de Chambonneau, "Traité de l'origine des nègres du Sénégal, coste d'Affrique, de leurs pays, relligion, coutumes et moeurs," in Carson I. A. Ritchie, "Deux textes sur le Sénégal, 1763–1767," *Bulletin de l'IFAN* 30, no. 1 (1968): 322.

11. Louis Moreau de Chambonneau, "L'histoire du Toubenan, ou changement de Royes, et Reforme de Relligion des Negres du Senegal Coste d'Affrique depuis 1673 qui est son origine, jusqu'en 1677," in Carson I. A. Ritchie, "Deux textes sur le Sénégal, 1763–1767," *Bulletin de l'IFAN* 30, no. 1 (1968): 339.

12. Ibid.

13. For the development of ceddo regimes, see Boubacar Barry, *Senegambia*, 81–93.

14. For a study of these safe havens, see Brahim Diop, "Traite négrière, desertions rurales et occupation du sol dans l'arrière-pays de Gorée," in *Gorée et l'esclavage: Actes du Séminaire sur "Gore dans la Traite atlantique: Mythes et réalités" (Gorée, 7–8 Avril 1997)*, ed. Djibril Samb (Dakar: Université Cheikh Anta Diop, Initiations et études africaines no. 38, 1997), 137–51.

15. Gajaga or Galam is a region located on the Senegal River east of Futa Toro. *Damel, buurba*, and *brak* are the titles given to the rulers, respectively, of the kingdoms of Kayor (North Senegal), Jolof (a region south of Futa Toro), and Walo (on the northern coast of Senegal).

16. Chambonneau, "L'histoire du Toubenan," 352.

17. Ibid., 351.

18. Jacques Joseph Le Maire, *Les voyages du Sieur Le Maire aux îles Canaries, Cap-Vert, Sénégal et Gambie* (Paris: J. Collombat, 1695), 100–101.

19. P. E. H. Hair, *Barbot on Guinea* (London: Hakluyt Society, 1992), 131.

20. Francis Moore, *Travels into the Inland Parts of Africa* (London: E. Cave, 1738). Philip Curtin, "Ayuba Suleiman Diallo of Bondu," in *Africa Remembered: Narratives by West Africans from the Era of the Slave Trade* (Madison: University of Wisconsin Press, 1967). Douglas Grant, *The Fortunate Slave* (New York: Oxford University Press, 1968).

21. For Ibrahima see Terry Alford, *Prince among Slaves: The True Story of an African Prince Sold into Slavery in the American South* (New York: Oxford University Press), 1986.

22. Gorée was also seized but returned to France under the Treaty of Paris in 1763.

23. Dominique Lamiral, *L'Affrique et le peuple africain considérés sous tous leurs rapports avec notre commerce et nos colonies* (Paris: Dessenne, 1789), 176. Brakna and Trarza were two Mauritanian emirates located in the Senegal River Valley.

24. Barry, *Senegambia*, 68.

25. William Plumer, "Meroh, a Native African," *New York Observer*, January 8, 1863, 1.

26. The captives rounded up by the Maures, who according to a 1783 French document

numbered about 9,000, were sold to the British. There has been controversy among historians as to the validity of those numbers. See Phillip Curtin, *Economic Change in Precolonial Africa: Senegambia and the Era of the Slave Trade* (Madison: The University of Wisconsin Press, 1975), 126, n.10; and Barry, *Senegambia*, 67–69.

27. The Trans-Atlantic Slave Trade Database, www.slavevoyages.org.

28. Oumar Kane, "Les Maures et le Futa-Toro au XVIIIe siècle," *Cahiers d'Etudes africaines* 14, no. 54 (1974): 250.

29. Trans-Atlantic Slave Trade Database.

30. For details about the ecological situation of Senegal at the time, see James Searing, *West African Slavery and Transatlantic Commerce: The Senegal River Valley, 1700–1860* (Cambridge: Cambridge University Press, 1993), 129–62.

31. John Ralph Willis, "The Torodbe Clerisy: A Social View," *Journal of African History* 19, no. 2 (1978): 195–212.

32. For general discussion, see Boubacar Barry, *Senegambia*; Martin A. Klein, "Social and Economic Factors in the Muslim Revolution in Senegambia," *Journal of African History* 13, no. 1 (1972): 419–41; David Robinson, "Abdul Kadir and Shaykh Umar: A Continuing Tradition of Islamic Leadership in Futa Toro," *International Journal of African Historical Studies* 6, no. 2 (1973): 286–303; David Robinson, "The Islamic Revolution in Futa Toro," *International Journal of African Historical Studies* 8 (1975): 185–221; Madina Ly-Tall, *Un Islam militant en Afrique de l'Ouest au XXe siècle: La Tijaniyya de Saïku Umar Futiyu contre les Pouvoirs traditionnels et la Puissance coloniale* (Paris: L'Harmattan, 1991).

33. Robinson, "Abdul Kadir and Shaykh Umar," 293.

34. Ibid., 292.

35. Kamara, *Florilège*, 324.

36. Curtin, *Economic Change*, 182.

37. For origin and election of Abdul Kader, see Sire Abbas Soh, *Chroniques du Fouta sénégalais* (Paris: Ernest Leroux, 1913), 43.

38. In 1787 it amounted to 4,333 pounds. The French also paid these "customs" to the kings of Kayor, Walo, Galam, and to the Trarza and Brakna Moors. The amounts varied. Prosper Cultru, *Histoire du Sénégal du XVe siècle à 1870* (Paris: Emile Larose, 1910), 243.

39. On Futa Toro and the Moors, see Kane, "Les Maures et le Futa-Toro."

40. Françoise Thésée, "Au Sénégal, en 1789. Traite des nègres et société africaine dans les royaumes de Sallum, de sin et de Cayor," in *De la traite à l'esclavage: Actes du colloque international sur la Traite des Noirs, Nantes 1985*, ed. Serge Daget (Paris: Société française d'histoire d'outre mer, 1988), 236.

41. Sylvester M. X. Golberry, *Travels in Africa Performed during the Years 1785, 1786 and 1787 in the Western Countries of this Continent* (London, 1803), I, 184.

42. Carl B. Wadstrom, "Observations sur la traite des nègres avec une description de quelques parties de la côte de Guinée durant un voyage fait en 1787 et 1788," in Robert Norris, *Voyage au pays de Dahomé* (Paris, 1790), 178.

43. Pruneau de Pommegorge, *Description de la Nigritie* (Amsterdam: Maradan, 1789), 14.

44. Boubacar Barry, *Le royaume du Waalo, le Sénégal avant la conquête* (Paris: François Maspero, 1972), 216.

45. Lamiral, *L'Affrique*, 174–75.

46. Baron Roger, *Kélédor, histoire africaine* (Paris: Nepveu, 1828), 6.

47. Ibid., 20.

48. Lamiral, *L'Affrique*, 174.

49. George Truman, *A Visit to the West Indies* (Philadelphia: Merrihew & Thompson, 1844), 109. For the Mohammedan or Mandingo Society or Trinidad, see Carl Campbell, "John Mohammed Bath and the Free Mandingos in Trinidad: The Question of Their Repatriation to Africa 1831–38," *Journal of African Studies* 2, no. 4 (1975–76): 467–95.

50. Roger, *Kélédor, histoire africaine*, 238–39.

51. West African Muslim hagiography states that El Hajj Umar Taal was born on the day Abdul Kader passed through his village on his way to Bunguye. See Kamara, *Florilège*, 336–37.

52. Ibid., 62.

53. Mungo Park, *Travels in the Interior Districts of Africa* (New York: Arno Press, 1971), 344.

54. Cultru, *Histoire du Sénégal*, 293–94; Robinson, "The Islamic Revolution in Futa Toro," 211; Barry, *Senegambia*, 104.

55. See Curtin, *Economic Change*, 55; Ly-Tall, *Un Islam militant*, 69–73; Barry, *Senegambia*, 105–6; Robinson, "The Islamic Revolution in Futa Toro," 211–14.

56. Soh, *Chroniques du Fouta sénégalais*, 54.

57. Kamara, *Florilège*, 344.

58. Cited in Ly-Tall, *Un Islam militant*, 71–72. For a similar version, see also Major W. Gray and Staff Surgeon Dochard, *Travels in Western Africa* (London: John Murray, 1825), 198–99. A version reported by Kamara mentions that Kane was captured by the people of Bundu and killed by the Bambara (*Florilège*, 349).

59. Kamara, *Florilège*, 351; Soh, *Chroniques du Fouta sénégalais*, 59.

60. Trade was conducted on the river during the rainy season. Boats left Saint-Louis in July to sail to Gajaga and came back with their captives in September/October.

61. Austin, *African Muslims*, 481. George H. Callcott of the University of North Carolina stated that Omar "was married and had one son" but does not mention any source ("Omar Ibn Seid," 59). Given the usual matrimonial patterns of African Muslim men at the time, it is doubtful that Omar would have had only one child and one wife. For a study of redemption during the transatlantic slave trade, see Sylviane A. Diouf, "The Last Resort: Redeeming Family and Friends," in *Fighting the Slave Trade: West African Strategies*, ed. Sylviane A. Diouf (Athens: Ohio University Press, 2003).

62. The Saint-Louis population was about 7,000 and more than half were enslaved domestics and sailors. A few European traders could accommodate a total of about 550 captives, but several smaller traders had *captiveries* that could accommodate from ten to twenty captives.

63. Why an American captain would have bought such an older man may be explained by the fact that these were the very last months of the legal trade and captains, in the scramble for slaves, may have put on board any captive they could find, so as to leave Saint-Louis on time in the last officially sanctioned American slave voyages.

64. The Trans-Atlantic Slave Trade Database, ships identification, 36926, 36921, and 25510. The website of the Davidson College Archives (http://library.davidson.edu/archives/ency/omars.asp), which owns materials that once belonged to Omar, states inaccurately that he arrived on the *Heart of Oak* on December 27. That ship sailed from Sierra Leone; see ship identification 25545. The international slave trade became illegal in the United States on January 1, 1808. It continued until 1860; see Sylviane A. Diouf, *Dreams of Africa in*

Alabama: The Slave Ship Clotilda and the Story of the Last Africans Brought to America (New York: Oxford University Press, 2007).

65. For an account of the Hausa and Yoruba in Bahia, see Joao Jose Reis, *Slave Rebellion in Brazil: The Muslim Uprising of 1835 in Bahia* (Baltimore: Johns Hopkins University Press, 1993); Sylviane A. Diouf, *Servants of Allah: African Muslims Enslaved in the Americas* (New York: New York University Press, 1998).

66. Kamara, *Florilège*, 323.

Representing the West
in the Arabic Language

The Slave Narrative of Omar Ibn Said

GHADA OSMAN and CAMILLE F. FORBES

In *From Behind the Veil,* a seminal text in African American literary studies, Robert Stepto posits that for African America, the "pregeneric myth"—a shared myth both predating the literary form and influencing the texts composing a culture's literary canon—is "the quest for freedom and literacy."[1] His study takes as its starting point four slave narratives that represent the earliest period in the history of the African American narrative as literary form. Introducing key phases in the slave narrative, Stepto charts the increasing independence of the slave's voice. He notes the plethora of voices, represented by appended documents, which serve to authenticate the narrative, and he subsequently analyzes slaves' strategies of gaining authorial control over their texts.

The work, a critical study of the slave narrative, could not have anticipated the 1995 rediscovery of a particularly significant text in the history of the African American narrative, which would trouble this proposed pregeneric myth: the 1831 slave narrative of Omar ibn Said. Commissioned to write in the Arabic language, Omar wrote the only existing autobiography of an American slave in Arabic, thereby complicating Stepto's statement regarding African American literature. Omar's narrative, written in the language of a slave already literate before coming to America, thus sets aside the driving myth of the quest for literacy. Furthermore, his having written in Arabic seems to dispense with the standard requirement for authenticating documents—endorsed by slaveholders or abolitionists—that historically proved the slave's capacity to write his or her own narrative.

Two other important distinctions of this text are (*a*) that it is written by a

182

Muslim, rather than a Christianized African American; and (*b*) that the author never gained manumission. The narrative was written while Omar was still enslaved.

This article is an analysis of Omar's manuscript, studied in the light of its importance as a unique text in the African American literary tradition, particularly in the slave narrative genre. Focusing on its most significant distinctions—its use of Arabic language and Qur'anic references—we observe the ways in which Omar's narrative reveals a different image of the "West" and the "Christian," not as that to which the African must aspire and with which he must necessarily affiliate, but rather as "Other" in the realm of this enslaved Muslim African's world.

Recent scholars have interpreted Omar's autobiography in relation to various manuscripts he wrote as evidence of his adherence to Muslim practices, or, conversely, to prove his renunciation thereof. Before the rediscovery of the document in 1995 and its retranslation, all previous translations had been carried out by Christian missionaries eager to view Omar as an enthusiastic adherent of their religion.[2] As a result, examiners of Omar's life could rely only on these interested translations.[3] This article, however, concerns itself with the narrative itself, studying the manner in which Omar strategically both identifies and disidentifies with the Christians/Westerners by whom he was surrounded and influenced. What we discover is that through his specific uses of Qur'anic references, he maintains a distinction between himself as Muslim and the Christians/Westerners with whom he interacts. These strategies seem to have affirmed for his American supporters his conversion to Christianity, which resulted in great interest in his life and writing, and some degree of freedom (though apparently not manumission).

Background on Omar Ibn Said's Life

Omar ibn Said was born and grew up in Futa Toro, a region between the Senegal and Gambia rivers in West Africa, where he became a scholar, teacher, and trader.[4] He learned Arabic for religious purposes and was said to have made the pilgrimage to Mecca, an indication of his position as a learned man in his society.[5] He was captured in his homeland in 1807 and transported across the Atlantic to Charleston, South Carolina, where he was sold to his first owner, the "evil" Johnson, a "small, weak, and wicked man who did not fear God at all, nor did he read nor pray."[6] Johnson reportedly was cruel to Omar, putting him to work in the fields.[7]

Apparently because of this cruel treatment, Omar ran away from his owner's rice plantation in South Carolina, hiding in what he describes as "houses." He headed north, but shortly thereafter was recaptured while praying and was thrown in jail in Fayetteville, North Carolina. Unable to communicate in English, he used coal to write on the wall petitions to be released. His literacy was a spectacle for the local people, who came to the jail specifically to see his writing. After Omar was put on the auction block by his jailer to pay for his keep, he was bought by General Jim Owen of Fayetteville, one of the many visitors who had gone to the jail to see him write. It appears that the Owens were kind masters, and Omar's literacy gave him an easier life as a house servant and gardener.[8]

It was while he was with the Owens that Omar was commissioned to pen his narrative, which he did in 1831. At the time he had been with the Owens for approximately twenty years.[9] The person who made the request was a "Sheikh Hunter"; no further information is known about this man. Ala Alryyes speculates that perhaps he was a member of the American Colonization Society (ACS), an organization dedicated to sending freed slaves to Liberia.[10] It is highly likely that his title of "sheikh" was one used by Omar as a sign of respect, rather than by the man himself.

Omar's literacy gained him general renown. Many were concerned about his fate: Pastor William Plumer, for example, wrote a full-length report about him entitled "Meroh, a Native African," which appeared in the *New York Observer* in 1863.[11] Several evangelists and members of the ACS also met Omar and wrote about him.

Fourteen of Omar's manuscripts are extant, thirteen others are quoted by interested parties. His writings include three Lord's Prayers, two Twenty-third Psalms, two lists of his masters' family's names, a commentary on Christian prayer, and several parts of the Qur'an. His last known manuscript is a copy of the Qur'anic *Sura* 110, *al-Nasr* (succor). All his writings begin with an invocation to God and His Prophet.[12] Omar actively sought his freedom through the written word and owed his improved situation to it. Many of his writings are testaments of faith. The renown Omar gained from his literacy was complemented by the recognition he received for his daily religious practices. Plumer mentions that he was a staunch "Mohammedan" who kept his fast of Ramadan at least the first year of his enslavement with great strictness. He wore a skullcap or turban, a visible sign of both his religious and cultural adherence.[13]

When he wrote his autobiography, Omar was about fifty-nine years old, and had been a slave for twenty-four years. He remained enslaved until the end of his life in 1864. There are no signs that he had any descendants in either Africa or America.[14]

General Contents of Omar's Narrative

Upon its rediscovery in 1995 in an old trunk in Virginia, the manuscript of Omar ibn Said's narrative was found to be in remarkably good condition: the document is easily legible to the naked eye. It was sold at an auction to the collector Derrick Beard, who lent it out for translation and display.

Omar's narrative is introduced by a single page in English: "The life of Omar ben Saeed, called Morro, a Fullah Slave, in Fayeteville, N.C., Owned by Governor Owen, Written by Himself in 1831 & sent to Old Paul, or Lahmen Kebby, in New York, in 1836, Presented to Theodore Dwight by Paul in 1836, Translated by Hon. Cotheal, Esq. 1848." This introduction conveys five pieces of information that relate to Omar's personal identification and relationships with those who played a part in the manuscript's production. Fullah is a reference to Omar's ethnic Fulbe background.[15] Lahmen Kebby was the freed slave also referred to as Lamine Kebe, with whom Omar exchanged letters, such as one beginning with "In the name of God, the compassionate," and continuing with apologies for Omar's forgotten Arabic before proceeding to matters of his earlier Islamic education.[16] Kebe had been a schoolteacher in his hometown in Africa, had been enslaved, and then had gained his manumission and was waiting in New York to be transported to Liberia.[17] Theodore Dwight (1796–1866) was a Free-Soiler opposed to the spread of slavery who had close connections at least with Kebe.[18] Cotheal was treasurer of the American Ethnological Society and an enthusiast of Arabic manuscripts.[19]

The narrative itself follows. Omar begins it with the Islamic formula "In the name of God, the Merciful, the Compassionate," a formula used to begin all but one *sura* of the Qur'an. He then continues with a rendition of *Surat al-Mulk* (Dominion), followed by an apology that he has "forgotten much of my talk as well as the talk of the Maghreb," presumably meaning his own language as well as Arabic. Although this is a common disclaimer in the slave narrative and has frequently been dismissed as such,[20] it is also a fact: Omar has forgotten parts of *Surat al-Mulk* that he records, sometimes confusing words. He then reiterates, "In the name of God, the Merciful, the Compassionate" before proceeding: "From Omar to Sheikh Hunter" and repeating his apology for having forgotten his Arabic. He continues here with a statement about his education and his teachers.

Omar gives very little information on the servile life he had to endure. Sylviane A. Diouf explains that this may have been due to his pride and dignity,[21] but there is the consideration that he wanted to please his master—a theme present throughout the text, such as in his Christian utterances—and therefore felt he should refrain from alluding too much to slavery. He talks a little about his journey to America, his adventures, upon arrival, in the hands of his first master, his escape from that master, and his transfer into the hands of Jim Owen. He highlights some principles of Islam, describing how he used to practice them in his native land. Notably, as Alryyes notes, he does not use the past tense in his descriptions, indicating his probable clandestine continuation of the practices.[22] At this point, he quotes the *Fātiha*, the opening *sura* that is recited in every prayer, and then the Christian Lord's Prayer.

Omar's main emphasis for the final portion of his narrative is praise for the Owen family. He proceeds to name all the members of the nuclear family, enquiring rhetorically, "O, people of America; O, people of North Carolina: do you have, do you have, do you have, do you have such a good generation that fears God so much?"[23] Thus the family is linked with religion, the major motif in the narrative. Omar ends his manuscript by extolling his master in particular: "I continue in the hands of Jim Owen who does not beat me, nor calls me bad names, nor subjects me to hunger, nakedness, or hard work. . . . During the last twenty years I have not seen any harm at the hands of Jim Owen."[24]

It must be stressed that, unlike other writings in the genre, Omar wrote his manuscript while still a slave. While very few understood his manuscript in the original,[25] it was immediately translated into English, becoming available to the public at large. Also, because it was in Arabic, no editor intervened between slave-author and reader, as Alryyes argues in the introduction to this volume. As Diouf highlights, Omar became the prime example of the literate African: "The literate Africans used their knowledge not only to remain intellectually alert but also to defend and protect themselves, to maintain their sense of self, to reach out to their brethren, to organize uprisings, and, for some, to gain freedom."[26] Therefore, while even as narrative it maintains certain conventions found in the slave narrative genre, such as the humility of the slave author regarding his command of the written word, it also evidences Omar's manipulation of the Arabic language, rendering various readings possible. For him, Arabic represented his freedom of expression, just as earlier it had won him his freedom from jail. Thus, although reluctant to state explicitly any negative points of view throughout his narrative, Omar none-theless feels free symbolically—and thus subtly—to express them.

Use of the Qur'an in Omar's Narrative

The most noticeable way in which Omar expressed his views is through his use of Qur'anic literary style and Qur'anic passages. Since he had learned the Qur'an for religious purposes, this was the style of writing with which he was intimately familiar. This comes across in his use of Qur'anic phrasing, such as "O, people of North Carolina; O, people of South Carolina; O, people of America."[27] This general vocative, translated into English as "O" with an accompanying subject, mirrors Qur'anic verses, such as "O You who have attained to faith!" (e.g., Q. 57:28; 58:11–12; 60:1, 10, 13; 61:2, 10, 14; 63:9), "O Prophet!" (60:12; 65:1; 66:1, 9), or "O humankind!" (4:1; 22:1; 49:13). The vocative evokes a sense of directness, emphasizing that the speaker is calling the attention of a specific and particular audience intended to hear the words.

Likewise, Omar mirrors the Qur'an's iterative style, for example, in repeating the aforementioned words in a later context: "O, people of America; O, people of North Carolina: do you have, do you have, do you have, do you have such a good generation that fears God so much?"[28] This use of the vocative combined with repetition is evident in such Qur'anic verses as 49:11–12: "O you who have attained to faith! No men shall deride [other] men: it may well be that those are better than themselves; and no women shall deride [other] women: it may well be that those are better than themselves . . . O you who have attained to faith! Avoid most guess-work [about one another]." Such usage has the effect of creating an emphasis and sense of urgency, drawing further attention to the words. Here the repetition is an emphatic tool: Omar juxtaposes the "people of America" and God by asking whether this particular people—who had so much power over him—feared God, the true holder of power.

In addition to its literary style, Omar's writing indicates a belief in the authority of the Qur'an, both when his linguistic skills fail him, as well as when they do not. Toward the end of his rendering of *Surat al-Mulk*, he confuses the order of its verses and then realizes his mistake. He cannot cross out his error since it is the Qur'an—the word of God—so he places dotted lines over it and continues with the correct verse. He omits a small part of the second to last verse, as Alryyes points out.[29] Conversely, his recital of *Surat al-Fātiha* is completely accurate; if indeed he continued to pray upon his arrival to the United States, it would have been a chapter that he would have recited five times a day, perhaps enabling his perfect retention of it.

Qur'anic passages evidence Omar's beliefs on both universal and personal levels. He begins by quoting *Surat al-Mulk* in its entirety, without giving its title. In a context where he has limited freedom of speech, Omar reveals his state of mind and his point of view through his quotation of this *sura*, the main theme of which is to recognize God as the sovereign of the world.[30] Slaves can be referred to in Arabic as *mamlūk* (possessed or owned), and thus by giving God dominion and ownership (*al-mulk*), Omar de-emphasizes the significance of his position as a slave by highlighting that all human beings are ultimately owned by God, rather than by a human slave master. Thus, although in the New World he is identified as a slave in contradistinction to his free white owner, he retains and affirms the understanding that he, his slave master, and all human beings are in turn subjects of God. In *The Message of the Quran*, the translator and commentator Muhammad Asad explains that "the fundamental idea running through the whole of this *sura* is man's inability ever to encompass the mysteries of the universe with his earth-bound knowledge, and hence, his utter dependence on guidance through divine revelation."[31] The chapter therefore provides solace to those in slavery in the recognition that supreme sovereignty rests with God alone, rather than with any slave master.

Since *Surat al-Mulk* is the first *sura* of the twenty-ninth part of the Qur'an, and Muslim children have often been taught to memorize the Qur'an beginning with the last three parts (which have much briefer and more easily memorizable chapters), this would have been a set of verses with which Omar was very familiar. It is interesting to note that the other Qur'anic chapter that Omar quotes and with which he was clearly familiar, *al-Fātiha*, also includes the word *Mālik* (derived from *mulk*) in *Mālik yawm al-dīn* (Owner of the Day of Judgment), thus once again referring to God as Owner. Earlier in his manuscript, Omar refers to God as "our Lord, our Creator, and our Owner and the restorer of our condition, health and wealth by grace and not duty."[32] Although it is a reference that could be taken by his slave owners to indicate the ascendancy of Christianity's grace over Islam's duties, and thus be seen as a confirmation of Omar's conversion to Christianity, the statement is also one that employs Qur'anic terminology, again using the word *Mālik* for "Owner." To Omar, a slave robbed of his wealth and to a large extent his health through his enslavement (he refers to himself as a "small, ill man"),[33] it was comforting to remember God's role as the true restorer.

The choice of *Surat al-Mulk* has further significance with regard to Omar's own situation. Asad paraphrases the following from the prominent twelfth-century Qur'anic commentator al-Zamakhshari: "Best known by the key-word *al-mulk* ('dominion') taken from its first verse, the *sura* has sometimes been designated by the Companions as 'The Preserving One' (*Al-Waqiyah*) or 'The Saving One' (*Al-Munjiyah*) inasmuch as it is apt to save and preserve him who takes its lessons to heart from suffering in the life to come."[34] The thirteenth-century commentator and imam Fakhr al-Dīn al-Rāzī elaborates that it is the *sura* that saves its reciter from the punishment of the grave and of the life to come, and the fourteenth-century commentator Ibn Kathīr narrates several *ahādīth* to this effect, including a couple where the Prophet specifically says, "I wish it [i.e., this *sura*] were in the heart of every person of my community."[35] The theme of being saved is clearly relevant here, just as it is in Omar's subsequent recitation of the Lord's Prayer, including the line "But deliver us from evil."[36] The *sura* as a whole serves as further affirmation of the primary importance of the eternal life to come, as opposed to present life struggle and suffering.

The Western Christian as Other

There has been much debate surrounding the possibility of Omar's conversion to Christianity. Some, such as Sulayman S. Nyang, have presented him as an example of those who "became freed men and reluctantly converted to Christianity."[37] This impression in part results from the missionary translators of his *Life*, as well as others, such as the authors of *The Christian Advocate* (the official periodical of the Methodist Episcopal Church), who clearly saw Omar as a member of the Presbyterian Church.[38] William Plumer reported that Omar had been baptized by the Reverend Dr. Snodgrass of the Presbyterian Church in Fayetteville and received into that church.[39]

Omar, like other Muslim slaves, had a Bible in Arabic, as well as a Qur'an.[40] His pastor mentioned that "through the kindness of some friends, an English translation of the Qur'an was procured for him, and read to him." The secretary of the American Colonization Society reported in 1837 that he had "retained a devoted attachment to the faith of his fathers and deemed a copy of the Qur'an in Arabic (which language he reads and writes with facility) his richest treasure."[41] Omar clearly read at least parts of his copy of the Bible. Alryyes postulates that perhaps Omar sought spiritual Christians to make up for the loss of community he suffered in his religious isolation as a slave.[42] Diouf suggests that he may have even read the Bible prior to his coming to America, since there is evidence that Muslims from his region had access to the book through the Arab teachers that they met in Mecca, Cairo, or their homelands.[43] In fact, Omar is quoted in the *New York Observer* as saying that the translation in his possession of the New Testament was not very good,[44] suggesting that he had encountered a previous one. Perhaps also this was an excuse for him not to adhere to the principles of faith outlined in it. Despite his reading of the Bible and his copying down of several fundamental Christian beliefs, Omar explicitly writes in his autobiography "I am Omar, I love to read the book, the Great Qur'an," before moving on to placate his masters by linking the Bible with "the path of righteousness." Yet even here, he follows up with Qur'anic terminology, quoting the second verse of *al-Fātiḥa* and of the Qur'an as a whole: "Praise be to Allah, the Lord of the Worlds."[45]

Throughout his narrative Omar refers to English as the Christian language. Being a native speaker of Fulfunde, a non-Arabic language written in Arabic letters,[46] he had learned Arabic for religious purposes. As a result, language and religion are conflated for him. He recounts that he was "sold to a Christian man" and "sold in Christian language" in a "Christian country," specifically in a place called "Charleston in the Christian language."[47] He explains the meaning of the

English word "jail" by referring to it as "jeel in the Christian language."[48] Upon his release from jail, he saw "many men whose language was Christian." They spoke to him, but he "did not understand [hear] the Christian language."[49] Based on this distinction, it makes sense that Omar never felt the need to really learn to speak this Christian language (English), since it was not his language culturally or religiously. The above-mentioned positing of Arabic and Islam *vis-à-vis* English and Christianity can be seen in other instances. As previously mentioned, Omar recites *Surat al-Fātiha* in one part of his narrative, then follows it immediately with the Lord's Prayer. In the old missionary translation this reads: "When I was a Mohammedan, I prayed thus," followed by quoting the *Fātiha*. "But now I pray 'Our Father,'" followed by quoting the Lord's Prayer.[50]

This suggests Omar's conversion from Islam to Christianity, and was the translation that was available until the 1995 rediscovery and retranslation of the document. Retranslating it, Alryyes rendered the passage as: "First, [following] Mohammed. To pray, I said: 'Praise be to Allah,'" followed by quoting the *Fātiha*. "And [but?] now, I pray in the words of our Lord Jesus the Messiah: 'Our Father,'" followed by quoting the Lord's Prayer.[51]

This rendering highlights the ambiguity in Omar's statement. In fact, word for word, the text reads: "First, Mohammed. To pray, he said," followed by quoting the *Fātiha*. "And now, the words of our Lord Jesus the Messiah," followed by quoting the Lord's Prayer.[52]

Here we note three points: the order in which the texts are written, the language used to discuss Christian beliefs, and the placement of these Christian beliefs in a larger Islamic context. The first is that Omar gives the *Fātiha* first, then the Lord's Prayer. This could be simply because of the chronological order in which he learned them, or it could be the order of importance he is assigning to them. He could also be signifying the second option under the guise of the first.

Furthermore, he uses Qur'anic terms to describe Christian beliefs, particularly the word "Messiah," which, in the Qur'an, refers to Jesus (e.g. Qur'an 3:45; 4:157, 171, 172; 5:17). The fact that he couples this with the word "Lord" (as in Lord Jesus the Messiah) does not indicate a recognition of the Messiah's divinity.

The third point is that these quotations of the *Fātiha* and the Lord's Prayer are prefaced by a reference to Moses: "Because the law (*Sharaʿ*) was to Moses given, but grace and truth were by Jesus the Messiah."[53] Omar situates Jesus alongside Moses, keeping the former within the framework of the Islamic Prophethood rather than that of Trinitarian Christianity. Thus Omar juxtaposes Moses and Jesus as equals in the Prophethood chain.

All these references point to the Qur'an as the center of Omar's weltanschauung. Omar's other writings confirm this adherence. Even when copying Christian passages, Omar's continuous use of Islamic invocations to Allah and His Prophet point to his unfailing adherence to his original religion. As previously mentioned, his last known manuscript is a copy of *sura* 110, *al-Nasr* (succor), a Qur'anic chapter that points to victory over one's enemies and people flocking to Islam. Remarkably, this last writing of Omar's happens to be the last complete *sura* of the Qur'an conveyed by the Prophet to the world, just over two months before his death.[54] Thus, Omar followed in the steps of the founder of his religion all the way until the end of his life.

Conclusion

From 1703 to the Second World War, about six thousand slave narratives were recorded in North America. Yet among these, very few are by African-born slaves, whose narratives generally were not sought after by the abolitionists. The disproportionate number of Muslim writers among the Africans can be attributed to the fact that as "non-Africans"—that is, as honorary Arabs in the imagination of white Americans—they were accorded more consideration than the "real" Africans. Journalists and other "objective" writers fantasized about their origins, imagining them as rich Arab princes for whom the tables had been turned in their transplant to the Americas.[55] Also, their background as intellectuals probably encouraged them to seize opportunities to express themselves with the written word.[56]

A textual analysis of Omar ibn Said's manuscript reveals the striking ways in which some Africans identified themselves in the new American context while retaining their prior sense of identification. This is particularly remarkable in a slave narrative, a genre often acknowledged more as propagandistic than as revelatory of slave identity. Through the use of Arabic and Qur'anic references, Omar reveals an image of the "West" and the "Christian" not as something to which the African must aspire, but instead as an "Other" in the realm of his enslaved Muslim African's world. Rather than being on the "double quest for literacy and freedom" typical of American slaves, Omar ibn Said is a newly rediscovered representation of the already literate and learned slave. His narrative also provides a critical connection between Islam during nineteenth-century American slavery and contemporary African American Islam, giving even more momentum to the concept of today's African American Islam as a "reversion" to a past religious adherence.

Notes

1. Robert B. Stepto, *From Behind the Veil: A Study of Afro-American Narrative* (Urbana: University of Illinois Press, 1979), ix.

2. Allan D. Austin, *African Muslims in Antebellum America: Transatlantic Stories and*

Spiritual Struggles (London: Routledge, 1997), 8. The two earliest translations of the autobiography were by Alexander Cotheal, treasurer of the American Ethnological Society, and the Reverend Isaac Bird (1793–1876) of Hartford, Connecticut, who had been a missionary in Syria during the years 1823–35 (Ronald T. Judy *(Dis)forming the American Canon: African-Arabic Slave Narratives and the Vernacular* [Minneapolis: University of Minnesota Press, 1993], 153; H. H. Jessup. *Fifty-Three Years in Syria* [Chicago: Fleming H. Revell Company, 1910], 42–46).

3. Previously, the most thorough examination of the primary documents of Omar ibn Said's life was carried out by Allan D. Austin in his *African Muslims in Antebellum America: A Sourcebook* (New York: Garland Publishing, 1984), 445–523. At the time he was writing this work, the original of Omar's autobiography had not yet resurfaced.

4. Sylviane Diouf, *Servants of Allah: African Muslims Enslaved in the Americas* (New York: New York University Press, 1998), 30, 141; Austin, *Transatlantic Stories and Spiritual Struggles*, 11. For more information about Islam in Futa Toro and its relevance to the Americas, see Michael A. Gomez, "Muslims in Early America," *Journal of Southern History* 60 (Nov. 1994), 671–709 [reproduced here, 95–132].

5. Diouf, *Servants of Allah*, 68.

6. *The Life of Omar Ibn Said, Written by Himself,* with introduction and translation by Ala A. Alryyes, in *The Multilingual Anthology of American Literature: A Reader of Original Texts with English Translations*, ed. Marc Shell and Werner Sollors (New York: New York University Press, 2000), 90–91 [76–77]. Unless otherwise indicated, all English renderings of the text are from Alryyes's masterful translation (henceforth this earlier translation will be referred to as *Life of Omar Ibn Said* and page numbers following in square brackets refer to Alryyes's introduction or translation in this volume). The only deviation is that we have used the word "God" where he uses "Allah," to render the text more religiously neutral, as the English term "God"—like the Arabic "Allah"—can be used by Muslims or Christians, whereas the term "Allah" in an English text strongly suggests adherence to Islam.

7. Alryyes, *Life of Omar Ibn Said*, 59 [6].

8. Diouf, *Servants of Allah*, 134–35; Alryyes, *Life of Omar Ibn Said*, 59 [7].

9. Alryyes, *Life of Omar Ibn Said*, 59 [7].

10. Alryyes, introduction to this volume, 17.

11. William Plumer, "Meroh, a Native African," *New York Observer*, January 8, 1863, 1. "Moro" was a common corruption of Omar's name.

12. Austin, *Transatlantic Stories and Spiritual Struggles*, 24, 136; Diouf, *Servants of Allah*, 138, 50.

13. Diouf, *Servants of Allah*, 66–67, 76.

14. Ibid., 141, 180.

15. Alryyes, *Life of Omar Ibn Said*, 713; see also introduction to this volume, 9.

16. Diouf, *Servants of Allah*, 139. Note the recurrence of these themes in Omar's autobiography, as discussed below.

17. Austin, *Transatlantic Stories and Spiritual Struggles*, 11; "Condition and Character of Negroes in Africa," *Methodist Review* 46:77–90, esp. 80–84.

18. Alryyes, *Life of Omar Ibn Said*, 712, n.1 [9]; Austin, *Transatlantic Stories and Spiritual Struggles*, 118. It is interesting to note that, as in the case of Omar, there was widespread belief that Kebe had converted to Christianity, but Theodore Dwight believed that he remained a staunch Muslim till the end of his life.

19. Jessup, *Fifty-Three Years in Syria*, 42–46.

20. See, e.g., Alryyes, *Life of Omar Ibn Said*, 59 [6].

21. Diouf, *Servants of Allah*, 142.

22. See Alryyes, *Life of Omar Ibn Said*, 713, n.15 [25–26].

23. Ibid., 84–85 [70–71].

24. Ibid., 92–93 [78–79].

25. Arabs did not start coming to the United States until the 1850s; for more on this see Ami Ayalon, "The Arab Discovery of America in the Nineteenth Century," *Middle Eastern Studies* 20, no. 4 (1984): 5–17.

26. Diouf, *Servants of Allah*, 144.

27. Alryyes, *Life of Omar Ibn Said*, 80–83 [66–69].

28. Ibid., 84–85 [70–71].

29. Ibid., 712–13 [57].

30. For an earlier treatment, see Alryyes, *Life of Omar Ibn Said*, 60 [18], and Ala Alryyes, "'And in a Christian Language They Sold Me': Messages Concealed in a Slave's Arabic-Language Autobiographical Narrative," in *American Babel*, ed. Marc Shell, Harvard English Studies 20 (Cambridge: Harvard University Press, 2002), 46.

31. *The Message of the Quran*, translated and explained by Muhammad Asad (Gibraltar: Dar al-Andalus, 1984), 879.

32. Alryyes, *Life of Omar Ibn Said*, 86–87 [72–73].

33. Ibid., 92–93 [78–79].

34. *Message of the Quran*, 879; see Abū-l-Qāsim Maḥmūd b. ʿUmar al-Zamakhsharī, *Al-Kashshāf ʿan Ḥaqāʾiq al-Tanzīl wa-ʿUyūn al-Aqāwīl*, 4 vols. (Cairo: Mustafā al-Bābī al-Ḥalabī Press, 1972), iv. 133 ff.

35. Fakhr al-Dīn al-Rāzī, *Al-Tafsīr al-Kabīr* (Beirut: Dār al-Kutub al-ʿIlmiyya, 1990), 30:46; Abu al-Fidā Ismāʿil ibn Kathīr, *Tafsīr al-Qurʾān al-ʿAẓīm*, 4 vols. (Beirut: Dar al-Maʿrifa, 1987), 4:421–22.

36. Alryyes, *Life of Omar Ibn Said*, 88–89 [74–75]; see below for more on Omar's recitation of the Lord's Prayer.

37. Sulayman S. Nyang, *Islam in the United States of America* (Chicago: ABC International Group, 1999), 13–14.

38. G. T. Bedell, *Christian Advocate* 5 (July 3, 1825), 306–7.

39. Plumer, *New York Observer*, 1.

40. His Arabic Bible is extant, though his Qur'an is not; see Austin, *Transatlantic Stories and Spiritual Struggles*, 130.

41. Diouf, *Servants of Allah*, 113; see also Ralph R. Gurley, "Secretary's Report," in this volume, 217.

42. Alryyes, *Life of Omar Ibn Said*, 60 [26].

43. Diouf, *Servants of Allah*, 39.

44. Plumer, *New York Observer*, 1.

45. Alryyes, *Life of Omar Ibn Said*, 86–87 [72–73].

46. Austin, *Transatlantic Stories and Spiritual Struggles*, 152.

47. Alryyes, *Life of Omar Ibn Said*, 74–75 [60–61], 76–77 [62–63], 80–81 [66–67], 90–91 [76–77]. All these are rendered *nasrānī* in Arabic.

48. Ibid., 76–77 [62–63].

49. Ibid., 78–79 [64–65].

50. Austin, *A Sourcebook*, 467.

51. Alryyes, *Life of Omar Ibn Said*, 88–89 [74–75].

52. Ibid., 88 [74].

53. Ibid., 88–89 [74–75].

54. *Message of the Quran*, 982.

55. See, e.g., Louis T. Moore, "Prince of Arabia," *Greensboro (North Carolina) Daily News*, February 13, 1927.

56. Diouf, *Servants of Allah*, 140.

Appendix 1

Omar's Earliest Known Manuscript (1819)[1]

Translated by JOHN HUNWICK

1. Omar's manuscript was sent as an accompaniment to a letter (dated 10 Oct. [?] 1819) from John Louis Taylor, Chief Justice, North Carolina, and vice-president of the Auxiliary Society of the American Colonization Society of Raleigh, North Carolina, to Francis Scott Key, in the hope that the latter could obtain a translation of it; see Allan D. Austin, *African Muslims in Antebellum America: A Sourcebook* (New York: Garland, 1984), 455. It is not clear how John Louis Taylor got hold of the letter, or why he thought Francis Scott Key could obtain a translation of it.

الحمد لله الذي خلق العلو للعباد في ... حتى جرى ... افعالهم واقوالهم وجد الصمم والاد نير

تبليغ الاسلام ... الى مبتدون ... وما معصم وفي جماعة النهي افني ... في مكان ... بيتقي

زولي ولاولى ... به ... ولا ... في ... انطلا بابا ... اقولى من بعد افع انقول

يجمع ... قول ... الحول ... ولانصوفه خمس بابي ... فا خمس البعل بان يتزيط

وينا ... ما ... عوا بابا ... او خمرت او ... بد سعتيار ... البغر ... الله لا لخيرت رد

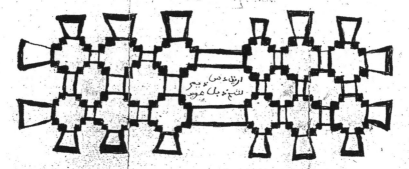

... دار ... تيس الاموال ... ولد الاللتي ذللرا اذ افسمة

الليى ... الاسما ... سمتنموا وانتروع ابا ... مكا ... انزل الله ... جها

الغير عنه الله لا لخير ... بند ... ابي لهب ... انغى عنه مال ... وما

ستكر بالله يا من شاب ما ... انتظ ... هل ... بنا ... اخذ من مكا ... م

امرانت ... ونوا امرانت اصمو ... وشع ... وفلبط اشو ... كى

اقول من بعد

أقول من بعد افتتح أقول بمحمد ﷺ ثم أقول آمن الرسول بما أنزل الله

له لغيره ﷺ من الرسول بما أنزل إليه من ربه وملائكته وكتبه ورسله لا نفرق

بين أحد من رسله وقالوا سمعنا وأطعنا غفرانك ربنا وإليك المصير لا يكلف الله نفسا

إلا وسعها لها ما كسبت وعليها ما اكتسبت ربنا لا تؤاخذنا إن نسينا أو أخطأنا ربنا

لا تحملنا ما لا طاقة لنا به واعف عنا واغفر لنا وارحمنا وأنت مولانا فانصرنا على القوم الكافرين

الكفي جرى أنه سمعت بقول الله تعالى ومن عمل صالحا فلنفسه وفي عندي جعلنا

سمعت بقول الله تعالى ومن قضى حاجة المؤمن فقضى الله حاجته يوم يرجع المرء من

أخيه وأمه وأبيه وصاحبته ونبيه لكل امرئ منهم يومئذ شأن يغنيه

سمعت بقول الله تعالى ومن قضى حاجة الموتى فقضى الله حاجته يوم لا نطال نبعث

لنبعث شيخا ولا من يوم يبعث لله يوم يبعثهم المرء ما أخذ من بعده وبقول الناس يا ليتني

محنت نراب الله إن أراد أن يقرأ في بطن كل جسم إلى آخر جسم في مكان اليمن يستقل ليبقى

بارك الله ببركة الصلاة وهو على كل شيء فقد يراه الله خلق الموت والحياة ليبلوكم أيكم أحسن

أحسن عملا وهو العزيز الغفور الله خلق سبع سموات طباقا ما ترى في خلق الرحمن من

تفاوت فارجع البصر هل ترى من فطور ثم ارجع البصر كرتين ينقلب إليك البصر خاسئا وهو

حسير ولقد زينا السماء الدنيا بمصابيح وجعلناها رجوما للشياطين وأعتدنا لهم عذاب

السعير وللذين كفروا بربهم عذاب جهنم وبئس المصير إذا ألقوا فيها سمعوا

لها شهيقا وهي تفور تكاد تميز من الغيظ كلما ألقي فيها فوج سألهم خزنتها ألم يأتكم

نذير قالوا بلى قد جاءنا نذير فكذبنا وقلنا ما نزل الله من شيء إن أنتم إلا

في ضلال كبير وقالوا لو كنا نسمع أو نعقل ما كنا في أصحاب السعير

فاعترفوا بذنبهم فسحقا لأصحاب السعير إن الذين يخشون ربهم بالغيب لهم

مغفرة وأجر كبير وأسروا قولكم أو اجهروا به إنه عليم بذات الصدور وهو على

Translation of Page 196

Line 1. Praise be to God who created creatures in order to worship Him, so that he might put to the test their deeds and their words,[2] and their circumstances in the world.

2. Conveyance of greeting to Major John Owen[3] and whosoever is with them from among the community of Christians in the place, town,[4] called

3. Rūlī [Raleigh]. And [God] is the First, the Unique without a beginning, and the Last, the Everlasting without an end. "I say after opening [my] speech

4. with praise of the One possessed of mastery, the Mighty in Power":[5] . . . . [*illegible*]

5. . . . . [*illegible*] Goodness comes from God, not from anyone else.

6. [Geometric design[6] with writing inside it, including the title and name Shaykh *Dh-b-l* / *J-b-l*[7] Jim Owen,[8]

2. This phrase is also used at the beginning of a copy of the Lord's Prayer written out by Omar, reportedly in 1840; see Austin, *African Muslims*, document X on 471. It is likewise found in an undated document of which only a fragment is reproduced in Austin, *African Muslims*, plate C on 507.

3. In the Arabic script this is written: *m-y-dh dh-w-n 'ū-'-n*. The Arabic letter *dhāl* is clearly to be read as "j." In the Autobiography Omar uses the same letter for "ch," which he doubtless heard as "j" (i.e., Jālustun = Charleston). Hence we can supply the vowels for the first word to get *mayja*, i.e., "Major." *Dh-w-n* is to be read *Dhūn* = *Jūn*, i.e., John, and appears again in this form in the Autobiography and in a list Omar wrote of Jim Owen's family (see Austin, *African Muslims*, document VII on 463), and *'ū-'-n as 'ū'in*, i.e., Owen. John Owen was the brother of James (Jim) Owen, Omar's master, and was later governor of North Carolina, December 1828 to December 1830.

4. Omar uses a transcription of the English word "town" (*t-w-n* = *tawn*).

5. This is the opening line, somewhat corrupted, of a poem on Arabic grammar, the *Mulḥat al-i'rāb* of al-Ḥarīrī (d. 1122), a popular textbook in West Africa.

6. An identical design appears in two other documents—both lists of members of the Owen family, reproduced in Austin, *African Muslims*, document VI on 462 and plate A on 506.

7. The letters *dh/j-b-l* were apparently written in error for *j-n-l* (a dot being placed below the middle letter rather than above it). This could then be read: *jin[r]al* = "general." James Owen was a commander in the state militia, and in the War of 1812 had been Adjutant General; see Austin, *African Muslims*, 447, 509–10, n.6. The form *dh-n-l* is used in another document where mention is made of *Mista Dhin-l 'ū'in* (Mister General Owen) in a list of members of that family; see Austin, *African Muslims*, plate A on 506, and in the Life, where it is clearly vocalized dhinal.

8. *Dh-y-m '-w-'-n*, i.e. Jim [James] Owen (1784–1865), Omar's master.

7. November 1419 (i.e. 1819). "Is the male for you and the female for Him? That is then a division

8. most unjust. What are they but names which you and your ancestors bestowed on them, for which God sent down {no authority}"9

9. Goodness comes from God, not from anyone else. "May the two hands of Abū Lahab perish and may he perish. His wealth shall not benefit him, neither what {he gained}."10

10. I ask you by God, O you who have grown gray-haired, what do you expect? * Have you reflected, O my brother, upon blame?11

11. Or are you mad or are you foolish? * And your hair and your heart are both black.

Translation of Page 197

Line 1. "I say after opening [my] speech with praise of the One possessed of mastery, the Mighty in Power." Goodness comes from God,

2. not from anyone else. "The Messenger believed in what was sent down to him {from his Lord, as did the believers. All believed in God}12 and His angels and His books and His messengers. We make no distinction

3. between any of His messengers. And they say, 'We hear and we obey. [Grant us] Thy forgiveness, O our Lord, for towards Thee is the [final] journey.' God does not burden a soul

4. with anything beyond its capacity to bear. It is rewarded for [the good] that it earns, and pays for [the evil] it commits. 'O our Lord, do not take us to task if we forget or fall into error.13 . . . O our Lord,

5. do not burden us with what we have no strength to endure, and pardon us and forgive us and have mercy on us. Thou art our Lord, so aid us against

6. the unbelievers.'"14 I heard the saying of God Most High, "Whoever does a good deed, it shall be accounted in favor of his soul, and whoever commits evil, it shall be accounted against it."15

9. Qur'ān, 53:21–23. Words in braces omitted in Omar's text.

10. Qur'ān, 111:1–2. Words in braces omitted in Omar's text.

11. The symbol * marks the division between two hemistichs in a verse of poetry. Lines 10 and 11 are written out like verse, though they do not fit a regular meter.

12. Words in braces omitted in Omar's text.

13. Omar omits here a sentence that begins with the same words as that following.

14. Qur'ān, 2:285–86, the last two verses of the second *sura* of the Qur'ān.

15. Qur'ān, 41:46. This phrase is also used at the beginning of a copy of the Lord's

7. I heard the saying of God Most High, "*Whoever looks after the need of a believer, God will look after his need*[16] 'on a day when a man shall flee from

8. his brother and his mother and his father and his wife and his sons. Every man on that day shall have a matter that preoccupies him.'"[17]

9. I heard the saying of God Most High, "*Whoever looks after the need of a believer, God will look after his need*[18] 'on a day when no soul shall have power to do anything for another soul

10. and the matter on that day shall belong to God.'"[19] "A day on which a man shall see what his hands have wrought and the unbeliever will say, 'Would that I

11. were dust.'"[20] [Pentacle] I wish to be seen in our land called Āfrikā, in a place [on] the river called K-bā / K-b-y.

12. "Blessed is He in whose hand is Dominion, and He has Power over all things. He who created death and life that you might be tested to see which of you

13. has performed best, and He is the Mighty, the Pardoner. He who created the seven heavens in layers. You see not in the Merciful One's creation any

14. disharmony. Look back again, then, do you see any flaw? Return your gaze yet again and again; it will return to you weakened and

15. enfeebled. We adorned the lower heaven with lamps and made them objects to be cast at the demons, for whom we prepared a punishment

16. of flames. And for those who disbelieved in their Lord is a punishment of Hell. What a terrible end! When they are cast in it they shall hear it

17. roaring as it wells up, almost bursting with fury. Whenever a group is cast therein its keepers shall ask them,

18. 'Did no warner come to you?' They shall say, 'Yes, a warner came, but we did not believe and we said, "God did not send anything down. You are

19. simply in great error."' And they will say, 'If we had listened or heeded we would not be dwellers in the Blaze.'

Prayer written out by Omar, reportedly in 1840; see Austin, *African Muslims*, document X on 471.

16. The quotation up to here does not form part of the Qur'ān, whereas what follows does.

17. Qur'ān, 80:34–37.

18. The quotation up to here does not form part of the Qur'ān, whereas what follows does.

19. Qur'ān, 82:19.

20. Latter part of Qur'ān, 78:40.

20. And they confessed their sin, but far removed [from God's mercy] are the dwellers in the Blaze. Those who fear their Lord in the Unseen shall enjoy

21. forgiveness and a great reward. Speak secretly or openly; God knows what is in your hearts."[21]

21. Qur'ān, 67:1–13. The text continues with the single Arabic word *'alā*, perhaps an error for *alā*, which is the first word of the following Qur'ānic verse. In his *Life* Omar quotes the entire *sura* as a sort of prelude to the account of his life. There he correctly writes *Alā [ya'lam man khalaq]*.

Appendix 2

Letter from Reverend Isaac Bird, of Hartford, Connecticut, to Theodore Dwight, of Brooklyn, New York (April 1, 1862)

My Dear Sir,

I received in due time, through our friends the Miss Perkinses, your Arabic Manuscripts. I have taken a good deal of pleasure in looking them over. I have been particularly gratified with the plain & symmetrical hand on the writers of No. 2, 3 & 4 & with the little difference there is between the forms of the alphabetical characters & forms prevailing in the nations of Arabs farther east. I have not by me any specimens of *Maghrebeen* or Morocco writing, but as far as my recollection serves me, their character differs considerably more from the eastern, than these which you have sent me.

You have here a hasty translation, such as I have been able to make out in the time I have had to devote to the object, of the three most interesting manuscripts. I should by no means be willing to stake my reputation, small as it is, upon the accuracy of what I have attempted.

[. . .]

In the religious portions of the composition there seems to have been an effort to imitate the style & language of the Koran. If I had been familiar with that book (the whole of which I have never read), I might have succeeded in my attempts more to my satisfaction.

When your expected manuscripts from Africa shall arrive, I should be very glad to see them, in case they can be spared for a short season.

With kind salutations to my respected friend, Mr. Cotheal, I am, dear Sir,

Very respectfully,
yours
I. Bird.

Appendix 3

"Uncle Moreau,"
from *North Carolina University Magazine*
(September 1854)

The town of Wilmington, though of much commercial importance to the good State of North Carolina, cannot boast of many notable personages, and is woefully destitute of "lions." Perhaps it may strike some strangely, and others ludicrously, that many persons inquire with most apparent interest, or at least curiosity, after the venerable coloured man whose name stands at the head of this article. The reason of this we will make an attempt to disclose by a short sketch of his life.

"Uncle Moreau" is now well stricken in years, being, according to his own account, eighty-four years of age. He was born in eastern Africa [*sic*], upon the banks of the Senegal River. His name, originality [*sic*] was Umeroh. His family belonged to the tribe of Foutahs, whose chief city was Foutah. The story that he was by birth a prince of his tribe, is unfounded. His father seems to have been a man of considerable wealth, owning as many as seventy slaves, and living upon the proceeds of their labour. The tribes living in eastern Africa are engaged almost incessantly in predatory warfare, and in one of these wars the father of Moreau was killed. This occurred when he was about five years old, and the whole family were immediately taken by an uncle to the town of Foutah. This uncle appears to have been the chief minister of the King or Ruler of Foutah. Here Moreau was educated, that is, he was taught to read the Koran (his tribe being Mohamedans) to recite certain forms of prayer, and the knowledge of the simpler forms of Arithmetic. So apt was he to learn, that he was soon promoted to a mastership, and for ten years taught the youth of his tribe all that they were wont to be taught, which was for the most part, lessons from the Koran. Those barbarians did not think, like the more Enlightened States of excluding their sacred books from their schools.

After teaching for many years, Moreau resolved to abandon this pursuit and become a trader, the chief articles of trade being salt, cotton cloths, &c. While engaged in trade, some event occurred, which he is very reluctant to refer to, but which resulted in his being sold into slavery. He was brought down the coast, shipped for America, in company with only two who could speak the same language, and was landed at Charleston in 1807, just a year previous to the final abolition of the slave trade. He was soon sold to a citizen of Charleston, who treated him with great kindness, but who, unfortunately for Moreau, died in a short time. He was then sold to one who proved to be a harsh cruel master, exacting from him labour which he had not the strength to perform. From him Moreau found means to escape, and after wandering nearly over the State of South Carolina, was found near to Fayetteville in this State. Here he was taken up as a runaway, and placed in the jail. Knowing nothing of the language as yet, he could not tell who he was, or where he was from, but finding some coals in the ashes, he filled the walls of his room with piteous petitions to be released, all written in the Arabic language. The strange characters, so elegantly and correctly written by a runaway slave, soon attracted attention, and many of the citizens of the town visited the jail to see him.

Through the agency of Mr. Mumford, then Sheriff of Cumberland county, the case of Moreau was brought to the notice of Gen. Jas. Owen, of Bladen county, a gentleman well known throughout this commonwealth for his public services, and always known as a man of generous and humane impulses. He took Moreau out of jail, becoming security for his forthcoming if called for, and carried him with him to his plantation in Bladen county. For a long time his wishes were baffled by the meanness and the cupidity of a man who had bought the runaway at a small price from his former master, until at last he was able to obtain legal possession of him, greatly to the joy of Moreau. Since then, for more than forty years, he has been a trusted and indulged servant.

At the time of his purchase by Gen. Owen, Moreau was a staunch Mohamedan, and the first year at least kept the fast of Rhamadan, with great strictness. Through the kindness of some friends, an English translation of the Koran was procured for him, and read to him, often with portions of the Bible. Gradually he seemed to lose his interest in the Koran, and to show more interest in the sacred Scriptures, until finally he gave up his faith in Mohammed, and became a believer in Jesus Christ. He was baptized by Rev. Dr. Snodgrass, of the Presbyterian Church in Fayetteville, and received into the church. Since that time he has been transferred to the Presbyterian Church in Wilmington, of which he has long been a consistent and worthy member. There are few Sabbaths in the year in which he is absent from the house of God.

Uncle Moreau is an Arabic scholar, reading the language with great facility, and translating it with ease. His pronunciation of the Arabic is remarkably fine. An eminent Virginia scholar said, not long since, that he read it more beautifully than any one he ever heard, save a distinguished savant of the University of Halle. His translations are somewhat imperfect, as he never mastered the English language, but they are often very striking. We remember once hearing him read and translate the twenty-third psalm, and shall never forget the earnestness and fervour which shone in the old man's countenance, as he read of the going down into the dark valley, and using his own broken English said, "Me, no fear, master's with me there." There were signs in his countenance and in his voice, that he knew not only the words, but felt the blessed power of the truth they contained.

Moreau has never expressed any wish to return to Africa. Indeed he has always manifested a great aversion to it when proposed, changing the subject as soon as possible. When Dr. Jonas King, now of Greece, returned to this country from the East, he was introduced in Fayetteville to Moreau. Gen. Owen observed an evident reluctance on the part of the old man to converse with Dr. King. After some time he ascertained that the only reason of his reluctance was his fear that one who talked so well in Arabic might have been sent by his own countryman to reclaim him, and carry him again over the sea. After his fears were removed he conversed with Dr. King with great readiness and delight.

He now regards his expatriation as a great Providential favour. "His coming to this country," as he remarked to the writer, "was all for good." Mohammedanism has been supplanted in his heart by the better faith in Christ Jesus, and in the midst of a christian [*sic*] family, where he is kindly watched over and in the midst of a church which honors him for his consistent piety.—He is gradually going down to that dark valley, in which, his own firm hope is, that he will be supported and led by the hand of the Great Master, and from which he will emerge into the brightness of the perfect day.

Appendix 4

Ralph Gurley's "Secretary's Report," from *African Repository and Colonial Journal* (July 1837)

The Secretary of the Society left his residence in March last, on a visit to several of the Southern and Western States, with the purpose of advancing the interests of the cause in that region. Subjoined is the greater part of a Report recently made by him to the Managers, in which are given some interesting particulars in relation to *Moro*, an African convert to Christianity. The concluding passage of the Report will not, we trust, be without its influence in animating the Ministers of the Gospel to exertions on behalf of the Society on, or about the Fourth inst:—

Augusta (Georgia) May 21st, 1837

To the Board of Managers of the American Colonization Society;

GENTLEMEN, I have the honor to submit a brief report of my proceedings since I left Washington early in March, with such suggestions and reflections as may occur during the relation of the incidents and observations of my tour up to this date.

I left Washington the 10th of March, and on Sunday the 12th addressed the friends of the Society in Fredericksburg, in the Methodist Church, on the views, state, and prospects of the Society, and of its settlements in Africa. Liberal contributions have been made in former times, by the citizens of this place, to the funds of the Society, and the recent appeals of the able Agent of the Society, Mr. Andrews, to the Episcopal congregation have been successful.

At Richmond, I attended a large meeting of the friends of the Society, in the Hall of the House of the Delegates, convened especially to hear statements from the Rev. Mr. Rockwell (late Chaplain of the United States' ship Potomac) who had then just returned from a visit to Liberia. In the month of November last this gentleman examined the condition and prospects of all the settlements within the limits of the Colony, and also the settlement at Cape Palmas under the exclusive direction of the Maryland Colonization Society, and his testimony, as publicly given before the citizens of Richmond, was adapted to animate the zeal, and strengthen the resolution and confidence of all the friends of African Colonization. A noble minded benefactor of the Society in that place expressed to me his purpose to subscribe $500 in aid of the cause, provided a few other individuals could be induced to unite with him in raising a liberal Fund to promote it. The great and enlightened Commonwealth of Virginia will sustain with increasing energy the operations of the Society, and Richmond, the centre of her power and influence, will give to it a constant and firm support.

In company with the Rev. C. W. Andrews, the very efficient Agent of the Virginia Colonization Society, the writer attended a meeting of the friends of the Institution in Petersburg on the 23d of March, when a subscription was received for the benefit of the Society. Among the generous inhabitants of that town prevails a general and active interest in the enterprise of the Society, and I feel confident it will continue to receive from them a liberal proportion of their regard. The Rev. Wm. M. Atkinson, of this place, is well known throughout Virginia and the Union, as an early, able, and devoted friend of the Society, who both by his pen, and eloquent addresses, has done much to recommend it to the confidence of his fellow citizens, and especially to present it to the South in those clear lights of truth and reason which command a favorable verdict of the judgment even when they fail to win the heart.

North Carolina will stand forth a powerful and decided friend of the scheme of Colonization. The State Society (over which Judge Cameron, one of the most intelligent, wealthy and respected citizens presides) has revived, filled with able and active friends of the cause, the vacancies in her Board of Directors, and resolved to employ an Agent to explain the views, enforce the claims, and solicit aid to the objects of the Society in the several counties of the State. The Society of Friends in this State, early turned their thoughts to the plan of African Colonization, encouraged the free people of colour under their protection to emigrate to Liberia, and supplied a generous fund to defray the expenses of such as consented to remove thither. Several hundreds, once under the guardian care of this Society, are now enjoying the freedom and privileges of that Colony. There are still in North Carolina numerous free coloured persons of respectable intelligence and moral character. Those in Fayetteville, Elizabethtown, and Wilmington, have probably no superiors, among their own class, in the United States. After careful reflection, some have resolved to remove to Africa, and others are anxiously directing their thoughts to the subject. Louis Sheridan, with whose reputation and views the Board are partially acquainted, is a man of education, uncommon talents for business, a handsome property, and the master of nineteen slaves. His determination to emigrate to Liberia with a company of from forty to sixty of his relations and friends has already been announced. The public meetings held in Raleigh, during my visit, were well attended and of much interest, and addressed with spirit and effect by several of the citizens of that place. Collections were made for the benefit of the Society. The Resolutions adopted by the citizens of Raleigh are before the public.

In Fayetteville, gentlemen of all political and religious opinions gave countenance and assistance to the cause. At several public meetings in the Methodist Church, attended indiscriminately by the members of the several religious denominations, one sentiment of confidence in the principles and policy and concern for the success of the Society was manifested. Gentlemen of different communions in the Christian Church, but of one spirit, addressed these meetings; and the measures adopted (already before the public) will result, I doubt not, in the awakening of a new and extended interest throughout a large portion of the State in the prosperity of the African Colonies and in the diffusion, through them, far over the barbarous territories of Africa, of knowledge, civilization, and the inestimable blessing of the Religion of Christ. Collections were made for the Society, both in the Presbyterian and Methodist Churches, and several donations received from individuals.

In Wilmington, the views, purposes, and prospects of the Society were submitted in the Presbyterian Church to the consideration of a large audience of different religious sects, which contributed in aid of its funds. It was the first time that public attention had ever, in that place, been invited to the scheme and interests of the Society. Several gentlemen expressed their purposes of endeavouring at an early day to organize an Auxiliary Colonization Society.

In the respected family of General Owen, of Wilmington, I became acquainted with a native African, whose history and character are exceedingly interesting, and some sketches of whose life have been already published. I allude to *Moro* or *Omora*, a Foulah by birth, educated a Mahometan, and who, long after he came in slavery to this country, retained a devoted attachment to the faith of his fathers and deemed a copy of the Koran in Arabic (which language he reads and writes with facility) his richest treasure. About twenty years ago, while scarcely able to express his thoughts intelligibly on any subject in the English language, he fled from a severe master in South Carolina, and on his arrival at Fayetteville, was seized as a runaway slave, and thrown into jail. His peculiar appearance, inability to converse, and particularly the facility with which he was observed to write a strange language attracted much attention, and induced his present humane and christian master to take him from prison and finally, at his earnest request, to become his purchaser. His gratitude was boundless, and his joy to be imagined only by him, who has himself been relieved from the iron that enters the soul. Since his residence with General Owen he has worn no bonds but those of gratitude and affection.

> "Oh, tis a Godlike privilege to save
> And he who scorns it is himself a slave."

Being of a feeble constitution, Moro's duties have been of the lightest kind, and he has been treated rather as a friend than a servant. The garden has been to him a place of recreation rather than a toil, and the concern is not that he should labor more but less. The anxious efforts made to instruct him in the doctrines and precepts of our Divine Religion, have not been in vain. He has thrown aside the bloodstained Koran and now worships at the feet of the Prince of Peace. The Bible, of which he has an Arabic copy, is his guide, his comforter, or as he expresses it, "his Life." Far advanced in years, and very infirm, he is animated in conversation, and when he speaks of God or the affecting truths of the scriptures, his swarthy features beam with devotion, and his eye is lit up with the hope of immortality. Some of the happiest hours of his life were spent in the society of the Rev. James King, during his last visit from Greece to the United States. With that gentleman he could converse and read the scriptures in the Arabic language and feel the triumphs of the same all-conquering faith as he chanted with him the praises of the Christian's God.

Moro is much interested in the plans and progress of the American Colonization Society. He thinks his age and infirmities forbid his return to his own country. His prayer is that the Foulahs and all other Mahomedans may receive the Gospel. When, more than a year ago, a man by the name of Paul, of the Foulah nation and able like himself to understand Arabic, was preparing to embark at New York for Liberia, Moro corresponded with him and presented him with one of his two copies of the Bible in that language. Extracts from Moro's letters are before me. In one of them he says "I hear you wish to go back to Africa; if you do go, hold fast to Jesus Christ's law, and tell all the Brethren, that they may turn to Jesus before it is too late. The Missionaries who go that way to preach to sinners, pay attention to them, I beg you for Christ's sake. They call all people, rich and poor, white and black, to come and drink of the waters of life freely, without money and without price. I have been in Africa; it is a dark part. I was a follower of Mahomet, went to church, prayed five times a day and did all Mahomet said I must but the Lord is so good. He opened my way and brought me to this part of the world where I found the light. Jesus Christ is the light, all that believe in him shall be saved, all that believe not shall be lost. The Lord put religion in my heart about ten years ago. I joined the Presbyterian Church, and since that time I have minded Jesus' laws. I turned away from Mahomet to follow Christ. I don't ask for long life, for riches, or for great things in this world, all I ask is a seat at Jesus' feet in Heaven. The Bible, which is the word of God, says sinners must be born again or they can never see God in peace. They must be changed by the Spirit of God. I loved and served the world a long time, but this did not make me happy. God opened my eyes to see the danger I was in. I was like one who stood by the road side and cried Jesus, thou Son of God, have mercy; he heard me and did have mercy. 'God so loved the world that he gave his only begotten Son, that whosoever believeth in him should not perish but have everlasting life.' I am an old sinner, but Jesus is an old Saviour; I am a great sinner, but Jesus is a great Saviour: thank God for it. — If you wish to be happy, lay aside Mahomet's prayer and use the one which our blessed Saviour taught his disciples — our Father, &c."

In another letter to the same, he writes, "I have every reason to believe that you are a good man, and as such I love you as I love myself. I have two Arabic

Bibles, procured for me by my good Christian friends, and one of them I will send you the first opportunity; we ought now to wake up, for we have been asleep. God has been good to us in bringing us to this country and placing us in the hands of Christians. Let us now wake up and go to Christ, and he will give us light. God bless the American land! God bless the white people. They send out men every where to hold up a crucified Saviour to the dying world. In this they are doing the Lord's will. My lot is at last a delightful one. From one man to another I went until I fell into the hands of a pious man. He read the Bible for me until my eyes were opened, now I can see; thank God for it. I am dealt with as a child, not as a servant."

I spent but a few days in South Carolina, and can express no very decided opinion in regard to the general sentiment towards the Colonization Society. A clergyman of high standing in the Episcopal Church, and who has ever resided in that State, said he believed some reaction had commenced in the public mind favorable to the Society. Such I judge to be the fact from conversations with many sensible and religious men, citizens of that community. The passions of men, inflamed and agitated almost to fury during the late conflict of political parties, are sinking to repose. All rejoice in the fact; the bands of social affection are reuniting, topics which would awaken unkind or painful recollections are sedulously avoided, and the general desire is for harmony and peace. Hitherto the press in South Carolina has excluded every thing in favor of Colonization. The subject is not understood. A few political men have frowned upon it, and this has been enough to prevent the multitude from examining its merits. Times are changing, and opinions also in South Carolina. We have warm and enlightened friends there. Many in that State do not and never will adopt the ultra doctrines of Gov. McDuffie on slavery.[1] A discreet and able Agent might, I think, render as important service to the interests of the Society in South Carolina as in any State of the Union. Even when mistaken, the citizens have a large share of honor, candor, and integrity.

The Board may recollect, that soon after the organization of the Society, several auxiliary associations arose in this State (Georgia,) that several valuable Reports were published in behalf of the Society, and some generous subscriptions made to its funds. In this place, Augusta, individuals have contributed liberally to sustain the institution. From many of the citizens of this place, the Society may expect aid; much will be done for it throughout this State. No time, however, could be more unfortunate than the present for applications to obtain pecuniary means for any object and in any section of the Union. The necessities of the Society

---

1. Editor's note: George McDuffie (1790–1851), a protégé of John C. Calhoun, was the fifty-fifth governor of South Carolina and a proponent of nullification.

are urgent, or I should certainly deem it wise to postpone such applications, until the public shall have recovered (in some degree at least) from the shock which they have of late, and are now experiencing in the overthrow of so many great commercial establishments, and the vast ruin of general confidence, of high expectations and enthusiastic hopes which has succeeded.

The slaves recently manumitted, conditionally, by the will of the late Mr. Tubman of this place, most of whom, are now about to emigrate to Cape Palmas, under the direction of the Maryland Colonization Society, are represented as intelligent, of good habits, and several of them of fair christian character. Six of their number preferred to remain in this country. Forty-two go from Mr. Tubman's estate, and four others, their relations, who have been emancipated by benevolent individuals, accompany them. One noble minded friend of the Colonization Society, aided by some of his wealthy relatives, purchased three of them at a cost of about two thousand dollars. Another was manumitted by a gentleman who has repeatedly testified his regard to the Institution by large donations.

In a time like this, of general depression in pecuniary affairs, increased liberality becomes those who are not deeply affected by the calamity. Without this, the resources of our charitable institutions must fail. But let those to whom Providence continues large means give much, and all of moderate ability something, and their operations will be with increasing power.

And may we not rely upon the Churches, generally, to unity in contributions for the benefit of the American Colonization Society on the Fourth of July, or on some Sabbath near that day? I hope that earnest appeals will be made to them, that they will understand that without their aid, at this period, the means of the Society must prove altogether inadequate to its necessities. I trust they will not close their ears to the cries of Africa, but realize the truth, that all the suffering now experienced in christendom by pecuniary failures and embarrassments, is small compared with those endured annually, in that land, since the slave trade first made merchandise of her children; and I fervently pray, that our whole nation may feel its obligations to conduct forward the scheme of African Colonization to those magnificent results, which from its vigorous prosecution, may reasonably be expected—the establishment of a free and christian empire on her shore, and the submission of her vast population to the dominion of Christ.

I have the honor to be,
With great respect,
Gentlemen, your obedient Servant,
R. R. GURLEY

Contributors

ALA ALRYYES is associate professor of comparative literature and English at Yale University. He is author of *Original Subjects: The Child, the Novel, and the Nation* (Harvard University Press, 2001) and several articles on eighteenth-century European literature and the Arabic novel.

ROBERT J. ALLISON chairs the History Department at Suffolk University in Boston. His books include *The Crescent Obscured: The United States and the Muslim Word, 1776–1815* (University of Chicago Press, 2000) and *The American Revolution: A Concise History* (Oxford University Press, 2011).

ALLAN D. AUSTIN received his PhD from the University of Massachusetts in English and Afro-American literature in 1975. He taught both subjects at both Springfield College and the University of Massachusetts at Amherst. He is author of *African Muslims in Antebellum America: A Sourcebook* (Garland, 1984) and *African Muslims in Antebellum America: Transatlantic Stories and Spiritual Struggles* (Routledge, 1997), as well as six relevant entries in *African American National Biography.*

SYLVIANE A. DIOUF is an award-winning historian of the African Diaspora and a curator at the Schomburg Center for Research in Black Culture. She is author of *Servants of Allah: African Muslims Enslaved in the Americas* (New York University Press, 1998), *Dreams of Africa in Alabama: The Slave Ship Clotilda and the Story of the Last Africans Brought to America* (Oxford University Press, 2007), and editor of *Fighting the Slave Trade: West African Strategies* (Ohio University Press, 2003).

CAMILLE F. FORBES is associate professor of African American literature and culture in the Department of Literature at the University of California, San Diego. Her research fields are African American performance and theatre history, and her latest work is titled *Introducing Bert Williams: Burnt Cork, Broadway, and the Story of America's First Black Star* (Basic Civitas Books, 2008).

MICHAEL A. GOMEZ is professor of history at New York University. He is author of, among other books, *Black Crescent: The Experience and Legacy of African Muslims in the Americas* (Cambridge University Press, 2005) and *Exchanging Our Country Marks: The Transformation of African Identities in the Colonial and Antebellum South* (University of North Carolina Press, 1998).

Contributors

GHADA OSMAN is associate professor of Arabic studies and chair of the Department of Linguistics & Asian/Middle Eastern Languages at San Diego State University. Her primary research areas are medieval Arabic and Islam and Arabic and Islam in the United States. She is author of "The Historian on Language: Ibn Khaldun and the Communicative Learning Approach," *MESA Bulletin* 37, no. 1 (2003): 50–57.

Wisconsin Studies in Autobiography

William L. Andrews
General Editor

Robert F. Sayre
The Examined Self: Benjamin Franklin, Henry Adams, Henry James

Daniel B. Shea
Spiritual Autobiography in Early America

Lois Mark Stalvey
The Education of a WASP

Margaret Sams
Forbidden Family: A Wartime Memoir of the Philippines, 1941–1945
Edited with an introduction by Lynn Z. Bloom

Charlotte Perkins Gilman
The Living of Charlotte Perkins Gilman: An Autobiography
Introduction by Ann J. Lane

Mark Twain
Mark Twain's Own Autobiography: The Chapters from the North American Review
Edited by Michael J. Kiskis

Journeys in New Worlds: Early American Women's Narratives
Edited by William L. Andrews, Sargent Bush, Jr., Annette Kolodny,
    Amy Schrager Lang, and Daniel B. Shea

American Autobiography: Retrospect and Prospect
Edited by Paul John Eakin

Caroline Seabury
The Diary of Caroline Seabury, 1854–1863
Edited with an introduction by Suzanne L. Bunkers

Cornelia Peake McDonald
A Woman's Civil War: A Diary with Reminiscences of the War, from March 1862
Edited with an introduction by Minrose C. Gwin

Marian Anderson
My Lord, What a Morning
Introduction by Nellie Y. McKay

American Women's Autobiography: Fea(s)ts of Memory
Edited with an introduction by Margo Culley

Frank Marshall Davis
Livin' the Blues: Memoirs of a Black Journalist and Poet
Edited with an introduction by John Edgar Tidwell

Joanne Jacobson
Authority and Alliance in the Letters of Henry Adams

Kamau Brathwaite
The Zea Mexican Diary: 7 September 1926–7 September 1986

Genaro M. Padilla
My History, Not Yours: The Formation of Mexican American Autobiography

Frances Smith Foster
Witnessing Slavery: The Development of Ante-bellum Slave Narratives

Native American Autobiography: An Anthology
Edited by Arnold Krupat

American Lives: An Anthology of Autobiographical Writing
Edited by Robert F. Sayre

Carol Holly
*Intensely Family: The Inheritance of Family Shame and the Autobiographies
    of Henry James*

People of the Book: Thirty Scholars Reflect on Their Jewish Identity
Edited by Jeffrey Rubin-Dorsky and Shelley Fisher Fishkin

G. Thomas Couser
Recovering Bodies: Illness, Disability, and Life Writing

John Downton Hazlett
My Generation: Collective Autobiography and Identity Politics

William Herrick
*Jumping the Line: The Adventures and Misadventures of
    an American Radical*

Women, Autobiography, Theory: A Reader
Edited by Sidonie Smith and Julia Watson

José Angel Gutiérrez
The Making of a Chicano Militant: Lessons from Cristal

Marie Hall Ets
Rosa: The Life of an Italian Immigrant

Carson McCullers
*Illumination and Night Glare: The Unfinished Autobiography
    of Carson McCullers*
Edited with an introduction by Carlos L. Dews

Yi-Fu Tuan
Who Am I? An Autobiography of Emotion, Mind, and Spirit

Henry Bibb
The Life and Adventures of Henry Bibb: An American Slave
Introduction by Charles J. Heglar

Diaries of Girls and Women: A Midwestern American Sampler
Edited by Suzanne L. Bunkers

Jim Lane
The Autobiographical Documentary in America

Sandra Pouchet Paquet
Caribbean Autobiography: Cultural Identity and Self-Representation

Mark O'Brien, with Gillian Kendall
How I Became a Human Being: A Disabled Man's Quest for Independence

Elizabeth L. Banks
*Campaigns of Curiosity: Journalistic Adventures of an American Girl
    in Late Victorian London*
Introduction by Mary Suzanne Schriber and Abbey L. Zink

Miriam Fuchs
The Text Is Myself: Women's Life Writing and Catastrophe

Jean M. Humez
Harriet Tubman: The Life and the Life Stories

Voices Made Flesh: Performing Women's Autobiography
Edited by Lynn C. Miller, Jacqueline Taylor, and M. Heather Carver

Loreta Janeta Velazquez
*The Woman in Battle: The Civil War Narrative of Loreta Janeta Velazquez,
    Cuban Woman and Confederate Soldier*
Introduction by Jesse Alemán

Cathryn Halverson
Maverick Autobiographies: Women Writers and the American West, 1900–1936

Jeffrey Brace
The Blind African Slave: Or Memoirs of Boyrereau Brinch, Nicknamed Jeffrey Brace
as told to Benjamin F. Prentiss, Esq.
Edited with an introduction by Kari J. Winter

Colette Inez
The Secret of M. Dulong: A Memoir

Before They Could Vote: American Women's Autobiographical Writing, 1819–1919
Edited by Sidonie Smith and Julia Watson

Bertram J. Cohler
Writing Desire: Sixty Years of Gay Autobiography

Philip Holden
Autobiography and Decolonization: Modernity, Masculinity, and the Nation-State

Jing M. Wang
When "I" Was Born: Women's Autobiography in Modern China

Conjoined Twins in Black and White: The Lives of Millie-Christine McKoy and Daisy and Violet Hilton
Edited by Linda Frost

Four Russian Serf Narratives
Translated, edited, and with an introduction by John MacKay

Mark Twain
Mark Twain's Own Autobiography: The Chapters from the North American Review, *second edition*
Edited by Michael J. Kiskis

Graphic Subjects: Critical Essays on Autobiography and Graphic Novels
Edited by Michael A. Chaney

Omar Ibn Said
A Muslim American Slave: The Life of Omar Ibn Said
Translated from the Arabic, edited, and with an introduction by Ala Alryyes